雜感自譯

——注释与解析——

（第3辑）

[澳] 林 巍 著

MY RANDOM THOUGHTS WITH
MY ENGLISH TRANSLATION

商務印書館国际有限公司
中国·北京

图书在版编目（CIP）数据

杂感自译：注释与解析 . 第 3 辑：汉英对照 /（澳）林巍著 . -- 北京：商务印书馆国际有限公司，2025.2.

ISBN 978-7-5176-1147-9

Ⅰ. H315.9

中国国家版本馆 CIP 数据核字第 2025NT4643 号

ZAGAN ZIYI: ZHUSHI YU JIEXI (DI 3 JI)

杂感自译：注释与解析（第 3 辑）

著　　者	［澳］林巍
出版发行	商务印书馆国际有限公司
地　　址	北京市朝阳区吉庆里 14 号楼 佳汇国际中心 A 座 12 层
邮　　编	100020
电　　话	010-65592876（编校部） 010-65598498（市场营销部）
网　　址	www.cpi1993.com
印　　刷	北京建宏印刷有限公司
开　　本	880mm × 1230mm 1/32
印　　张	11.75
字　　数	300 千字
版　　次	2025 年 2 月第 1 版第 1 次印刷
书　　号	ISBN 978-7-5176-1147-9
定　　价	88.00 元

前　言

《杂感自译：注释与解析》（第 2 辑）于 2023 年由商务印书馆国际有限公司出版后，受到读者欢迎，从而激励我继续写下去，故现在有了第 3 辑。

比起长篇大论来，短文要灵活很多，涉及的面也可更广，如时事、政治、经济、文化、艺术、教育、心理、历史、医学、科技等等，但杂感写作并不轻松，要积攒很多材料，把问题想通透后，才敢下笔，所谓“厚积而薄发”。

由于本人长期从事翻译教学和研究，一向重视相关翻译的注释与解析，故将本书的文章和译文以“一般注释篇”和“深度解析篇”分为两大类：前者就原文的某些理解和翻译技巧做了解释，后者则除此之外还涉及相关的翻译理论和历史背景等。

总之，此类文章和译文，大都是作者所独创，力求做到思想性、知识性、可读性和翻译理念与技巧相结合，专业性与普及性相融汇，从而雅俗共赏。

目　录

一般注释篇

深度解析篇

附录

一般注释篇

原 文

法律的温度

贺岁片《第二十条》近来在社会上引起热议。该片讲述了三个颇具法律争议的故事：受害者丈夫捅死了放高利贷的强奸犯、公交车司机重伤调戏妇女的流氓、高中生打伤校园霸凌的同学。其焦点为，如何避免误判正当防卫与防卫过当，以及因此而导致的对所谓罪犯和受害者的不公正的司法判决。[1]

所谓“第二十条”，是指《中华人民共和国刑法》第二十条：“为了使国家、公共利益、本人或者他人的人身、财产和其他权利免受正在进行的不法侵害，而采取的制止不法侵害的行为，对不法侵害人造成损害的，属于正当防卫，不负刑事责任。正当防卫明显超过必要限度造成重大损害的，应当负刑事责任，但是应当减轻或者免除处罚。对正在进行行凶、杀人、抢劫、强奸、绑架以及其他严重危及人身安全的暴力犯罪，采取防卫行为，造成不法侵害人伤亡的，不属于防卫过当，不负刑事责任。”这条看似明确的法律条文，实施起来却迷雾重重、处处陷阱，导致了众多的冤案。[2]

在我看来，这当中体现的一个核心问题是：法律的温度。[3]

我们的法学教育认为法律思维是一种有别于常人、常理的思维定势，是完全根据法律的品性进行抽象、推理、概括的程序，排除了任何人情世故，否则就失去了法律的尊严。然而，这部电影中所反映的典型社会事件，却对此提出了极大的质疑。[4]

其实，法律既应该冷酷无情，也可以温暖怡人。“冷酷”主要体现为在法律面前人人平等，权贵犯法与庶民同罪；或无论某人曾做过多少好事，但犯法后应按同样的法律尺度判刑，这体现了法的客观性。然而，法律又并非是不食人间烟火的冷冰冰的条文，其生命不在于合乎逻辑，而在于遵循情理，这属于法本身应具有的人性。[5]

典型的例子如影片中的受害者丈夫，在明知施暴者要去车中取凶器再次施暴的情况下，首先出手了结了对方，这不是常人的一种自卫本能吗？为什么要被判罪？在另一个例子中，公交车司机见义勇为打伤流氓，结果被判刑三年。无论法院按照怎样的法律逻辑解释其行为有罪，都不能服众，因为这有悖于情理，从而损害了法律的信誉和尊严。[6]

法律的逻辑与情理往往是叠加在一起的。举个例子：一个在美国留学的日本学生，傍晚带着假面具去参加朋友的化装晚会，误闯进了隔壁邻居家，做着各种怪异的动作。由于语言沟通不畅，在几次警告无效后，主人开了枪，打死了日本学生。这似乎不近人情。然而，法官依据法律和情理——私人财产神圣不可侵犯及房主当时的恐惧感——判定房主为正当防卫，无罪。再如，世界上“最善良的法官”弗兰克·卡普里奥在判案时，并不是机械地拘泥于法律条文，而是从当事人的具体困境考虑，作出相当人性化的判决，在没有受害人的情况下更是如此。这使被告和群众感动不已。[7]

我在澳大利亚时，曾有幸入选过一次法院的陪审团。我们一共 12 名成员，都是从法律界以外的行业里被随机抽中。当时要求我们从自己的最初直觉、而不是从任何法律条文来判断一起家暴案的被告是否有罪，然后再由法官作具体结论。人们广泛认为，这种制度能在一定程度上使法律判决更为人性化。[8]

所以，法律人要做的其实是用人之常理来体现法律逻辑，让法律具有“温度”。难以想象，一个完全违背人之常情的判案会具有正当的法律逻辑。具体而言，法律中的“不法侵害”是机械逻辑，但如何判断“正在进行的不法侵害”却是个情理问题。[9]

归根结底，法律是以人为中心，而不是以逻辑为中心。法律所暗含的自然正义来自于人类的基本情理，而机械的法律逻辑只会导致相反的效果。[10]

正如电影《第二十条》的结尾台词所言：“什么是法律？是天理、是国法、是人情。我不相信没有天理的国法，也不相信没有人情的天理。”“要让天底下每一个人都明白这件事：法律，是让坏人犯罪的成本更高，而不是让好人出手的代价更大！”[11]

译 文

Humanity in Applying the Law

The Chinese New Year film “Article 20” has recently sparked heated discussions widely in China. The film tells three controversial legal stories: about the victimized husband who stabbed and killed a rapist who lent out loans at an exorbitant rate of interest, the bus driver who seriously injured a hooligan harassing a lady, and a high school student who wounded a bully on campus. The key issue involved here is how to avoid wrongly identifying "legitimate defense" with "excessive defense" , leading to unfair judicial judgments against the suspected "criminals" and "victims" .[1]

The so-called "Article 20" actually refers to Article 20 (Legitimate Defense) of the *Criminal Law of the People's Republic of China*: "An act that a person commits to stop an unlawful infringement in order to prevent the interests of State and the public, or his own or other person's rights of the person, property or other rights from being infringed upon by the on-going infringement, thus harming the perpetrator, is legitimate defense, and he shall not bear criminal responsibility. If a person's act of legitimate defense obviously exceeds the limits of necessity and causes serious damage he shall bear criminal responsibility, however, he shall be given a mitigated punishment or be exempted from punishment. If a person acts in defense against an on-going assault, murder, robbery, rape, kidnap or any other crime of violence that seriously endangers his personal safety, thus causing injury or death to the perpetrator of the unlawful act, it is not undue defense, and he shall not bear criminal responsibility." This seemingly clarified article, however, can actually cause tremendous hassles, misorientations and injustices in its practice.[2]

The central issue to me here is how to handle the humanity in applying the law.[3]

In our legal education, it has always been believed that legal thinking is a mindset alienated from ordinary people and common sense; it is a procedure that abstracts, infers and summarizes based solely on the definitions of the law, excluding any worldly wisdom, otherwise the authority of the law will no longer be maintained. However, the typical social events reflected in this movie have raised great doubts about this.[4]

In fact, the law should be both cold, heartless and warm, pleasant. Its former attribute is mainly manifested in the equality of everyone before the law—when the powerful and the common people are guilty of the same crime; or no matter how many good deeds a person has done, once he/she commits a crime, he/she should be sentenced according to the same legal standards, which reflects the objective nature of law. However, the law is not a dehumanized provision caring nothing about human desires, thus its latter attribute lies not in logic but in reasons integrated with human nature.[5]

Typically, the victimized husband in the film, knowing that the perpetrator was going to pick up a weapon from the car and commit violence again, took preemptive action to end his opponent's life. Isn't this the instinct of ordinary self-defense? Why should he be convicted? In another example, the bus driver bravely injuring a rogue was sentenced to three years' imprisonment. Regardless of the legal logic applied by the court to interpret his guilt, it does not convince the public; because it goes against reason, thus damaging the credibility and dignity of the law.[6]

Legal logic and reason are often intertwined. For instance, in the United States, a Japanese student, wearing a mask to attend a friend's costume party in the evening, accidentally broke into the next-door neighbor's house and acted weirdly. Communicating poorly due to the language barrier, after several ineffective warnings, the homeowner opened fire, killing the student. It seemed so inhuman. However, based on the law and reason—the sanctity and inviolability of private property, as well as the homeowner's fear at the time—the judge ruled that the homeowner was not guilty based on legitimate defense. Another case can be found in Frank Caprio, the "kindest judge" in the world. When adjudicating cases, he does not rigidly abide by the relevant legal provisions, but considers carefully the specific plights of the parties, especially in cases where there are no victims, to make a very humane judgement, so that the defendants and audiences are deeply moved.[7]

I had the privilege of sitting on a jury once in a court in Australia. Twelve of us, drawn at random from outside the legal profession, were asked to judge whether the defendant was guilty or not in a case of domestic violence, based on our initial intuition rather than any legal provisions, before the judge made a specific conclusion. In this way, the system is still widely believed in and to some extent its legal judgements can be made more human to the public.[8]

Therefore, what legal professionals have to do is to reveal legal logic through their common sense, that is to manifest the law's humanity. It is inconceivable that a judgement that goes completely against human nature contains any legitimate legal logic. Specifically, "unlawful infringement" is rigidly logical, but how to determine "ongoing unlawful infringement" is an issue of reasoning.[9]

Ultimately, law is centered around people rather than logic. Natural justice within the law is derived from basic human reasoning, while rigid legal logic can only result in its inversion.[10]

As the film's closing line says, "What's the nature of law? It should embrace natural law, national law and human nature. I don't believe in a national law that is not infused with any part of natural law, nor do I believe in any natural law without human nature." "We ought let everyone understand this: the law should make the cost of bad people committing crimes higher, rather than cost good people in preventing crimes." [11]

注 释

[3] 这里的"温度"不是通常的temperature，而是指法律执行过程中应具有的人性，故可用humanity、humane等，又如："让我们的产品质量更高，更简约，也更具'温度'。"（Let's

make our products better, with added quality, simplicity and humanity.）

［4］“人情世故”似乎还可译成 the ways of the world、traditional code of conduct、the ways of people 等。

［5］“不食人间烟火的冷冰冰的条文”，此处没有直译为 are otherworldly and cold clauses，而是将其分解、变通为 dehumanized provision caring nothing about human desires。

此处的“生命”，实则为“生命力”（vitality），但又不宜刻板，而是应该结合上文的法的客观性（the objective nature of law）来理解，故用了 attribute，其本义为 an inherent characteristic，表述的是一种法律的属性。

［7］“叠加”似乎是 superposition、overlay，但此处未能体现出二者你中有我、我中有你的性质，故用了 intertwine，其本义为 are closely connected with each other in many ways。

［9］此处的“机械”不宜套用 mechanical，而是 rigid，其本义为 deficient in or devoid of flexibility，故结合“逻辑”，译为 rigid logic、rigidly logical 等。

［11］此处的“法律”不是简单指法律的定义，而是指其性质，故变通为 the nature of law。

原 文

自然疗法与中医

我在澳大利亚留学时，读的第一个学位是自然疗法。其中的课程竟然有中医的内容，这使我很惊讶。后来慢慢发现，这二者之间其实有着深层的渊源。[1]

“自然疗法”的概念最早源于西方，近几十年来颇为流行。这固然顺应了西方人回归大自然的趋势，同时也是由于其疗法的有效性。西方自然疗法的哲学基础是对生命力的信仰，认为新陈代谢源自、适应、生长于自然，人体有着天然的自愈本能，因而要力戒外科手术和不必要的药物。其实，这与中医的根本理念不谋而合。[2]

中医的哲学理念是“天人合一”，即认为人是大自然的一部分，人体就是一个小宇宙。“神农尝百草”的传说、《黄帝内经》，莫不是人与宇宙、天地自然最直接的感应与互动。由此而论，早在五千年前的神农、黄帝时代，中国已经建立起了极其完整的自然医学体系。[3]

当然，由于传统文化和科技背景的不同，中西自然医学体系存在诸多差异。[4]

对于治愈疾病，西方自然疗法有“微生物”的概念，认为微生物是地球生命的一部分，而所有生物的最佳生存方式是找到其恰当的共生位置；疾病是生物在生存链中错位的结果。例如，微生物不断攻击人体，突破一定界限时便会引起发烧；发烧是身体调整和自疗的本能方式。在某些情况下，用药物抑制发烧则阻碍了身体痊愈。[5]

中医讲求的是整合天地的正气，“正气存内，邪不可干；邪之所凑，其气必虚”。“邪气”是指风雨不调、温凉寒热，感之于身，同时亦有因内而生的喜怒忧思。所谓治愈，就是要“正本清源”，善养浩然之气，从而以一正而压百邪。[6]

西方的自然疗法医师主张“非药物”、“非创伤”疗法，这些概念与中医原则又有出入。中药基本都是天然、完整自然之物，但一些中成药却不被西方自然疗法医师所认可，因为他们无法理解中医在食物、药物方面所进行的各种性能搭配及炮制原理。同样，许多西方自然疗法医师所使用的从植物中提取出来的有效成分，在中医看来，则完全违背了药物完整性的原则。至于中医的拔罐、刮痧、针灸等的“有创性”与“无创性”，则更存争议。[7]

此外，西方自然疗法所强调的“无毒副作用”，亦与中医理念完全不同。在中国人的自然观里，万物相生相克，有一毒物，则必有一相克之物，从而可达平衡。因而，“毒”在中医里是个相对概念。一杯凉开水，对于健康人来讲，无毒有益，但对于阴虚者而言，则有毒无益；砒霜，对于健康人是绝对毒品，但对白血病患者则有特殊疗效。“以毒攻毒”的概念，在西方并不那么容易接受。因而，许多中药，至今在西方被认为是有毒的。[8]

通过在西方自然疗法学院的学习，我亲身体会到了中西方对于“自然疗法”概念理解与实践的异同。而那里，之所以有越来越多的人对自然疗法感兴趣，主要是看到了正统医学的局限性，而同时感受到这一对立疗法的疗效性。[9]

然而，从根本上来讲，中医的“自然疗法”植根于中国人的传统思维与生活方式，是数千年来的主流医学，而在西方世界，自然疗法至今也只能是西医的一种补充疗法。[10]

译 文

Natural Therapies and Traditional Chinese Medicine

When I studied in Australia, the first degree I obtained was in Natural Therapies. One thing impressed me was that some ingredients of traditional Chinese medicine (TCM) were integrated with the course. Later it was discovered that the two are actually deeply interrelated.[1]

"Natural therapies", a concept that originated in the West, has become popular in recent decades, which is surely in line with Westerners' leaning toward the natural world, but is also due to its curative effects. Western naturopathy philosophically believes in vitality, that metabolism comes from, adapts to and grows in nature, and that the human body has a natural immune system for self-healing. It is therefore imperative to abstain from excessive surgeries and drugs. This idea in fact coincides well with that of TCM.[2]

Philosophically, TCM is rooted in the traditional Chinese theory of the "unity of man and nature" , believing that man is part of nature and the human body is a mimi universe. The legend "Shennong tasted hundreds of herbs" and the *Inner Canon of the Yellow Emperor* were full of direct responses and interactions between man and nature. In this sense, China had established quite a comprehensive system of natural medicine in the eras of Shennong and the Yellow Emperor five thousand years ago.[3]

However, there are also many discrepancies between the two natural medical systems based on different traditional cultures and scientific and technological backgrounds.[4]

In treating diseases, naturopath in the West employs the idea of "micro-organisms" which are believed to be part of terrestrial life, and the best way for all living things to survive is to find their proper symbiosis. A disease may be seen in this way as being misplaced in its chain of existence. Microbes keep attacking the human body, for example causing a fever, when certain boundaries are crossed. Fever is thus an instinctive way to adjust for self-healing, whereas suppressing fever by taking drugs in some cases may prevent the body from healing.[5]

In TCM, *zheng qi* (vital *qi*) , integrating the positive energy of heaven and earth, is upheld, believing that "so long as this kind of *qi* is stored inside, evil *qi* has no way to intrude into the body; otherwise, it will become vulnerable to being targeted by any disease" . The so-called "evil *qi*" refers to pathogenic factors, including some adverse conditions (e.g. inadequate rain and winds, abnormal cold and heat) affecting the body and causing unhealthy emotions, such as atypical joy, anger, anxiety and contemplation. To cure, is in fact to cultivate the good *qi* and defeat all the evil ones.[6]

Western natural therapists advocate "non-drug" and "non-surgery" treatments, which are not totally compatible with the principles of TCM. Basically, Chinese herbs are made completely from plant materials and vegetables, but some Chinese patent medicines are not accepted by Western natural therapists, since they do not comprehend the ways in which various ingredients of plants and foods are processed philosophically in Chinese medicine. By the same token, some of the "curative components" extracted from plants by Western natural therapists are completely contrary to pharmaceutical integrity in the view of TCM. The surgical nature of common practices in TCM, such as cupping, scraping, acupuncture and so on, has also long been controversial.[7]

In addition, the "non-toxic side effects" stressed by Western naturopathy are completely different from those of TCM. In the Chinese view of nature, all things in the universe mutually reinforce and neutralize each other: every poison must have its antagonist, so that equilibrium can be achieved. The concept of "poison" is therefore dependent on its context. A cup of cold water, for healthy people is non-toxically beneficial, but for people with "*yin* deficiency" , it is poisonous and harmful. In the same way, arsenic is a lethal drug for healthy people, but has some special curative effects for leukemia patients. It may not be so easy to accept the idea of "combating poison with poison" in the West. As a result, many Chinese herbal medicines are perceived as being toxic.[8]

By studying Natural Therapies in a Western college, I have witnessed the similarities and differences between the two kinds of natural therapies in terms of ideas and practices. People there have become more and more interested in natural therapies, because it has indeed cured some chronic diseases and ailments that orthodox medicine has failed to.[9]

Nevertheless, fundamentally speaking, the "natural therapies" of TCM, if we can use the term indiscriminately, is rooted in the traditional thinking and way of life of the Chinese people, and has been the mainstream medicine for thousands of years; whereas so far in the West, natural therapies as an alternative medicine seem to be only complementary to western medicine.[10]

注释

[2] "顺应了……趋势"，似应译成 has complied with...、has conformed to... 而此处变通为一般现在时的 is surely in line

with；“不谋而合”，还可译为 happen to have the same view、happen to hold the same opinion 等。

［3］“哲学理念”，似乎是 philosophical idea/concept，但此处根据前后语境译为副词 Philosophically 放在句首，以更为顺畅。

［6］此处的“正本清源”并非 radical reform，而是要在“养浩然之气”的语境下，融汇为 ... to cultivate the good *qi* and defeat all the evil ones。

［7］“有创性”与“无创性”与 invention 无关，而是医学上的 surgical nature。

［8］“相对概念”可以是 relative concept，但此处用了 dependent on its context，用以说明，在中医里同一种物质在不同的条件下会有不同的属性。

［9］“局限性”，一般可译成 limitations、boundedness、confinements 等，但此处的定语是“正统医学的”，故变通为 orthodox medicine has failed to。

［10］严格说，“中医”与“自然疗法”分别是东西方的两个概念，而此处“中医的‘自然疗法’”是个合成词，代指中医疗法，故采用增译法，加上了 if we can use the term indiscriminately。

原 文

生命之“应”

中国俗语说，“生死有命，富贵在天”。这句话虽然有些消极，容易陷入宿命论，但它指明了“命”与“天”的相关性。[1]

人生于大地，是自然的一部分。宇宙运行，是生命存在的摇篮和基础；生命不能违背自然规律而独立存在。《素问》说：“呜呼！远哉，天之道也，如迎浮云，若视深渊，视深渊尚可测，迎浮云莫知其极。”[2]

自然之道是天道，生命之道是人道；后者只能认识、顺应而不能改变前者。整个生命过程，就是一个人道“应”天道的过程。如《素问》所言，从出生到死亡，女子“三七，肾气平均，故真牙生而长极”，男子“三八，肾气平均，筋骨劲强，故真牙生而长极”；之后，肉体组织由盛而转衰。无论哪个生命阶段，生命之“应”的活力始终处于动态变化之中，饥而食，冬而寒，夜而眠……[3]

人道和天道之间的联系以“气”为中介，以生命感应性为根本，通过生命之“应”，把握《素问》中所说的“至而至者和；至而不至，来气不及也；未至而至，来气有余也”的基本规律。“应”之力，上通宇宙，外应四时，内和五脏，表现出各种各样的生命现象。这是一个高度微妙的协调过程，其协调质量决定了人的健康和寿命。[4]

中医里的人由“形”和“神”两部分组成。《灵枢》说，人的形体“外可度量切循而得之，其死可解剖而视之”。生命之“应”丧失后，肉体组织仍会在一定时期内存在，但那是解剖意义上的“尸”，而非生物意义上的“人”。因而，“应”是中医区别生命与非生命的本质所在。[5]

同时，中国传统文化又历来推崇“天行健，君子当自强不息”，这是生命之“应”的积极性一面，即在有限之内，争取最大限度。就天道与人道的关系而言，“应”的最高境界，是《黄帝内经》上讲的“形与神俱，尽终其天年”。[6]

从某种意义上讲，健康长寿才是生命的最大成功，而现代社会物质文化的高度发展，容易使人们把物质利益放在首位，甚至为名利牺牲健康，这与中医的理念是背道而驰的。[7]

中医的适应性，并不是对这种社会氛围的随波逐流；相反，人应逆流而上，强调文化发展的生命属性，在横流的物欲中，守住顺应生命时空的底线。[8]

译 文

The Biotic Response

A Chinese saying goes that “One’s life and fortune are determined by heaven” . Despite its negativity towards life, which may easily fall into fatalism, this adage reveals the connections between fate and nature.[1]

Born on the earth, humans are part of nature and life cannot be separated from but has to be nurtured and underpinned by laws of the Universe. As the *Plain Questions* says, "Alas, the laws of heavens are so far-reaching! It's like looking up at clouds in the sky—no one knows its ultimate location; unlike when looking into the abyss, where, though deep, place can still be detected." [2]

The so-called "way of heaven" refers to natural laws, and the "way of man" to biotic laws, which throughout the life process can only realize and conform to, not change, the former. According to the *Plain Questions*, from birth to death, "women's kidney-*qi* matures and consequently their bodies reach a peak at the age of 21" , while "men's kidney-*qi* functions normally and their muscles and bones are most robust at 24" . Subsequently, both their body tissues gradually decline. The biotic response is always dynamically changing at every point in life, such as eating to slake hunger, donning clothes to combat coldness, sleeping at night...[3]

The connections between the way of heaven and the way of man are mediated by *qi* based on the responsive nature of life. In this way, as the *Plain Questions* goes that "when timing and *qi* are coordinated, harmonious living will result; when timing arrives without *qi*, the *qi* response will be insufficient; when *qi* arrives at the wrong time, the *qi* response will be surplus." The power of biotic response communicates with the Universe functionally, reacts to the four seasons externally and regulates the viscera internally, as manifested in various life phenomena. The quality of this highly delicate, coordinated process determines one's health and life span.[4]

According to traditional Chinese medicine (TCM), a biological body consists of physique and soul. As *The Spiritual Pivot* points out, flesh and blood, if alive, can be observed, but when dead can be dissected and looked at in detail. After the loss of the biotic response, physical tissues can still exist for a certain period of time, but an anatomical "corpse", is no longer a biological "human". Therefore, biotic response is the intrinsic distinguishing quality between "life" and "non-life" in TCM.[5]

Meanwhile, Chinese traditional culture also endorses the idea of "As heaven's movement is vigorous, so must gentlemen constantly strive for self-renewal", which is the positive spirit of biotic responses in achieving the maximum within their limits. As far as the relations between the way of heaven and the way of man are concerned, the highest realm of biotic response is to live up to one's "heavenly age" in a perfect match of physique and soul, as the *Inner Canon of the Yellow Emperor* holds.[6]

In a sense, maintaining a healthy life into longevity is the greatest success in life. However, the highly developed materialistic culture of modern times tends to motivate people to put material interests first, even to pursue wealth and fame at the expense of health, which runs counter to the idea of TCM.[7]

The so-called biotic response in TCM in fact is not to drift with such a social atmosphere. Instead, one should go against the current, cherish the living nature of cultural development, so as to hold the bottom line of biotic response in conforming to the time-space of life even in a materialistic society.[8]

注 释

[1]“生死有命，富贵在天”，一般似可译成 Life and death are destined, wealth and fortune are determined by the heavens./The life and death has the life, the riches and honor depend on the appointment of heaven./It is one’s destiny that decides life or death; it is the God that governs rich or poor./Life or death is by one’s fate, while wealth and honor by God. 等，但分析起来，此处的“生死有命”可与后面的“富贵在天”作互文翻译。所谓“互文”，是“参互成文，合而见义”，即是一种互辞形式——前后两句，看似说两件事，实则是互相阐发，互相补充，如“烟笼寒水月笼沙”，并不是“烟雾笼罩着寒水，月光笼罩着沙”，而是“烟雾笼罩着寒水也笼罩着沙，月光笼罩着沙也笼罩着寒水”。因而，不妨将两句融合为 One’s life and fortune are determined by heaven。

[3]“人道”似可译为 human way、humanity、human sympathy

等；此处对应前面的“天道”（way of heaven），译为 way of man，含指生命之道（biotic laws）。此段中的第一个“应”融合在了 realize and conform to... 之中，第二个“应”则是本文主旨的 biotic response。同时，“饥而食，冬而寒，夜而眠”，此处的“饥”、“冬”、“夜”是动词，作状语，而在英文里，则转译为名词，即 hunger、coldness 和 night。

[5]“‘形’和‘神’”，不宜简单地音译成 *xing* and *shen*, 而可意译为 physique and soul。

[6]“天行健，君子当自强不息”，还可译成 As heaven is moving vigorously, gentlemen should strive constantly to become stronger! / Strengthen self without stopping, and hold world with virtue. / While the universe keeps rolling on orbit, a superior man makes untiring endeavor for advancement. 等。相关的，清华大学的校训“自强不息，厚德载物”，英文是：Strengthen self without stopping, and hold world with virtue；其完整句出自《周易》：“天行健，君子以自强不息；地势坤，君子以厚德载物”，可译为 As Heaven's movement is ever vigorous, so must a gentleman ceaselessly strive along; as the environment is steady, so the gentleman should hold world with virtue。此处加以变通为 As heaven's movement is vigorous, so must gentlemen constantly strive for self-renewal。

[8]此处的“适应性”，不是一般意义上的 adaptation、adaptability 等，而要在中医的语境下去理解，仍为 biotic response。“强调”的一般意思为 emphasize、stress、underline，此处

为了强调其“生命属性”，用了 cherish，其本义为 to love somebody or something very much and want to protect them or it。同时，“横流的物欲”，还可译为 our abundant world、materialistic age、the era with flashy and material desires、the material-focused society 等。

原 文

情绪疗法的哲学认知

情绪疗法，已经成为现代医学的一个重要内容。它的出现体现了治病中对于人的本质认识的深化，是西医从过度分科趋向整合意识的一种标志。其原因在于，西医终于认识到，人体毕竟不是一堆器官的简单组合，而是充满感情与情绪的有机体。然而，更深的原因又不止于此。[1]

植根于中国传统哲学的中医，对情绪疗法的认识和重视源远流长。中医将人体分为不同层次，那些看不见的理性部分处于顶层，而可见的感性部分处于底层；意识引导能量（精、气、神）在二者之间流动；这种流动的形态和质量，就决定了人体的生存状态。[2]

感情和情绪是人性的本质特征。根据《说文解字》，“心，人心，土藏”，即点明了其物质属性，但心又可“藏神”，这是指其精神属性；二者可在某种情况下高度融合。中医认为，当人被赋予一颗真正的“心”时，人便处于一种两难境地，即在属地的动物性欲望与属天的灵性精神范畴之间挣扎。这亦是一种形与神的矛盾动态协调。[3]

因而，人的情绪波动是正常的；但当情绪波动到一定限度，量变引起质变，又会导致人体的失衡，产生疾病。据《释名》解释：“病，疾加也。”从字形上看，“病”字由两部分组成：“疒”代表一个卧床不起的人，而“丙”与心有关，二者加在一起，意为由情绪或精神问题所引起的身体上的疾患。[4]

然而，这种变化，在某种程度上，又是可以控制的。中医认为，无形的精气神，控制着有形的物质。如北齐哲学家刘昼所论：“故神静而心和，心和而形全；神躁则心荡，心荡则形伤。将全其形，先在理神。”[5]

《吕氏春秋》总结道：“圣人之所以异者，得其情也。由贵生动，则得其情矣，不由贵生动，则失其情矣。此二者，死生存亡之本也。”可见，掌控情绪对于健康长寿十分重要。[6]

在西方，“合理情绪疗法”创立者、美国心理学家艾利斯，通过对于有关功能障碍的观念和情感之间关系的研究，发现引起人情绪困扰的，不是外界事件，而是人们对于事件的态度、看法、评价。因此，通过改变非理性的观念，可以改进性格，缓解焦虑情绪。[7]

应当说，这当中所涉及的感性与理性认识、量变与质变、物质与精神、部分与整体、外因与内因等，都属哲学范畴——人类的最高认知层次。其实，这也是生命及生活中的基本道理：情绪来源于想法和观念；面对同一件事，不同素质的人会产生不同的情绪，从而带来千差万别的结果。因而，不断提高人的哲学认知，可以在很大程度上调整人的负面情绪，提高生活和生命的质量。[8]

译 文

The Philosophical Understanding of Emotional Therapy

As an important part of modern medicine, the emergence of emotional therapies embodies the progressive understanding of human nature in the treatment of diseases and a sign that western medicine has moved towards an integrated approach from its excessive divisions. The reason is that western medicine has finally realized that the human body is not, after all, simply an assembly of a bunch of organs; rather, is an organism motivated by sensitivities and emotions, and the underlying causes have yet to be further explored.[1]

Rooted in traditional Chinese philosophy, traditional Chinese medicine (TCM) has long practiced and valued emotional therapy. In TCM, there are different levels in the human body, with the invisible rational part at the top, while the perceptional and touchable part at the bottom, interacting with the energy in the form of *jing* (essence), *qi* (inner vitality) and *shen* (spirit), and the state and quality of the interaction determine the conditions of an individual's existence.[2]

Feelings and emotions are essential features of human nature. According to *Origin of Chinese Characters*, "Heart, virtually meaning people's heart, is the organ of the earth" , denoting its physical nature, while heart is also the place where the "spirit" is stored, and the two can sometimes be highly integrated in a body under certain conditions. TCM believes that when a person is endowed with a "true heart" , he or she is actually being put in a dilemma, struggling between bodily instincts and divine desires, which constitutes a dynamic adjustment and coordination between the physical and spiritual parts of the body.[3]

People's mood fluctuations are thus considered normal. However, when they reach a certain limit, quantitative changes cause qualitative changes, they will lead to an imbalance in the human body, which would result in sickness. As *Shi Ming*, a classical work about Chinese characters interprets: "Sickness means a disease is induced." The configuration of the Chinese character *bing* (sickness) indicates that it is composed of a sick person and a heart, the combination of the two meaning a physical illness caused by emotion or spirit.[4]

These kind of changes, however, are somewhat controllable. TCM holds that the invisible essence, *qi*, and spirit can manipulate the tangible things. As the philosopher Liu Zhou (514-565) in the Northern Qi Dynasty pointed out: "When your spirit is quiet, your heart is calm as well, which will generate a physical and mental harmony in your body. When you are internally upset, on the contrary, your body will be disturbed. In order to have a perfect body and health, the first thing is to properly manage your mental order." [5]

Lü's Spring and Autumn Annals concluded that "The reason why saints are different from others is because they understand their own hearts. Namely, an action initiated by decency will result in gaining heart; otherwise, will be losing heart. The difference between the two determines how you survive" . Clearly, emotional control is vital for a healthy life and longevity.[6]

In the West, Allis, an American psychologist and founder of Rational Emotional Therapies, has found, through a study of the relationship between dysfunctional perceptions and emotions, that people's emotional disturbances are normally caused not by external events but by their attitudes, opinions and evaluations of those events. Consequently, by changing our irrational concepts, we can improve our personalities and ease our anxieties.[7]

As mentioned above, issues involved here, such as perceptual and rational knowledge, quantitative and qualitative changes, the material and the spiritual, its parts and their whole, external and internal causes and so on, are actually in the realm of philosophy, which is at the highest level of human cognition. In fact, this is also the basic truth of life. Confronting an event, people of different aptitudes are motivated by their moods manifested in various ideas and concepts, which lead to diverse consequences. In this sense, by constantly improving our philosophical cognition, we can certainly better the quality of our lives.[8]

注释

[2] 中医的“精、气、神”有其特指，故宜先以拼音 *jing*、*qi*、*shen* 出现，再译其意。具体而言，“精”主要是指肾中所藏之精，这种精秉受于先天，并受后天精气的滋养。肾精化生元气，运行全身，促进人体的生长发育和生殖，并且推动和调节全身的生理活动功能，是人体生命活动的原动力；“气”是指肾精所化生之气、水谷精气和自然界的清气，三者共同组成人体的精气，它是生命活动的动力；“神”是指人体内一切生命活动的主宰者。三者关系非常密切，精可化气，气可化精，精气互化。精气生神，精气养神，而神则统驭精与气，故三者可分而不可离。翻译时可分译为 essence、inner vitality、spirit。

[8]“不同素质的人会产生不同的情绪”，似还可译成 different emotions of people with different qualities/different emotions generated by individuals with different qualities，此处根据其具体语境和句式，变通为 people of different aptitudes are motivated by their moods manifested in various ideas and concepts, which...。

原 文

哲学的困惑与价值

“哲学”其实是一个蹊跷的概念，其涵义随着不同的文化、历史语境甚至个人的阅历而演化。[1]

我在学生时代所记下的哲学的定义是，自然科学、社会科学及思维科学的概括和总结，是关于世界观的高深学问。由此，也不免产生疑问：哲学有什么具体用处？[2]

阅读中国哲学史，我发现老子、庄子、孔子、孟子、朱子等都一概被称为“哲学家”。然而，研读中国古代典籍，却找不到“哲学”、“哲学家”、“哲学史”的概念，有的是“经学”、“道学”、“理学”、“心学”、“玄学”、“义理之学”、“心性之学”等。[3]

后到国外留学，选修了哲学课，发现这不是一门令人生畏的学科，倒是吸引了不同专业的学生来旁听。这里讲的和世界观、人生观、方法论等没有关系，而涉及的是形而上学、逻辑学、伦理学、认识论，甚至宇宙论。其内容并不玄奥。简单一句话，哲学就是“求智慧”，并且其中点缀着许多格言警句和给人启示的小故事。[4]

参阅西方哲学史，我惊奇地发现，那些大哲学家们并不认为中国古代有哲学，因为那里没有思辨和推理，有的只是劝人为善、理智处事的道德箴言。因而以孔子为代表的那群人，更确切地说是“智人”，而非“哲人”。[5]

从词源上讲，这种观点似乎并不错，因为中国古代并无“哲学”一词。这个词是由日本学者西周在19世纪从英语的philosophy翻译而来，后经晚清学者黄遵宪转译到中文。因而，后人写中国哲学史，将“诸子之说”及“诸子”一概冠以“哲学”和“哲学家”，不免有些生硬。[6]

从中西传统文化和思维方式看，的确不能这样简单地对号入座。例如，“气”是中国传统哲学里的一个重要范畴，但用于表达的意涵过于丰富和泛化，诸如正气、阴气、阳气、邪气、淫气、厉气等，似乎任何事物都可用气来解释，因而令其涵义异常复杂，难以分辨；从逻辑学角度看，“气”概念歧义交错，与逻辑基本规律相悖；再如，“易”可同时释为“简易”、“变易”、“不易”等等，这几乎在任何语境下，都会让西方人一头雾水。[7]

那么，中西在“哲学”意义上就没有交集了吗？当然有，不过是更深意义上的。[8]

从根本上讲，哲学探究的是主观与客观之间的关系与意义。叔本华说，“我们可以做我们想做的，但却不能想我们所想的”，意思似乎很抽象，但若将“所做的”和“所想的”分别对应为“客观的”和“主观的”，就不难理解了。而认识到这种矛盾，本身就是一种智慧。这与孔子所说的“知之为知之，不知为不知，是知也”（最后的“知”通“智”），及庄子的“知天之所为，知人之所为者，至矣”，又不谋而合。[9]

再如，先秦名家公孙龙的“离坚白”论，其中“坚”是抽象的，不固定于某物，因而其各种共相是可以互离而隐藏的。坚不必是石的坚，也不必是任何物的坚；它不固定在某一特殊事物上，因而并不依赖特殊的事物，但可以是具体事物具有“坚”的性质。这里提出的是“一般性”和“特殊性”的思辨，与两千余年后黑格尔的辩证法相疏通，不过仍矛盾重重，似乎愈陷愈深。[10]

生活中充满了矛盾，因而就需要思辨，就需要哲学。中国古代诸说探讨的是天地、阴阳、生死、胜败、进退、攻守、兴衰、祸福、善恶、高下、前后、长短、大小、轻重、难易、音声、美丑、刚柔、强弱、损益、智愚、巧拙等等。而西方近代哲学研究的是物质与精神、思维与存在、灵魂与肉体、性善与性恶、理性与信仰、经验与超验、自由与责任、有限与无限、人类与上帝、哲学与神学、哲学与科学等问题。其实，无论是在更宏观或更微观的层面，这两类系统中的问题都有着某些内在的关联。上千年来，这些哲学的基本问题，几乎没有变化。有答案了吗？既有，也没有，其实这正是哲学的价值所在。[11]

归根到底，哲学是要让人们活得更明白。这样看来，黑格尔的“绝对精神”，康德的“道德理性”，马克思的唯物辩证法，笛卡尔的“普遍怀疑”，胡塞尔的“悬置判断”，维特根斯坦的“语言分析”，萨特的“存在主义”，索绪尔的“结构主义”，德里达的“解构主义”，不过是从不同的角度，为人们提供了不同的思维方式。其思考的结果，不在于找到了某种答案，而在于从中进行自我反思，更加清晰地认识自我与世界的关系，从而使自己当下的存在和努力更有意义。[12]

据说，生活中既要有低头看路的人，也要有仰望星空的人。那么，这两种素质可不可以集中在同一个人身上？完全可以。不妨这样理解，低头看路是“才”，仰望星空是“智”；“才”源于专业知识，“智”在于思辨、融通的能力和宏观视野。观察成功人士，他们无不具有这两方面的优势。功夫大师李小龙在美国学的是哲学专业，科技精英乔布斯信奉佛学教义，投资奇才罗杰斯平时看得最多的书是哲学和文学。据调查，在美国 100 强企业 CEO 的书柜里，超过 90% 的书都与经济无关，而是哲学、宗教、心灵方面的。[13]

对一般人而言，我们不一定立志做哲人，但一定希望避免做愚人。那么，就不妨在获得专业知识和技能的同时，培养一些哲学头脑，从而做一个有所作为而又合情合理的平凡智人。[14]

译　文

The Perplexing Value of Philosophy

“Philosophy” is actually a peculiar concept with shifting meanings that have evolved with different cultures, historical contexts, even personal experiences.[1]

The definition of philosophy written down when I was a student was “the generalization and summary of natural, social and thinking science”, a profoundly knowledgeable view about the world. Hence I began to wonder what's the actual application of philosophy.[2]

Reading the history of Chinese philosophy, I found that Lao Tzu, Zhuangzi, Confucius, Mencius, Zhuzi and others were called "philosophers". However, when delving into Chinese classics, the terms "philosophy", "philosopher" and "history of philosophy" cannot be found. Instead, what we confront is some very Chinese teachings, including "Classical Confucianism", "Taoism", "Neo-Confucianism", "Heart-Mind Theory", "Metapsychology", "Argumentative Theory", "Study of Disposition" and so on.[3]

Then I studied abroad and an elective "philosophy" was chosen to gratify my curiosity. Surprisingly, I found it was not a formidable subject at all, but rather it was quite approachable, attracting students from different majors. The subject has nothing to do with world views, outlooks on life or methodology; instead, it involves metaphysics, logics, ethics, epistemology, even cosmology. The idea of philosophy in this context is not abstruse. In a simple sentence, "philosophy is to pursue wisdom" which is often crystalized in aphorisms or storiettes inspiring people in their daily lives.[4]

Referring to the history of Western philosophy, it is astonishing to read that its great philosophers did not believe that there was any such thing as "philosophy" in ancient China, where there was no speculation or reasoning, but only moral proverbs urging people to be good and wise. Therefore, the bunch of people represented by Confucius were more precisely "wise men" rather than "philosophers" .[5]

Etymologically, this view might not be wrong, since there were indeed no such characters in Chinese to match "philosophy" in ancient China. In fact, "philosophy" , in its modern sense, was translated from the English "philosophy" in the 19th Century by Japanese scholar Nishi Amane as *tetsu gaku* (哲学), which then, as the same characters, was introduced into China in the late Qing Dynasty by Chinese scholar Huang Zunxian. When later people wrote the history of Chinese philosophy, they named all ancient Chinese scholars and their doctrines as "philosophers" and "philosophies" , which was bound to be incondite.[6]

From a cross-cultural perspective between China and the West, it is true that there is no room for such a simple alignment. For example, *qi* (气), an important Chinese philosophical category, was used very extensively and diversely, including *zheng qi, yin qi, yang qi, xie qi, yin qi, li qi*—for just about everything. As a result, it's hard to specify the exact connotations of *qi* in some contexts. So diverse and even contradictory are its meanings, that *qi* is logographically undefinable. So is the idea of *yi* (易), since it could be interpreted as *jian yi* (simple), *bian yi* (change) and *bu yi* (hard) almost concurrently, which in almost any context will confuse Westerners.[7]

So, is there any "philosophical intersection" between China and the West? Surely, there is, but in a much deeper sense.[8]

Fundamentally, philosophy explores the relations and meanings between subjectivity and objectivity. Schopenhauer said, “We can do what we want to do, but we can’t think that we have no idea to think” , which seems to be abstract. However, it may not be so difficult to understand when “what to do” and “what to think” are correlated with “objectivity” and “subjectivity” respectively. The realization of this contradiction presents a kind of wisdom, which in some way coincides with Confucius’ maxim that “Knowing what your unknown is a kind of knowing itself” , and Zhuangzi’s saying, “Understanding heavenly fortune and man’s mission is the highest wisdom” .[9]

Another example is Gongsun Long’s theory of “Discourse on Hardness and Whiteness” in the pre-Qin Period, which posited the theory that, as an abstract concept, hardness is not tied to certain materials but can be extracted and recognized in any interrelated substances apart from concrete ones. The dialectical nature of generality and specialty, in this way, was properly analyzed, which, two thousand years later, related to Hegelian Dialectics in both contradictory and profound senses.[10]

Human life brimming with contradictions entails speculation, or so-called “philosophy” . In traditional Chinese culture, the issues explored were virtually all in pairs, such as heaven-earth, *yin-yang*, life-death, win-lose, advance-retreat, offence-defense, rise-decline, weal-woe, good-evil, high-low, front-back, long-short, big-small, heavy-light, hard-easy, voice-sound, beauty-ugliness, hardness-weakness, powerfulness-powerlessness, profit-loss, wisdom-foolishness, smartness-awkwardness and so on. Issues in modern Western philosophical studies, however, are mainly abstract—matter vs spirit, thinking vs existence, soul vs flesh, good vs evil, reason vs faith, experience vs transcendence, freedom vs obligation, finite vs infinite, human beings vs God, philosophy vs theology, philosophy vs science and so on. In fact, the problems and issues in both systems are somehow intrinsically interrelated, whether at the macro or micro levels. These fundamental questions of philosophy have remained almost unchanged for thousands of years. Have we found any solutions? Yes and no. It is this unending process that philosophy values.[11]

Ultimately, philosophy is about making people live more consciously. In this way, Hegel's "Absolute spirit", Kant's "Ethical rationalism", Marx's "Materialist dialectics", Descartes' "Universal skepticism", Husserl's "Suspended judgment", Wittgenstein's "Linguistic analysis", Sartre's "Existentialism", Saussure's "Structuralism", Derrida's "Deconstructionism", are nothing except providing people with thinking tools from various perspectives. All this is not about finding answers, but about reflecting "the self". By realizing more one's self-position in the world, one's current situation and endeavors will become more meaningful as well.[12]

It is said that in life there should be men who look down at the way and these who look up at the starlit sky. Then can these two kinds of qualities be acquired by the same person? Surely they can when understood in this way: "looking down" signifies practical skills, training in one's vocational field, while "looking up" equips a person to think more broadly and dialectically at a macroscopic level. Reviewing successful persons around us, almost all of them possess these two kinds of advantages: Kungfu master Bruce Lee majored in philosophy at an American University; technology elite Steve Jobs believed in Buddhist philosophy; Rogers, the investment prodigy, usually reads philosophy and literature more than anything else. According to a survey, in bookcases owned by CEOs of America's top 100 companies, 90% of books have nothing to do with economics but are in the fields of philosophy, religion or spirituality.[13]

Generally speaking, most of us may not aim to be a "philosopher" as such, but surely we wish to avoid being seen to be foolish. In a way, everyone should, apart from acquiring professional knowledge and skills, develop a philosophical mind, so as to be a generally competent and reasonably wise person.[14]

注　释

[1]"蹊跷"似还可译为 strange、queer、odd、fishy，但 peculiar（意为 strange or unusual, sometimes in an unpleasant way）更适合"哲学"带给人们的困惑。同时，"演化"不是一般意义上的 evolution，而是有 changed understanding or opinion...

的意思，可考虑使用 shift 这个词，如 Public attitudes towards marriage have shifted over the past 50 years.（50 年来，公众对婚姻的态度已经改变。）The line of thought involved in this shift can be pursued further.（可以进一步探讨这一转变所涉及的思路。）等。

[2]“高深学问”，还可译为 depth of learning、higher learning、advanced knowledge、profound knowledge 等，此处用了“副词＋形容词”，即 profoundly knowledgeable 作定语，以修饰后面的宾语 view about the world。同时，“具体用处”，不宜按字面译成 concrete application，应理解为“实际应用”，译为 actual application。

[3]“心性之学”，属传统国学的范畴，涉及儒家、道家、佛家思想等，虽有“本心”，但不是现代心理学意义上的“心”，而更多指的是“本性”，故不宜简单对译成 psychology。

[6]“这个词”是指现代意义上的“哲学”概念（因中国古代并无此概念），故应进行解释说明，增译为 in its modern sense，以更明确；而“生硬”此处亦可变通为 inaccurate。

[9]“知之为知之，不知为不知，是知也”，有着不同的译法，直译的如：Presenting what you have really known and admitting what you have never known, that is really knowing. /To know what you know and know what you do not know—this then is wisdom. 等；意译的如：Be certain of what you know and don’t pretend to know things you don’t. / No pretending to know what you actually don’t know. 等。本文采取了较为中和的译法。

[10]“愈陷愈深”，还可译成 ... get bogged down deeper and deeper、plunge deeper and deeper、sink more and more deeply into the mire 等；此处结合前面的“矛盾重重”融合成一句 in both contradictory and profound senses。

[12]“归根到底”还可译为 after all、in the long run、in the final analysis 等。同时，“自我与世界的关系”，似乎是 the relationship between me and the world，但结合后面的“自己当下的存在”，不妨一并译为 one’s self-position in the world, one’s current situation...

[14]“做愚人”，实则是“在别人看来是愚人”，故译为 being seen to be foolish。

原 文

加速奔向未知

无论你是否意识到，我们正处在一个空前的科技加速度发展时代，用“一日千里”都不足以形容。然而，奔向何方？却似乎是个未知问题。[1]

就人类演化历史看，从单细胞进化到生物人，大约用了30亿年；从石器时代到农业时代，大约用了4万年；从农业时代到工业时代，大约用了3000年；从工业革命到信息时代，大约用了100年；从信息时代到人工智能时代，只用了40余年；而从一维的GPT到二维的SORA，却用了不到区区一年！这期间，OpenAI就两次震惊了世界。[2]

放眼看来，人类出现在地球上，总共300余万年，而世界这几十年的发展却比过去几百万年发展的总和还要快。所谓“加速度”，是指速度变化量与发生这一变化所用时间的比值；决定加速度的因素是物体所受合力和物体的质量。随着现代社会各种物质和非物质积累的剧增，这种加速度只会更快。[3]

如果，这种加速度始终沿着由某种超级智慧设定好的轨道前行，对人类或许是种福音；但是，分析起来，好像未必如此。[4]

特别是2020年以来，人工智能在医疗、教育、金融、军事等领域取得了突破性进展，如谷歌的深度思维利用深度学习解决了蛋白质折叠问题；百度的飞桨成为首个通过工业互联网创新发展项目评审的深度学习平台；特斯拉推出了全自动驾驶测试版本，实现了无人驾驶汽车的部分功能；微软发布了MUM，创造了一种能够理解多种语言和多种媒体的多模态通用模型；美国国际商用机器公司推出了神经符号概念学习机，完成了一种能够从图像中学习概念并用自然语言表达的神经符号模型。[5]

然而，所有这些，在我看来，都没有美国科技奇人马斯克2024年1月30日宣布的一项成功更应令世人警觉，那就是他旗下脑机接口公司“神经连接”已完成首例人类大脑设备植入手术。大脑在被植入“心灵感应”的芯片后，只需通过意念便可控制电脑、手机等所有设备，而脑机接口通过连接大脑的电极收集与运动意图相关的神经活动信号，又可回传到电脑进行解密。马斯克并声称，在神经元尖峰检测方面已经取得了良好结果，即可以从受验者的大脑中获取信息。[6]

这意味着，人类意识与数字虚拟世界之间的壁垒被打通了，人脑和电脑合二而一了。可以说，这是人类自300万年前出现在地球上以来，最为震撼的事件，因为这将颠覆人类有史以来对于自身和自身之外的世界的所有认知。[7]

如果这项技术成熟、普及开来，那么以后青少年为什么还要上学、受教育、积累知识、丰富经验？各种专业人士为什么还要进行多年的勤学苦练？做一次手术、植入芯片就好了。从解剖学上讲，人们的所有意识和行为，不过是大脑中各种神经元接通、支配的结果，而最能胜任此项任务的莫过于与人脑神经突触融为一体的人工智能芯片，而且它可以源源不断地得到体外电脑最强大、最及时的更新。[8]

理论上讲，这种手术可以在一个人的任何年龄段进行，于是人类自古以来对于人生“在什么年龄做什么事”的安排整个被打乱了。[9]

人的身躯不过是意识的载体，如果一个人的思想和情感可以被移植、转存在电脑里，并且继续存活、发展下去，并不随着肉体的消失而失去任何功能，那么人不就在这个意义上得到了永生？这样，自然和社会中的新陈代谢机制也便不复存在了。[10]

既然人脑和电脑中的信息、图像可以随时流通、互换，人的任何想法、念头也便即时成文、成像地展示在电脑屏幕上，那么从此以后就没有了个人隐私？[11]

这不正是“福兮祸所伏，祸兮福所倚”吗？[12]

有种心理学说将人的智力分为“流体智力”和“晶体智力”，前者指处理信息的速度，即算力；后者指所获得的所有信息，即数据。而统计表明，在这两方面，人工智能都远胜于人脑。人工智能一旦汲取了人脑的精华，更新换代，具有了超强的自我学习能力，便已不再是机器，而是质变为一种硅基生命，成为一种有了自我意识的新的智能和文明，同时，它会将其赖以衍生的物种降低为次等生物。[13]

问题的关键在于由谁来控制以及以怎样的方式来控制中枢神经系统，而这当中存在着极大的不确定性。因而，就完全有可能出现一些我们不愿意看到的情景：由于从莫名其妙的终端发来的指令，一个乐观性格的人，突然有了抑郁、自杀倾向；本该和平相处的人们突然自相残杀起来；正常的人突然失去了理智……特别是，随着非侵入式脑机接口技术的发展，不再需要植入手术；只需采用脑电图仪、蓝牙遥控即可，一切变得更加轻而易举。于是，以往所有的医学、伦理、法律、社会规范、安全措施等方面的内容，可能都要被改写。[14]

最终，我们所能仰仗的似乎只有这个信念：进化毕竟总是从低级向高级发展的，尽管其间会生成各种各样的曲折。[15]

译 文

Speeding Up into the Unknown

Believe it or not, we are in an unprecedented era of technological acceleration, well beyond the "at seven league strides" description. However, where are we heading to? The answer to that question seems to be unknown.[1]

Tracing back into the history of human evolution, it took approximately 3 billion years to evolve from single cells to biological humans, about 40,000 years from the Stone Age to the Agricultural Age, 3,000 years from the Agricultural Age to the Industrial Age, 100 years from the Industrial Revolution to the Information Age, only about 40 years from the Information Age to the Artificial Intelligence (AI) Age. However, it took less than a year to evolve from a one-dimensional GPT to a two-dimensional SORA! During this year,

OpenAI has twice broken through itself and shocked the world.[2]

To put it in perspective, humans have been on Earth for about 3 million years, and the world has grown faster in the last four decades than the total development of the last few million years combined. "Acceleration", so to speak, refers to the ratio of the change in velocity to the time taken for this change to occur; the factors determining acceleration are the resultant force on the object and its mass. With the dramatic increase in the accumulation of all kinds of tangibles and intangibles in modern world, this acceleration will only speed up exponentially.[3]

If this acceleration always follows a trajectory set by some "superintelligence", it may be a blessing for humanity. However, evidence shows that it may not always be the case.[4]

Especially since 2020, AI has made various breakthroughs in medicine, education, finance, the military and many other fields. Typically, Google's Deep Mind uses deep learning to solve the problem of protein folding; Baidu's PaddlePaddle has become the first in-depth learning platform to pass the evaluation of the industrial Internet innovation and development projects; Tesla has launched a fully autonomous driving test version, implementing some of functions of a driverless car; Microsoft has released MUM, creating a multimodal universal model that can understand multiple languages and media; International Business Machines has invented a neural symbol concept learning machine, running a neural symbol model that can learn concepts from images and consequently convey them in a natural language.[5]

However, none of these, in my view, should be more alarming than an achievement announced by American tech prodigy Elon Musk on 30th January, 2024, that his brain-computer interface company, Neuralink, has completed the first human brain device implantation surgery. After being implanted with a "telepathic" chip, the brain can control all electronic devices such as computers and mobile phones simply by thinking, and the brain-computer interface collects neural activity signals related to movement intentions through electrodes connected to the brain, which can then be transmitted back to the computer for decryption. Musk also claimed that some good results have been achieved in detecting neuronal spikes, enabling information to be obtained from the subject's brain.[6]

This means that the barrier between human consciousness and the digital virtual world has been broken down, where the human brain and computer are merged into one. This is arguably the most shocking event since humans first appeared on Earth three million years ago, as it will overturn almost everything relating to humanity.[7]

When this technology becomes mature and popularized, why would teenagers still need to go to school, receive education, accumulate knowledge and enrich their experience in the future? Why would various professionals still have to study and practice hard for years? It could all be achieved by a simple operation, implanting a chip in the brain. Anatomically, all of a person's consciousness and behaviors are manipulated by neural connections in the brain, while nothing will be more capable in performing this task than an artificial intelligence chip integrated with human brain synapses, especially when it can be instantly updated and empowered by the extracorporeal brain-computer link.[8]

Theoretically, this type of surgery could be done on a person of any age, thus it will cause a total rearrangement of previous human life sequencing since civilization began.[9]

As a matter of fact, the human body is nothing more than a carrier of a person's consciousness. Once a person's thoughts and emotions can be transplanted and stored in computers, and continuously survive and develop without losing any function when the body disappears, then won't human beings get "eternal" life in this sense? If that is the case, the metabolic mechanism embedded in nature and societies will also be interrupted.[10]

Since the information and images in the human brain and its related computer can be circulated and exchanged simultaneously, any person's thoughts and ideas can then immediately be displayed either in writing or imaging on a computer screen, so will there consequently be no more personal privacy from then on?[11]

Isn't it true that "blessings and misfortunes go hand in hand" ?[12]

In psychology, human intelligence can be divided into "fluid intelligence" and "crystallized intelligence" , with the former referring to the speed of processing information, the so-called "computing power" ; while the latter refers to all information obtained, namely data. According to statistics, AI far outperforms the human brain in both aspects. Once AI draws on the know-how of the human brain, it can constantly renew itself with a super self-learning power. In a way, it's no longer a machine, but has been transformed into silicon-based life, a new intelligence and civilization with self-awareness. Meanwhile, it will have downgraded the species it derived from to a lesser creature.[13]

The key issue here lies in who will and how to control the central nervous system, which is obviously at risk of tremendous uncertainty. Consequently, some rather unpleasant scenarios may become very real: a person with an optimistic personality suddenly becoming depressed and suicidal caused by instructions from an unidentifiable terminal; by the same token, peace-loving people starting to kill each other, perfectly normal folks losing their rationality...In particular, with the advance of nonsurgical brain-computer interface technology, an implant surgery may no longer be needed. Everything happens so easily simply by remote control through an electroencephalogram and Bluetooth. As a result, all previous legitimacy in medicine, ethics, laws, social norms, safety measures and so on will have to be redefined.[14]

Ultimately, it seems that all we can still rely on is the belief that evolutions, after all, always move progressively from lower to higher, despite all the twists and turns along the path.[15]

注释

[1]“一日千里”似还可译成 cover a thousand *li* a day、advance at a high speed、advance at a tremendous pace 等，而此处用了英文里的惯用语“at seven league strides”，其中 league（里格）是旧时长度单位，约等于 5 公里。

[3]“物质和非物质”，一般是 materials and non-materials, 但还有更好的选择。tangible 意为 clear enough or definite enough to be easily seen, felt, or noticed，如 tangible evidence（明晰证据）；intangible 意为 is abstract or is hard to define or measure，如 intangible cultural heritage（非物质文化遗产），更符合文中意思，故此处用了 tangibles and intangibles，以包括更广泛的内容。

[4]“分析起来”，表面上是 on/upon analysis, 但此处可变通为 evidence shows，意思更为确切。

[7]“自身和自身之外的世界”不宜对译成 human perceptions of themselves and beyond，而可概述为 almost everything relating to humanity。

[9]“自古以来”，似乎是 since ancient times，但此处其实际内涵是“自有人类文明以来”，故译为 since civilization began。

“在什么年龄做什么事”，直译是 doing certain things at a certain age，此处译为 previous human life sequencing 是一种实质性的概括。

[10]“不复存在”，一般译成 no longer exist、cease to exist 等，但此处实际指的是在自然和社会中的新陈代谢规律被打破了，故用了 will be interrupted。

[12]“福兮祸所伏，祸兮福所倚”一般还可译成 Misfortune may be a blessing in disguise. /No weal without woe. /Luck and misfortune comes in turn. 等，此处的译文加强了语气。

[13]“精华”似乎是 essence、quintessence，但在此处的科技语境里，know-how（specialized knowledge and skills）更为确切。

[14]“莫名其妙的”，似乎是 inexplicable，但此处实际涵义是“难以鉴别”，故用了 unidentifiable。

“内容”，一般是 content、aspect 等，但此处实际指的是在医学、伦理、法律、社会规范、安全措施等领域的相关规范，故用了 legitimacy，其本义为 validity by virtue of being authorized or in accordance with law。

“被改写”，一般是 to be rewritten，但此处搭配前面的 unidentifiable，故译为 to be redefined。

原 文

跨越时间维度

世间最令人感叹的，莫过于时间的流逝。因为生命由时间组成，过一秒少一秒，全部过完，便是生命的终结。[1]

但是，时间又不是绝对的：不同的空间有着不同的时间；时间可以弯曲、膨胀；时间既能加快，也可缓慢；甚至失去的时间可以补救。最主要的是，时间有着不同的维度，而时间的流逝并不是全方位的，人们可以在相当程度上跨越时间维度，……了解这些，对人们岂不是莫大的慰藉！[2]

在亚里士多德、牛顿时代，时间是平面、直线、绝对的，人们永远可以准确地测量出两个事物之间的时间间隔，而无论是谁、怎样测量，只要钟是准确的，时间总是一样的。一百多年前，爱因斯坦将时间放在了空间里，于是一切都改变了。实验证明，由于引力和光速的作用，宇宙中时间的分布并不均匀，时空可以扭曲，即时间随着空间和参照物的不同而变化。[3]

著名的“双生子佯谬”将深奥的理论简单化了：老大在平原，老二去山顶生活，过相当时间后，经测定，二者的实际年龄出现了差异；而根据爱因斯坦的公式，若老二以每秒 24 万公里而非 20 万公里的速度去旅行，于 2023 年离开地球，2043 年返回，这一行程将只花费 12 年，而留在地球的老大则老了 20 岁，其中出现了8年的时间差距！[4]

根据爱因斯坦的广义相对论，时间膨胀可以减慢时间的速度，因而使我们可以穿越未来。想象一艘往返于地球的飞船，时间膨胀告诉我们，由于飞船的移动，飞船上的时间变慢，飞船上的乘客所经历的时间将少于地球上的人所经历的时间。所以，当飞船返回时，旅行者会发现他们已经穿越到了未来的地球。[5]

其实，在“宇宙大爆炸”之前，并没有时间，而根据量子物理学的研究，时间最终也会在空间消失。所以时间从来都既是客观的，也是主观的。爱因斯坦更有通俗的解释：当你在夏天守着火炉待上一分钟，就像过了一小时；而在漂亮姑娘身边，坐了一小时，却如一分钟。[6]

人们普遍感觉，少年时期的一年似乎很长，中老年之后越来越短了，“光阴似箭”，这与参照物和年龄比例有关。少年初出茅庐，事事新鲜，正如航海家去寻找新的目的地，多费周折，但回程就觉得很快；而且，6岁时，一年在生命中的占比是六分之一，而60岁时，则是六十分之一，自然短暂很多。当然，这是指时间的平面维度而言，在立体维度则未必如此。[7]

现代物理学研究的一个前沿领域是平行宇宙，即有各种证据表明，生活中的确会有某种“穿越现象”，但只有处于高维度者可见到低维度者，正如恒温鱼缸里的鱼，游弋在自己的世界，不会想到是谁创造了这样的环境，有谁在什么角度在观看它们。据物理学研究，宇宙中的第四维度，其实不是物质的，是意识的，而意识的穿越性可说是无边无际、无拘无束。[8]

根据英国著名物理学家霍金的理论，当人以超光速飞行时，就可以看到过去发生的事。至今，人类还未能造出这种飞行器，故暂无法证其真伪。但有一种途径可以做到，那就是在人们的意识里。当回看陈年照片和影像时，特别是在梦中，时间的秩序便不复存在，顷刻之间任意驰骋、剪接，不但可以穿越回过去，而且可以穿越到未来。这在经典文学作品中，也一直有所体现，比如，中国有《枕中记》，西方有《睡美人》。甚而，发展到了现今的人体冷冻技术，希冀能以这种方式“活”到未来。[9]

在本质上，人是活在意识里，身体不过是承载意识的躯壳。于是又有当代生物学家，研究如何将人类大脑结构的副本上传到电脑，在AI作用下继续发展，形成个体独特的时间维度；而一旦意识可与身体分离，人类便实现了在时间意义上的永恒？[10]

所有这些理论和实践，其现实意义在于，它们使人打开脑洞，多角度地看待生命和生活。爱因斯坦说，纯粹思维足以理解世界，因为自然界存在着精确的逻辑上的必然一致性。所以，不必为逝去的时间而悔恨，因为“失之东隅，收之桑榆”。时间其实可以人为地慢下来，静静地，人们能够抚摸其走过的一分一秒。回首过去，无论多少年，都是瞬间的事，那么不妨多些计划，因为对于未来的期盼会把时间拉长。[11]

在某种意义上，生活在地球上的人，每人都被赋予了一个“时间银行”。每天凌晨0点，时间会给你86400秒，到晚上12点全部清零；若无效利用，便是亏本。国外近年兴起的时间银行业务——将自己相对年轻的时间支付给需要帮助的人，而在自己力所不能及时，按相应比例提取储存在那里的时间（接受别人的服务）——是一种对时间秩序和容量的重新调整。[12]

一千多年前苏轼曾感悟，“盖将自其变者而观之，则天地曾不能以一瞬；自其不变者而观之，则物与我皆无尽也，而又何羡乎？”现在看来，这更是一种超前的对于时间立体维度的跨越了。[13]

译 文

Transcending Time's Dimensions

There is nothing in the world more lamentable than the passage of time, since life is made up of time—life will end when every second of your time has passed.[1]

However, time is not absolute. The following facts may provide people with great comfort: time varies within different spaces, and can be bent, expanded, accelerated or slowed down, even compensated for after its loss. Most importantly, since time has multiple dimensions, its passing is not all-encompassing and its boundaries can be transcended.[2]

In the days of Aristotle and Newton, time was linear, unidirectional, absolute, and its intervals could always be precisely measured by anyone at any time so long as the clock was accurate. More than a hundred years ago, however, Einstein changed all that when he put time into space. Experiments have proved his theory that time is not evenly distributed in the universe but, affected by both gravity and the speed of light, it varies with both space and its own referent, consequently space-time can be bent as well.[3]

The famous “Twin Paradox” simplifies this profound theory: the older twin brother stays in the plain, while the younger twin goes to the top of a mountain to live. After a considerable period of time, when they come together again, their actual ages are measurably different. According to Einstein’s formula, if the younger brother were to depart Earth in 2023, travelling at 240,000 instead of the speed of 200,000 kilometers per second, his journey would take just 12 years within its time-frame of reference. But returning to this planet in 2043, having actually experienced only 12 earth years, he would be surprised to find his older twin brother had aged 20 years, while he himself was eight years younger.[4]

Based on Einstein’s general theory of relativity, time dilatation slows down the speed of time, making it possible for us to travel through the future. Imagine a spaceship going from and to the Earth, as the spaceship moves within time, time dilatation slows it down and the passengers on the spaceship will experience less time than people on Earth. In that way, when the ship returns, its travelers will find that they have already travelled once through the future on Earth.[5]

In fact, there was no such thing as “time” before the Big Bang, and quantum physics predicts that it will eventually disappear altogether. In a way, time has always been both objective and subjective. Einstein once explained his theory in a very simple way: if you were taken to a furnace room in summer for a minute it may seem like an hour; while sitting with a pretty girl, an hour passes as a minute.[6]

There is a general feeling that a year in our childhood seems rather long, while it becomes increasingly shorter as we age and “time flies” , which has something to do with reference and an age ratio. Being young and inexperienced, people are responsive to almost everything, like navigators searching for new destinies. On their return journey, however, they seem to skip a lot of things with a light heart, so as to “shorten” the time. In terms of relative proportions, one year for a six-year old is one-sixth, while it’s one-sixtieth at the age of 60, reflecting a time difference. But of course, all this happens in a linear dimensional concept of time and not necessarily in its stereoscopic dimensions.[7]

One of the frontiers of modern physics is the parallel universe, where all sorts of evidence reveal the “transitional experience” , with the proviso that only those in the higher dimensions can perceive those in the lower, just as fish in a thermostatically-controlled tank, swimming in their own world, can never be able to realize the creators and observers who are just beside them. Exploring this fourth dimension, physics has found nothing in any material sense, just unrestrained and boundless consciousness.[8]

When flying at the speed of superlight, one would see what had happened in the past, as Stephen Hawking, the famous British physicist, suggested. As so far humans haven't been able to build such aircraft, it's virtually impossible to prove its validity; however, there is a way to achieve it—that is in our minds. Looking back at old photos and images, and most especially in dreams, the linear order of time exists no longer—we can pitch ourselves freely into any slice of time either in the past or the future. This phenomenon has also been reflected in traditional literary works, such as *A Dream In A Pillow* in China and *Sleeping Beauty* in the West. Today's cryonics is the technology attempting to preserve dead people's living time that may be revived in the future.[9]

In essence, humans live in their consciousness, with the body as its carrier. Some biologists nowadays are keen to study the potential of uploading a copy of a human brain into computing to develop "individual time dimensions" that can continuously evolve assisted with AI. Once consciousness can be separated from the body, however, will human beings achieve eternity in terms of their time dimension?[10]

All these theories and practices can sensibly blow our minds, perceiving life and daily living from different approaches. Einstein believed that pure thought is competent enough to comprehend the world, since there is after all mathematical and logical consistency in nature. As the old Chinese saying goes, "if you lose something at sunrise, you may gain something at sunset" , so you should never regret the passing of time; instead, we should sometimes calm down to enjoy the clock ticking with some greater anticipations. Everything in the past, regardless of how long it actually took, is in the twinkling of an eye when we recall it, while everything planned for the future "prolongs" our time through expectations.[11]

In a sense, everyone living on Earth is given an account in the "time bank" . At 0 a.m. every day, time gives you 86,400 seconds, and by 12 p.m. it will be all zeroed. You may suffer a deficit if you don't use it efficiently. "Time banking business" has therefore emerged abroad in recent years, which means depositing your time in helping others when you are fit and withdrawing it when you are old and infirm by way of receiving others' help accordingly. Somehow, time's order and capacity are thus, in a sense, reversible.[12]

More than a thousand years ago, Su Shi (1037-1101), the well-known poet in the Song Dynasty, realized that "Perceived through the eyes of transformation, everything in the world changes in a transient period shorter than the blink of an eyelid; when seen through the eyes of consistency, however, everyone and everything is blessed with immortality. Why then should we be envious of things?" From today's viewpoint, his observation might well have wisely transcended the many dimensions of time.[13]

注释

[2]“全方位的”未必是all-around、all-wave、omni-bearing，而encompassing意为broad in scope or content、broad extensive panoptic wide等，故不妨用all-encompassing。同时，“跨越”似可用shift cross、bridge、step over，但transcend的本义为to extend notably beyond ordinary limits，如：Dreams can transcend cultural differences.（做梦可以跨越文化差异。）The internet was supposed to transcend color, social identity and national borders.（互联网被认为能够超越肤色、社会身份和国界。），故文中选用了transcend。

[3]“直线”一般用straight line、plane等，但linear意为involving a single dimension，故此处用它来译“时间维度”更确切。

[4]“时间差距”，可直译为lead time或time lag，但此处没有直译，而体现在对比的形式：...while he himself was eight years younger。

[7]“时间的平面维度”，其实际含义是指“从时间的平面维度的概念理解”，故增译concept一词。

[8]“穿越现象”似乎是the crossing phenomenon，但这里意指一种个人体验，故更宜译为transitional experience。

[11]古语“失之东隅，收之桑榆”还有多种译法，如What we lose in hake we shall have in herring./What you lose on the swings you get back on the roundabouts./Loses on one side

and gains on the other. / Lose in the east and gain in the west. / It gains on the swings, it will lose on the roundabouts. 等。同时，这里的“抚摸”是指一种心态，即静下来慢慢享受时间，故不宜译成 touch；而 clock ticking，一般是指时间的消失，如 He was conscious of a clock ticking.（他意识到了时间正在消逝。），但此处用其正面含义。类似的如：In the silence we could hear the clock ticking.（寂静中，我们能听到钟表滴答作响。）。此外，“多些计划”是就对未来的期待会使时间放慢而言的，故没有译成 should have more plans，而是融合在 ...with some greater anticipations 中。

[12] 此处的“重新调整”不是简单的 readjustment、redress、retune 等，而是指对时间的一种回溯，故用了 reversible。

[13]“立体维度”一般可用 three-dimensional 或 stereoscopic，此处不妨在古今含义上再扩展一些：...transcended the many dimensions of time。

原 文

安慰剂效应与文化因素

安慰剂效应在中西医里同样存在，且数据证明，对病人的治疗有益。然而，其效应，却因文化因素而有所不同。[1]

“安慰剂”一词源自拉丁文中的“我会满足”。第二次世界大战前，该词意味着用糖或面包制作的无害药丸和补养药。医生有时会用安慰剂去满足那些没有明显疾病但仍需要治疗的病人。战后，随着双盲随机对照实验的进步，越来越多的人承认安慰剂具有显著的疗效。[2]

1955 年，哈佛医学院的亨利·比彻博士率先提出“安慰剂效应”，认为安慰剂可引起“明显的身体变化”，包括一些原本归因于有力的药物反应的变化。特德·卡普特查克博士则把安慰剂的身份从“谦卑的欺骗”变成有效的神秘物质，而这种物质则足以模仿有效药物。[3]

简单说，安慰剂效应是指病人虽然获得无效的治疗，但却“预料”或“相信”治疗有效，而使症状得到缓解的现象。尽管如此，通过大量医学实验，现已有十余种关于安慰剂效应的机制，从可减轻疼痛感的内源性阿片类物质和多巴胺释放，到免疫系统介导的调节等。对于既定的医疗状况，一种或多种安慰剂效应的参与，足以产生相当明显的治疗效果。[4]

然而，安慰剂效应在不同的种族和文化环境里疗效是不同的。大致而言，对于南美人群效果较差，在非洲稍好，对盎格鲁-撒克逊族群效果更好，而在接受中医治疗的华人地区，效果最佳。[5]

俗语说，“甲之良药，乙之砒霜”。中医的安慰剂效应之所以更强，似有多种人文因素。[6]

中医信奉者普遍认为，西医有时虽诊断、见效快，但治标不治本，而中医虽缓慢，但治病求本，能带来更彻底的治愈。例如，中医理论将头痛归因于一系列潜在病症，或因气虚导致头失濡养，或因肝火上冲于头而引起疼痛。在中医疗法上，前者可用补气法，后者可予以清热，而在实施两种疗法时都常可辅之以安慰剂效应，以有效减缓患者的痛感。[7]

比之西医医生，中医的望、闻、问、切，需花更多时间在患者身上，需对患者的个人生活背景有更多的了解，有的还需更多的肢体接触。这种对患者的更高“同情感知度”，无疑会产生更强的安慰剂效应。[8]

医药的化学性质，普遍被认为具有毒性和副作用，而中医在世界医学体系中属“自然疗法”，有“天人合一”性质。特别是对于一些慢性病的治疗，中医效果更好，而这正是西医的短板。从某种意义上说，时间在中医一边，这是一种放大安慰剂效应的心理因素。[9]

安慰剂所以起作用，其实质是心理因素，而心理因素植根于具体的文化土壤。中国自古有言，“医者，仁心”。由此，便不难理解，何以西方医学里的安慰剂与中医的传统做法相结合，便可产生其特有的强大效应。[10]

译 文

The Placebo Effect and Cultural Factors

The placebo effect occurs in treatments both of Western medicine (WM) and traditional Chinese medicine (TCM), yielding benefits for patients as data shows. However, it varies with different cultural factors.[1]

The word "placebo" was derived from the Latin phrase "I shall be pleased" , and meant harmless pills, such as those made from sugar or bread and tonic before World War II. Doctors sometimes used placebos to treat patients who had no symptoms of any disease while still requiring treatment. In the postwar period, with the progress of double-blind, randomly controlled experiments, more and more people realized the significant effects of placebos.[2]

In 1955, Dr. Henry Beecher of Harvard Medical School pioneered the "placebo effect" , arguing that placebos could cause "significant physical changes" , including certain extras that had previously been attributed to potent drug effects in medicine. Dr. Ted Kaptchuk further turned its status from "humble deception" into an "efficient mystical substance" that mimics effective drugs.[3]

In simple terms, the placebo effect is a phenomenon in which patients receiving ineffective treatments "anticipate" or "believe" them to be effective and consequently their symptoms are relieved. Through extensive medical tests, nevertheless, there are now more than a dozen mechanisms causing placebo effects, ranging from the release of endogenous opiates and dopamine to reduce pain, to immune system-mediated regulations. For a given medical condition, the involvement of one or more placebo effects are sufficient to manufacture certain therapeutic effects.[4]

However, placebo effects vary across ethic and cultural settings. In general, it works less well for the South American population, slightly better in Africa, much better for the Anglo-Saxon population and best for Chinese receiving TCM treatments in the Greater China Region.[5]

As the saying goes, "A good remedy for A may be arsenic for B." The causes for TCM's placebo effects may have much to do with some humanistic factors.[6]

There is a general belief among TCM believers that WM is speedy in diagnosing and treating certain diseases, though it cures the symptoms rather than the root causes. Comparatively, TCM treatment is more gradual than WM but with the effect of a permanent cure. For example, TCM attributes headache to a series of underlying conditions in which a deficiency of *qi* may cause loss of nourishment, or the liver fire flooding the head may cause pain. According to TCM theory, the first issue requires a treatment to replenish *qi*, while the latter is about clearing heat. The implementation of both treatments can often be supplemented with placebo effects, so as to effectively alleviate patients' pain.[7]

In comparison with WM doctors, TMC practitioners need to spend much more time on patients in conducting the "four diagnostic methods"—inspecting, listening, inquiring and feeling pulses, as well as getting into patients' personal details and, in some cases, making physical contact. This greater degree of "sympathetic perception" of patients would undoubtedly boost sounder placebo effects.[8]

The chemical nature of WM is widely regarded as being toxic and causing side-effects, whereas TCM is a special kind of "natural therapy" in the category of alternative medicine, characterized by the combination of nature and humans. It's especially effective for treating certain chronic diseases that WM often fails to. In a sense, time, a psychological factor, favors TCM in manifesting the placebo effect.[9]

Essentially, placebos work through their psychological implications, which are rooted in specific cultural contexts. There is an old Chinese saying from ancient times: "Doctors should be persons with benevolent hearts." In this connection, it's not hard to understand why the combination of WM's placebos and the old practice of TCM can generate such uniquely great curative effects.[10]

注释

[3]“率先”，似可译成 to be the first doing something、the person who takes the lead in doing something 等，此处用了动词 pioneer，其本义为 to be the first to study and develop a particular area of knowledge, culture, etc. that other people then continue to develop。

[5]此处的“华人地区”，是泛指的“大中华地区”，故译为 the Greater China Region。

[6]此处的“更强”，没有按字面意思译成 stronger 或 more effective，因上一段已有 it works... best for Chinese...，故只以 TCM's placebo effects 代之。

[7]中医指的“治标不治本”，还可译为 cure the symptoms not the disease、temporary medical relief、palliative care 等。同时，“上冲于头”似可译成 rush to the head，但此处用了 flood，该词并不专指 water，还有 to affect somebody suddenly and strongly，即 overwhelm 之意，如 A great sense of relief flooded over him.（他深感宽慰。）Memories of her childhood came flooding back.（她童年的往事涌上心头。）等。

[10]“起作用”似可译为 function as、acting as、contributing to、living on 等，但此处用了 work through，以表示“通过” psychological implications 而起作用。

原 文

重新定义“万金油”

传统意义上的“万金油”，是指某人在职业技能上样样通，但样样松，是个贬义词。然而，现在情况有了变化，在西方，该词正在转向褒义。[1]

人们历来认为，术业有专攻，要学有所长。但随着科技的发展，信息和技能更新的加速，当你在某一行业的专业知识达到预期水准时，发现相当一部分已经过时或被替代。据本·哈默博士的《如何在未来工作中取得成功》一书研究，在过去5年里，职场上平均37%的内容发生了这种变化。[2]

自21世纪以来，各领域的重大突破，在依靠高度专业化的同时，亦仰仗高度的综合化。在美国，跨学科的研究进展突出，它鼓励文理交叉，特别重视许多领域间出现的“软技能”。[3]

就发展趋势而言，越是专业的知识与技能，越容易被科技所取代。固然，会计、工程师、医生、护士等职业还会存在，但他们的工作内容和性质会有很大变化。在其任务不断被自动化替代的同时，跨部门的合作、团队精神、技术间的调整与转化、人际沟通与人文关怀，即“人类技能”将更为重要。[4]

美国法学院的毕业生，平均年薪为9.4万美元，但如果他们同时具有语言、宗教或其他领域的学位，其平均年薪约为 13 万美元。新闻专业的毕业生平均需有三个不同领域的专业知识，才具备在大媒体间赢得岗位的竞争力。[5]

更有专家预计，未来人们在职业生涯中，平均一生会从事五种不同性质的工作。因而，在西方，有人提出了“教育是为寻找第三个职业做准备”的口号，即要有迎接新工种的心态与储备。[6]

在此背景下，知识早已不再是力量（“知识就是力量”为培根所提），运用和转化知识的能力才是。从这个意义上讲，“通才”的价值并不低于“专才”。[7]

人们的知识与技能，大致可概括为“内化”与“外化”两种，前者一般从专业培训中获得，应用于当下任务；后者通常用来在毕业后应对新的变化，可通过各种信息和技术系统地来实现。随着信息技术的发展，“围墙内学习”将逐渐成为过去，而“移动设备学习”将伴随人们终身。[8]

事实上，走出大学校门后，完全从事自己所学专业的人不到一半，即大部分人都要根据职业需要作出某种调整。一个人的事业乃至人生是否成功，某种意义上，就取决于能否在这种“内化”与“外化”之间不断进行充实与更新。[9]

所以，“万金”不是浅薄；而“油”，若取其柔润之意，则是适应能力。“适者生存”，仍为法则。由此重新认知“万金油”，对于求学和从业，都不乏现实意义。[10]

译 文

Redefining "Jack of All Trades"

Traditionally, the derogatory saying "Jack of all trades and master of none" refers to someone who is seemingly capable of doing a lot of things but not specialized in anything. However, its connotations have now started shifting more positively in the West. [1]

It's always believed that one in pursuit of a career should acquire specialized skills in a particular field. With the rapid development of technologies, information and know-how, however, when reaching the expected professional level, one may find that it has been partially outdated and replaced. According to a book entitled *How to Succeed in the Future of Work* (2022) by Dr. Ben Hammer, an average of 37% of workplace content underwent this kind of change over the previous five years. [2]

Since the beginning of the 21st century, significant breakthroughs in various fields have come out of both highly specialized and generalized skills. In the United States, for example, interdisciplinary research which promotes the intersection of arts and sciences has made prominent progress, with a special emphasis on "soft skills" emerging in many aspects. [3]

As a developmental trend, the more specialized the knowledge and skills are, the more easily they can be replaced by technology. Surely, there will still be professionals such as accountants, engineers, doctors and nurses, but the nature of their jobs and responsibilities will undergo significant transformation. While their technical tasks will constantly be replaced by automation, "human skills" —collaboration across sections, teamwork spirit, competence in synchronizing and transforming technical issues, interpersonal communicative skills and humanistic care—will be valued more.[4]

On average American law school graduates earn $94,000 a year, but if they concurrently hold degrees in foreign languages, or religion or some other fields, their average annual salary is about $130,000. Similarly, for graduates majoring in journalism, three areas of expertise are their prerequisite to compete for positions in big media.[5]

Moreover, some experts predict that in future people are likely to engage in five different types of jobs over the course of their careers. Thus in the West, the motto "Education is to prepare for the third profession" has been put forward, laying the foundation for mindset and mental reserves to meet the challenge of newly emerging work opportunities.[6]

Against this backdrop, Bacon's suggestion that "Knowledge is power" no longer holds water; instead, the ability to apply and transform knowledge does. In this connection, the value of generalists is no less than that of specialists.[7]

People's knowledge and skills can roughly be categorized as "internal" and "external". The former is generally acquired from professional training and applied to current undertakings, while the latter usually responds to new experiences after formal education by way of deploying information and technologies systematically. Furthermore, with the development of information and technologies, "campus study" will gradually become a thing of past, while "learning on mobile devices" will accompany people for life.[8]

As a matter of fact, less than half of college diploma holders currently engage in jobs that perfectly match their majors; most of them have to make certain adjustments to meet the requirements of the job market. In a sense, the success of a person's career, or even life, largely depends on their continued efforts in enriching and renewing their internal and external knowledge and skills.[9]

In Chinese, *wan jin you* literally meaning "a balm" and is analogous to "Jack of all trades and master of none", should no longer be regarded as superficial. But if we view balm as a kind of oil to smooth things out, it perfectly connotes "adaptability" as well. Given the still valid law of "survival of the fittest", re-emphasizing the literal Chinese meaning, therefore, by no means lacks practical applicability in terms of studying and working.[10]

注 释

[3]“文理交叉”，一般译成 the cross of liberal arts and science、combination of subjects in social science and natural science 等，此处结合前面的“跨学科的研究进展突出”，译为 interdisciplinary research which promotes the intersection of arts and sciences。

[4]“更为重要”，似乎应译成 more important、more significant、more crucial 等，此处强调的是，在新形势下，相对科技而言，人际沟通、人文关怀等显得更为可贵，故用了 will be valued more。

[5]“需有”是动词，一般译成 should have、have to possess、ought to hold 等，但亦可转译为名词；“竞争力”为名词，competitive power、competitive force、competitiveness 等，但亦可转译为动词，故此处将二者结合，变通为 three areas of expertise are their prerequisite to compete for positions in big media。

[6]“心态与储备”不宜简单地分开，译成 psychology、mental state、mentality 及 reserve、store 等，而宜结合前面的内容，融合为 ...laying the foundation for mindset and mental reserves to meet...。

[7]此处的“知识已不再是力量”是活用培根的名言“知识就是力量”，翻译时可不必拘泥于原文的形式，而可将其简化、整合为 Bacon’s suggestion that “Knowledge is power” no longer holds water。

原 文

“法自然”与“自然法”的本质区别

中西传统文化里都有“法自然”与“自然法”的说法，其中都有“自然”，似乎雷同。然而，分析起来，发现它们之间有着本质的区别。[1]

老子说“人法地，地法天，天法道，道法自然”(《道德经》第25章)，但他讲的“自然”并不是现代意义上的“客观自然界”，更非自然界的普遍规律，而是事物本来状态的“自然而然”，即摒弃任何的“人为”，而崇尚“无为”。[2]

源于古希腊的“自然法”，认为客观世界中存在着自然法则，其灵魂是理性，因而自然也是人的理性来源，使人能够辨别是非，明智地进行推理和判断价值，是人神之间的桥梁。遵循理性去生活，就是遵循自然而生活。只有基于自然理性，才会产生自然正义。法律是最高的理性，因而必遵自然法则而产生。[3]

概括而言，“法自然”与“自然法”的本质区别，主要体现在以下诸点。[4]

首先，“法自然”源于天人合一理念。二程理学家说，“天人未始有二”、“道未始有天人之别，天地人只是一道”(《二程集》二、十八)，即自然秩序就是人的秩序，二者彼此交融，不可分离；故人类应刻意效法、因循自然，而不可过分自作主张。

相反，“自然法”则认为，随着人类理性知识的积累，便形成了独立于自然之外的纯理性体系；而人们独立意识的不断强化，使得他们逐渐与自然区分开来，并日益试图以人为之力作用于自然界。[5]

其次，“法自然”是一种感性的顿悟，而非理性的实证。正如老子的论断，“天下万物生于有，有生于无”（《道德经》第40章）、“道生一，一生二，二生三，三生万物”（《道德经》第42章），但这些并非基于任何客观的论证，而是出于主观神秘的冥想。有意思的是，现代科学研究竟然在某些方面对此作出了某些佐证，如英国科学家霍金的“宇宙大爆炸”理论、量子力学中的“模糊测定原理”、“真空能量”学说等。就性质而言，“自然法”是利用实证主义方法进行的逻辑推理、演绎和论证。[6]

最后，“法自然”中的“道”不是现代意义上的客观规律，更不是理性和正义的价值标准，而是一种“不可名”之物，看不见，摸不着，却又无处不在。它既存在于天之上（“天之道”），又游移于人之中（“人之道”），且二者永远不可能完全统一。“自然法”则不然，它认定基于自然法则的人类理性是一个永恒不变的法律。当人们遵守代表人类理性的自然法时，公理便会主导，秩序变得井然，社会变得稳定，一切向好发展。[7]

归根结底，二者是植根于两种不同文化传统的道德价值判断体系。当然，在当今全球化时代，在二者之间进行不同层面的沟通与整合，亦不失是一种有益的探究。[8]

译 文

The Essential Differences Between "Following Nature" and "Natural Law"

"Following nature" and "Natural law" , rooted in traditional Chinese and Western cultures respectively, seem to have something in common, since both refer to "nature/natural" . However, a careful scrutiny will reveal their essential differences.[1]

Lao Zi said that "Man follows the earth, the earth follows the heavens, the heavens follow the *Dao*, and *Dao* follows nature" (Ch. 25 of *Dao De Jing*). The "nature" he referred to here, however, is not an objective natural world in the modern sense, nor a universal law of nature as such, but rather it is the original state of things, meaning that humans should abandon any intentional actions and adore "inaction" .[2]

Originating from the ancient Greek, "Natural law" believes that there is a natural rule in the objective world with reason as its soul. In that connection, nature also provides humans with reason, enabling them to know what is right and wrong, how to reason and judge a value wisely, bridging godly and human consciousness. Following reason to live is to live naturally. Only by being based on natural reason can there be natural justice. As law is supposed to be the highest form of reason, so it must comply with the law of nature.[3]

Generally speaking, the essential differences between "Following nature" and "Natural law" may be summarized as follows.[4]

Firstly, "Following nature" originates from the concept of the unity of heaven and humans. As Neo Confucianism believes that "In the beginning, heaven and humans could not be separated" ; "They are integrated by the very same *Dao*" (quotations from the *Two Chengs' Selections*), so the natural and human orders are intertwined as one. One should therefore avoid any deliberate actions but rather follow the natural way. On the contrary, in the West, "Natural law" has gradually formulated its own rational system distinguished from nature with the accumulation of human rational knowledge. As people's consciousness became more independent, it separated them more from nature, encouraging them even to enforce their power on nature.[5]

Secondly, "Following nature" is a perceptual epiphany rather than a rational empirical approach. As stated by Lao Zi, "All things under heaven are born of existence, while existence comes from nothingness" (Ch. 40 of *Dao De Jing*); "Dao produced unity, unity produced duality; duality produced trinity, and trinity produced all existing objects" (Ch. 42 of *Dao De Jing*)... but none of these were based on any objective argument, simply on mysterious subjective meditation. Interestingly, modern scientific research has provided some supporting evidence for this in certain respects, such as the "Big

Bang" theory proposed by British scientist Hawking, the "Fuzzy Measurement Principle" in quantum mechanics, "Vacuum Energy" theory and so on. In nature, "Natural law" is logical reasoning, deduction and argumentation using an empirical approach.[6]

Finally, the *Dao* in "Following nature" is not an objective law as stated in any modern sense, nor is it a value judgment for nationality and justice, but it is unnamed, invisible and ubiquitous. It exists both in the heavens (the "way of heaven") and among humans (the "way of humanity") and the two can never be completely unified. "Natural law" , on the other hand, holds that human rationality based on natural rules is an eternal law. When such kind of rationality prevails, axioms will dominate, everything will be in order, society will be stabilized, all will be progressing smoothly.[7]

Ultimately, the two are moral value judgmental systems rooted in two different cultural traditions. Surely, in the current era of globalization, it is advisable to communicate between the two and combine their merits.[8]

注 释

[2] "人法地，地法天，天法道，道法自然"，似还可译成 Human follows land, land follows sky, sky follows Taoism, Taoism follows nature.，但 man 是相对 nature 而言的，同时"道"是中国哲学特有的概念，故宜译为 *Dao*。同时，"无为"还可

译为 inactivity 或 letting things take their own course。

[3]“桥梁”本为名词，但此处根据具体语境，不妨变通为动词 bridging，作伴随状语。

[5]“彼此交融”，似还可译成 mingle/blend/fuse one another、they cross barriers and their identities are flexible 等。同时，此处的“自作主张”不必特意译成 self-assertion、decide for themselves、take liberties、handle matters on their own 等，而应融合在 should therefore avoid any deliberate actions 之中。

[6]“顿悟”似还可译成 insight、sudden enlightenment、aha 等，此处根据“法自然”的中国传统哲学性质，选用了 epiphany，其本义为 a moment of sudden insight or understanding。

[8]“有益的探究”，字面意思似可译成 a useful inquiry 或 profitably explore into... 等，此处将其含义融汇在 it is advisable to（communicate between the two and combine their merits）之中。

原　文

“轴心时代”的启示

公元前 500 年前后，在中国、希腊、印度同时产生了一批大思想家，如孔子、苏格拉底、释迦牟尼等，奠定了人类文明的三大中心。德国哲学家雅斯贝尔斯在《历史的起源与目标》（1949 年）中称此时期为“轴心时代”。[1]

就此现象的成因，学术界的研究至今莫衷一是，但所持共识是，“轴心时代”对之后中西文化的性质，乃至整个社会的发展，具有巨大而深远的影响。[2]

在“轴心时代”，中国文化先是经历了从殷商时代的尊神事鬼的巫觋精神向周代的尊礼敬德宗法精神的转化，之后又过渡到了春秋战国时期的注重内省的伦理精神，而这些是在孔子的“仁”与孟子的“四端之心”教化下完成的。从此，中国文化走上了一条道德内敛的道路，修身、齐家、治国、平天下，即“内圣而外王”。[3]

同样在“轴心时代”，西方文化主要发生了从自然崇拜的希腊多神教、律法主义的犹太教向唯灵主义的基督教的转化，即是一个外在的灵魂超越过程。由于人们把眼光转向了天国，于是从此形成了西方文化的一种注重彼岸世界的进取精神。[4]

在学术界，由于中国传统文化注重人与人之间的伦理规范，故而称为“伦理文化”，而西方传统文化注重人与上帝之间的信仰关系，又被称为“宗教文化”。由此，形成了中西文化的分水岭。[5]

不同文化对社会发展带来的影响，诚如梁漱溟在《东西文化及其哲学》(1921年)所论:“中国人随遇而安，得到一点快乐便享受一点快乐，不像西方人那样风驰电掣般地向前追逐。”由此，中国传统文化的主体精神，既对中国封建文化的繁盛起到积极促进作用，也对中国在近代的发展起到某些消极作用。[6]

特别是15世纪后，欧洲兴起的文艺复兴运动和宗教改革，进一步发扬光大了这种进取精神，促进了人性的复苏，推动了社会的转型。从17世纪开始，新兴的资产阶级在政治领域全面取代封建贵族统治后，又在经济领域掀起了变革高潮，这便是工业革命。18世纪后，西方社会正式进入了工业文明时代。[7]

与此同时，与世界上其他非西方国家和地区一样，中国开始受到西方文化的渗透。从利玛窦等人的来华传教，到鸦片战争的爆发，打破了华夏紧闭的国门和保守的心理。其应对的方式，先是“师夷长技以制夷”、“中学为体，西学为用”、洋务运动等技术变革，后有戊戌变法、辛亥革命等政治变革，最后导致“新文化”等中国式的思想启蒙运动。[8]

当然，中国最大规模的思想启蒙始于20世纪70年代末的改革开放，随后带动了全面的经济体制改革。经过40余年的艰辛探索，终于走上了中国式现代化之路。[9]

在某种意义上，如今世界正经历着“新轴心时代”。回顾历史，审视中西文化的发展历程，汲取过往宝贵的思想资源，对于把握规律、更有效地应对新时代的各种挑战，意义重大。[10]

译 文

Implications of the "Axis Age"

Around 500 BC, a group of great thinkers, such as Confucius, Socrates and Shakyamuni, emerged in China, Greece and India at roughly the same time, forming three major centers of human civilization. This period of time was referred to as the "Axis Age" by the German philosopher Jaspers in *The Origins and Objectives of History* (1949).[1]

Concerning the causes of this phenomenon, while there are still different insights among academics, the consensus is that the "Axis Age" had a profound and far-reaching impact on shaping the nature and development of Chinese and Western cultures, even their societies, as a whole.[2]

In the "Axis Age", Chinese culture first underwent a transformation from the much older spirit of respecting gods and ghosts in the Shang Dynasties (1600 BC-1046 BC) to the spirit of respecting etiquette and morality in the Zhou Dynasty (1046 BC-256 BC), and then transitioned to the ethical ethos of introspection in the Spring-Autumn and the Warring States periods (770 BC-221 BC) under the doctrines of Confucius' "benevolence" and Mencius'

"Four-Instinctive Kindnesses" , before it embarked on the path of moral soul searching. Namely, following the way of "sageness within and kingliness without" —cultivating the moral self, managing both family unity and order in the state, and bringing peace to the world.[3]

Roughly during the same period, Western culture mainly transformed from the Nature worship of Greek polytheism, through legalist Judaism to spiritualist Christianity, which was an external process of making the soul transcendent. As people's inspiration shifted towards the Heavenly Kingdom, a kind of enterprising spirit focusing on the other world was encouraged in the West.[4]

In academic circles, traditional Chinese culture is also called an "ethical culture" since it is rooted in people's relationships, while Western culture is known as a "religious culture" due to its relationship of faith between people and their God. As a result, a watershed was formed between Chinese and Western cultures.[5]

In his book entitled *Eastern and Western Cultures and Philosophies* (1921), Liang Shuming commented on the impact of the two cultures on social development: "Chinese people are so easily satisfied and enjoy whatever happiness they get, unlike Westerners who always chase forward like lightning." In this sense, while the subject spirit of traditional Chinese culture might have played a positive role in promoting the prosperity of Chinese feudal culture, it has also influenced its social development, partly negatively, in modern times.[6]

Especially after the 15th century, the Renaissance and Religious Reform in Europe further carried forward this enterprising spirit, and thus promoted the recovery of human nature and social transformation. Since the 17th century, having replaced the feudal aristocracy in politics, the emerging bourgeoisie set off a revolution in the economic field—the "Industrial Revolution". The late 18th century witnessed the entire Western society entering into the era of industrial civilization.[7]

At the same time, like other non-Western cultures and regions in the world, China began to be infiltrated by Western culture. From Matteo Ricci and others' early missionary work in China to the outbreak of the Opium War, China's closed doors and conservative mentality were being broken through. Confronted with the challenge, China initially adopted the strategies of "learning advanced technologies from the opponents and using them to fight back", "Chinese learning is required for fundamental principles, while Western learning is to be acquired for practical purposes", followed by the Westernization Movement and other technological reforms, which finally led to a certain kind of Chinese "enlightenment" represented by the "New Culture Movement".[8]

Surely, the largest ideological enlightenment in China began with the reform and opening up in the late 1970s, followed by sweeping economic reforms. After more than 40 years of painstaking exploration, China finally embarked on the road of Chinese-style modernization.[9]

In a sense, the world now is experiencing a "New Axis Age". Reviewing the histories of Chinese and Western cultures, examining their respective developmental processes, and drawing valuable ideological resources from the past, are all of great significance in mastering the inherent "developmental law" involved and dealing with various challenges more effectively in the new era.[10]

注 释

[3] "修身、齐家、治国、平天下"，可有多种译法，如 cultivate oneself, regulate the family, govern the state, and pacify the world/self-cultivation, a well-managed family, and the ability to administer the state and to bring peace to the nation 等，但应更强调 self 的性质，而"齐""治"可用同一词 managing；至于"天下"，实有狭义和广义之分，分别指中国与世界，故变通为 cultivating the moral self, managing both family unity and order in the state, and bringing peace to the world。

[4] "彼岸世界"似乎是个神秘词语。在中国古代文化里，彼岸世界指的是人死后灵魂所在之地，而在现代西方文化中，彼岸世界则被赋予了更广泛的含义，指的是一个超越现实的世界，是一种超自然的存在；在那里，人们可以看到超越现实的景象，感受到超越现实的存在。对此，有的译成 on the other side of the world、our different worlds 等，此处简化为

on the other world。

[8]“师夷长技以制夷”有着多种译法，如 beat someone by playing his games in better ways、learning merits from foreign to conquer the foreign、studying the foreign skills to deal with them、learn from foreigners to compete with foreigners 等，此处为更加符合其历史语境，译为: learning advanced technologies from the opponents and using them to fight back ;“中学为体，西学为用”似亦可译成 Chinese learning for the essence and western learning for practical use、traditional Chinese values aided with modern Western technologies、Chinese ideology is maintained as foundation while Western technologies are acquired as useful tools 等，此处将其变通为 Chinese learning is required for fundamental principles, while Western learning is to be acquired for practical purposes。

[10]“……意义重大”，此句不宜按原文顺序译成 ...are very important/significant，而可将其语序调整，译为 Reviewing the histories of Chinese and Western cultures, examining..., and drawing..., are all of great significance in..., 以求更符合英文的表述方式。

原 文

中国文化里的“醉”与“醒”

汉字的“醉”与“醒”都是“酉”字旁;“酉”原指酒器。《说文》:“醉,酒卒也”;“醒,醉解也”。换言之,“醉”指饮酒过量,“醒”则是酒醉之后脱离酒的控制、回归平静之态。故在中国传统文化里,“醉”与“醒”都基于“酒”;“醒”直接源于“醉”,因若无“醉”便无所谓“醒”,于是“醉”成了理解“醒”的前提。[1]

醉的过程,如《庄子·大宗师》所述:“堕肢体,黜聪明,离形去知,同于大通。”可以说,一场醉便是一种“形而上”,即形之飘忽;而醉之醒,则是一种“形而下”,即形之复原,回到现实。[2]

过度饮酒而醉,便会失去自我意识和正常的行为能力,飘然地忘身、无我,直至无知、无为、无欲。经历醉而醒,并不是脱离醉,而是植根于醉,从醉的体验中提炼新知;醒是对醉的升华。深沉的醉留存在意识里,而醒不过是游历醉体验后的残余。醒的程度,取决于醉的深度。醒是身体和精神秩序在生理机能上的恢复。因而,植根于醉的醒,并非醉前意识的简单恢复,而是飘飘然后无我状态的一种新认知。[3]

最初的醉是指在酒作用下，人对外界失去辨别能力，物我一体。之后是对特定对象的沉入、迷陷，失去独立的自我判断力，人与对象距离完全消弭，踏入“沉醉”。相应地，最初的醒，是指身心摆脱酒和相关对象的影响而恢复理性，进而复原之前独立分辨、判断的能力，称为“觉醒”。[4]

醉醒之后也会有“悔”，映衬出醉酒中精神活动之丰富。后悔的本质是因醉与醒之间存在某种价值观或理想状态的对立。醒虽基于醉，但醒者走出醉后，往往开始否定醉。醉是“迷失的我”，醒是“更新的我”。[5]

就道德和理想而言，“醉”是消极、逃避的，而“醒”则是积极、进取的。因而，在屈原看来，尽管绝大多数人并不饮酒，似是“醒着”，但其实却是“醉着”，故曰“举世皆浊我独清，众人皆醉我独醒”（《楚辞·渔父》）。虽然屈原并不反对饮酒，也不反感“酎饮尽欢”，但他更知摆脱酒醉而保持清醒的可贵。[6]

另类的是，道家欣赏“醉”，不提倡“醒”，甚至“但愿长醉不愿醒”，因为“醒者多苦志，醉者多欢情”，认为只有在“醉”中才能使分化的身心得以“神全”。这不免体现出其对现实世界认知的局限。[7]

孟子将“是非之心”作为人性之一端，而酒醉之后，可使人心智昏扰，确有迷乱人本性一面。明代大儒徐阶说：“人未饮酒时，事事清楚；到醉后，事事昏忘；及酒醒后，照旧清楚。乃知昏忘是酒，清楚是心之本然。人苟不利欲迷其本心，则于事断无昏忘之患。克己二字，此醒酒方也。”[8]

当今，基于传统文化和现代科技的认知，在日常生活中，对于酌饮的程度、“醉”与“醒”的把握，人们自然应当作出更为理智的决断。[9]

译 文

“Intoxication” and “Sobriety” in Chinese Culture

The characters for “intoxication” (*zui*) and “sobriety” (*xing*) both have the *you* radical, originally referring to wine vessels. According to the *Analytical Dictionary of Characters*, *zui* means the end process of drinking, while *xing* denotes sobering up from drunkenness. In other words, “intoxication” refers to excessive drinking, while “sobriety” signifies returning to tranquility after getting over the influence of alcohol. Therefore, in traditional Chinese culture, both “intoxication” and “sobriety” are related to the concept of “wine”, where the latter directly stems from the former, and the two are coexistent.[1]

The process of being drunk is described in “Great Master” of Zhuang Zi’s *The Book of Master Zhuang* as “losing physical sensations, intellectual stagnation, departing from both norms and common sense, as well as merging with the great *Dao*”. In a sense, it may be said that intoxication involves things “metaphysical”, while sobriety implies return to a “physical” state.[2]

Excessive drinking and intoxication will lead drinkers to loss of self-awareness and normal everyday competence, resulting in a state of oblivion, only to find themselves lacking cognition, action and desires. Meanwhile, awakening from drunkenness does not mean completely breaking away from intoxication, but rather it derives new insights from the experience of being intoxicated. In a way, sobriety is sublimation of intoxication. As the haunting experience of drunkenness remains in consciousness, awakening from it is merely the residue of traversing the intoxicated state, in which the degree of awakening depends on the degree of drunkenness. Biologically, awakening signifies the restoration of bodily and mental order. In this way, sobriety emerges from intoxication not simply as a refurbishment of the previous consciousness, but as a new vision refreshed within the oblivion.[3]

Initially, getting intoxicated refers to losing the ability to discern things linking the self to others under the influence of alcohol. Subsequently, it involves immersion in and enthrallment with specific objects, losing independent judgment, and erasing the distance between the ego and its surroundings, leading to "ecstasy". Similarly, the initial state of sobriety suggests regaining the sense of reasoning, free from any influence of alcohol and related objects, and furthermore to restore the abilities to self-sufficiently discern and judge, described as "awakened consciousness".[4]

Being awakened from drunkenness, one may feel guilty, reflecting the plenitude of mental activities during intoxication.

Essentially, this kind of regret is caused by the conflict between values or ideal states during intoxication and sobriety. Although the latter is rooted in the former, as mentioned above, those who awaken tend to negate things fancied in drunkenness after coming out of it. Really, intoxication embodies the "lost self" , while sobriety symbolizes the "renewed self" .[5]

In terms of morality and ideology, "intoxication" is seen as negative and escapist, while "sobriety" is viewed as positive and proactive. To Qu Yuan (340 BC-278 BC), a renowned poet in ancient China, even though most of people do not drink alcohol, appearing to be "awakened" , they are actually "intoxicated" in one way or another. As he described in his poem: "Contrasting with the murky world, my purity is brought out; as the crowd is intoxicated, I solely retain my sobriety" ("Fisherman" from *The Songs of Chu*). Despite Qu Yuan did not opposing drinking and even enjoying "drinking to the fullest" , he truly valued the sober mind remaining during intoxications.[6]

In an alternative view of the issue, Taoism strongly advocates intoxication with no mention whatsoever of sobriety. Taoists even express a wish to remain drunk forever, and never to be awakened by anyone, as "the sober-minded are often burdened with aspirations, while the intoxicated revel in joy" , believing that only in a state of intoxication, can the fragmented body and mind achieve their spiritual wholeness. Inevitably, this kind of perception in fact reflects a limited comprehension of reality.[7]

Mencius considered the "core of distinguishing right and wrong" as part of human nature, and that intoxication can actually confuse the mind and distort human nature. Xu Jie (1503-1583), a renowned Confucian in the Ming Dynasty (1368-1644), remarked that "Before drinking, everything is clear; when drunk, everything is confused. Upon awakening, clarity is restored. It is understood that clarity is inherent in the mind, which can be bewildered by alcohol. Once people are in control of their desires, in no way can they be muddleheaded. Self-control is thus the key to sobering up from any intoxication".[8]

Nowadays, with the blend of traditional culture and modern scientific understanding, people are surely capable of making more rational judgments on how much alcohol to consume and the balance between "intoxication" and "sobriety" in their daily lives.[9]

注 释

[1]"醉"与"醒"似可译成drunk和wake，但译文中选用的intoxication和sobriety更合适。其中，intoxication意为the state of being seriously drunk，sobriety意为the state of being sober rather than drunk。

"平静"一般可译成calmness、serenity、quietness、stillness等，但tranquility的本义为a disposition free from stress or emotion，

故此处更宜使用 tranquility。

［2］“大通”，似可译成 the great flow，但此处的“通”实则指的是“道”，故译为 *Dao*。

［3］“忘身”不是简单的 lost the self，而是指失去自我意识，译为 loss of self-awareness。

［4］此处的“觉醒”对应前面的“沉醉”，故有别于 awakening、sobriety，用了“awakened consciousness”。

［5］此处的“悔”固然有 regret、remorse、repent 之意，但更进一层的为 feel guilty。

［6］“举世皆浊我独清，众人皆醉我独醒”，字面意思固然是 Everyone is turbid, I am alone and clear; Everyone is drunk, I am the only one who is awake.，但还应有前后对比，以更加连贯：Contrasting with the murky world, my purity is brought out; as the crowd is intoxicated, I solely retain my sobriety.

［7］“但愿长醉不愿醒”，似还可有多种译法，如 Hopes to be drunk long and not willing to awake、I only wish to get drunk and never to be awake 等，此处简化为 a wish to remain drunk forever。

［8］此处的“心”固然可译成 heart、conscious、consciousness；但亦不妨译出更深一层含义，即其核心、实质，故用了 the core（of distinguishing right and wrong）。

［9］“酌饮的程度”，不宜简单译成 the degree of discretionary drinking，而可变通为 how much alcohol to consume。

原　文

国难中的学术追求

读完巨著《南渡北归》（三部），不禁掩卷长叹！当年中国知识精英在战火纷飞的民族危难中，不断逃亡，却从未放弃过学术追求，其中一幅幅悲壮画面，难以忘怀。[1]

1937 年 7 月 7 日卢沟桥事变爆发，北平（今北京）旋即沦陷。此时的日本侵略者十分清楚，要彻底击垮一个民族，除动用武力在政治、经济、军事诸方面予以摧毁，更重要的是精神上的彻底征服。7 月 29 日下午，日军窜入北平城西北郊树木参天的清华园，数次以参观为名，将窃取的大批珍贵图书、仪器设备用卡车装运出校园。与此同时，南开大学校园内弹如雨下，几十万册宝贵图书和珍稀资料灰飞烟灭。这所由著名教育家张伯苓创办、靠各界人士赞助，经过千辛万苦发展起来的中国当时最杰出的私立大学，成为一片废墟；时已转往南京的张伯苓闻此凶讯，老泪纵横，当场昏厥。7 月 31 日，蒋介石约见张伯苓，悲愤地表示："南开为中国而牺牲，有中国即有南开。"[2]

随即，中国开始了史诗般的学界大转移。平津科学界、教育界人士纷纷南迁；同时，坐落在上海、南京的国立同济大学、国立中央研究院、国立中央大学等科学机关、教育机构，也纷纷启动了西迁历程。这当中，发生了多少可歌可泣的事迹！[3]

梁思成、林徽因仓皇收拾了几箱学术资料及简单的随身换洗衣服，便领着年幼的儿女，告别北平北总布胡同三号，踏上了艰难的逃难之旅。此前医生曾警告林徽因，说她病弱的身体难以承受千里奔徙的颠沛流离之苦，但面对严酷的现实，她悲戚地答道："我的命是由天的了！"在天津乘船前，梁思成无法预料自己和家人的前途命运，遂将他此前用英文写就的几篇关于发现古建筑的学术论文及林徽因写的信，一同寄给美国朋友费慰梅，请她设法帮助在国外发表，并附上一张纸条："我们打算坐船到青岛，从那里途经济南，去到换车船不超过五次的任何地方——最好是长沙，而这期间尽可能不要遇上空袭。等到战争打赢了，我们就可以结束逃难生涯。"没想到，他们到了长沙后，再转昆明，最后流落到一个未曾听说过的偏僻地方——四川南溪李庄，隐居了下来。[4]

李庄地方闭塞，生活条件极其艰苦，学术研究遭遇的困难比想象的大得多。林徽因刚到此地时，主要整理几年前在山西五台山佛光寺考察所作的记录及其他古建筑材料，想写一部古代建筑史，但因肺结核病多次复发，常常低烧，进展缓慢。之后，即便在种种病痛折磨中，她还是完成了学术价值极高的论文《现代住宅设计的参考》，在《中国营造学社汇刊》第七卷第二期发表。[5]

国学大师陈寅恪在这场逃难中，历尽艰辛，饱受磨难。他曾将一批花费无数心血、用蝇头小楷批注的珍贵书籍，装箱运往云南，但到达之后打开，发现箱内只有砖头数块，书籍全无！见此惨状，陈寅恪当场昏倒。如同一场大病恢复后，他并未被当时贫瘠、不断跑警报的恶劣条件所打垮，而是拖着病体，靠一只几近失明的眼睛，备课、写讲义，承担起历史语言研究所历史组、西南联大、燕京大学文科研究所等职责内的各门课程，而且还居然完成了奠定其世界级学术大师地位的不朽名著——《隋唐制度渊源略论稿》。[6]

甲骨学大师董作宾，随逃难队伍来李庄后，蛰居在板栗牌坊巷里，在极其简陋的条件下，继续他过往十几年的艰苦研究，终于完成了在甲骨学史上具有里程碑意义的鸿篇巨制《殷历谱》，并在李庄镇石印出版。陈寅恪阅毕，盛赞："抗战八年，学术界著作当以尊著为第一部书，决无疑议也。"[7]

同样迁到李庄的中央研究院历史语言研究所所长傅斯年为该所拟定的目标是："培养学术研究的种子，为国家学术事业延续香火。"著名诗人徐志摩说，那时青年学者心中装的是"新文化，科学救国，振兴民族"一类的理想抱负。[8]

27 岁的李济，在哈佛大学拿到了哲学博士学位，此为第一位中国人获此殊荣，但他旋即收拾行装，告别了风景秀丽的查尔斯河畔，穿过波涌浪滚的浩瀚大洋，作为"海归"回到了多灾多难的祖国。多年后他说，"那时的中国留学生，都是在毕业之后就回国的。他们在回国之后，选择职业的时候，也没有人考虑到赚多少钱和养家糊口的问题。我就是在当年这种留学风气之下，选择了我所喜爱的学科——人类学"。之后，他到各地进行田野发掘，风餐露宿，采集了数十箱出土器物，完好保存到清华国学研究院，奠定了中国现代考古学的基石。[9]

童第周在比利时获得科学博士学位（生物学）后，达克教授让他再等一年，写一篇论文，便可再得一个特别博士学位，但他急于归国效力，婉言拒绝了。回国不久，他便加入了逃难大军。在李庄，只有简陋的仪器，没有电，点菜油灯，只能利用下雪天的光线或太阳光在破旧的显微镜下做点实验。他带着学生下稻田，捕捉青蛙，收集蛙卵，进行胚胎实验，写出了数篇高质量的论文并得以发表，引起了国内外生物学界的瞩目。当时，英国著名生物化学家李约瑟来到李庄，惊讶地问童第周："你就是用这样的器材在这片空地上完成了那样高难度的实验吗？简直不可思议！"[10]

同济大学迁来李庄之前，川南一带流行一种当地人称之为"麻脚瘟"的疾病，一旦染上该病，患者就会从脚部开始发麻，并伴有呕吐、腹泻等症状；当麻的感觉蔓延到胸部以上，立即死亡。同济大学医学院唐哲教授经与其他医生会诊，并通过对动物反复实验、研究，查明其病因是食用盐中的氯化钡所引起的慢性中毒，于是找到了根治办法。李庄人们欢欣鼓舞，奔走相告。该研究成果《痹病之研究》，荣获国民政府教育部 1943 年全国应用科学类发明一等奖，因而挽救了成千上万人的性命。[11]

多年后，李约瑟写出了闻名于世的皇皇巨著《中国科学技术史》。他说，当年他在中国的穷乡僻壤里，见到了一群中国最杰出的学者。的确，他们无论是在物质上还是精神上，都赢得了那场战争。[12]

《南渡北归》的封面题目下方写着"大师远去再无大师"。其实，大师虽去，但他们并未走远。他们当年留下的文化、学术种子，历经磨难，没有枯萎，而是深植土壤，开花结果，惠及至今。[13]

译 文

Academic Pursuits in National Crises

After reading the magnum opus *Strategic Transferrals* (3 volumes) I can't help but sigh deeply. Many historical scenarios depicted in this book, where Chinese intellectual elites were constantly fleeing in the midst of national crises while never giving up their academic pursuits, are truly unforgettable.[1]

On July 7, 1937, the Lugou Bridge Incident occurred, and Peiping (now Beijing) soon fell. The Japanese aggressors knew very well at that time that in order to completely defeat a nation, apart from conquering its people militarily, politically and economically, it was even more important to subjugate them in their minds. On the afternoon of July 29, the Japanese army stormed into Tsinghua University in the northwest suburbs of Peiping City and, under the pretext of visiting the place, stole a large number of precious books, instruments and equipment from the tree-covered campus using trucks. At the same time, Nankai University, the most outstanding private university in China, founded by the famous educator Zhang Boling, sponsored by people from all walks of life and developed through uncountable hardships, was bombarded and ruined by the

Japanese, with hundreds of thousands of valuable books and rare materials going up in smoke. Upon hearing the bad news, Zhang Boling, who had already returned to Nanjing at the time, burst into tears and fainted on the spot. On July 31, Chiang Kai-shek, then the national leader, made an appointment with Zhang Boling and expressed his grief and indignation: "Nankai sacrificed for China, and China will never give up on Nankai." [2]

Consequently, China began an epic academic shift. Professionals from scientific and educational circles in Peiping and Tianjin were moving one after another to the south; meanwhile, scientific and educational institutions such as National Tongji University, the National Academy of Central Research, and the National Central University, all located in Shanghai and Nanjing, had also started their westward migration process. During this historical period, many touching stories transpired.[3]

Liang Sicheng and Lin Huiyin hastily packed up several boxes of academic materials and simple personal clothes, then took along their young kids to bid farewell to No. 3 Beizongbu Alley in Peiping and embarked on a difficult journey of escape. Previously, a doctor had warned Lin Huiyin that her poor health couldn't withstand the hardships of thousands of miles of migration. Facing the harsh reality, however, she could only reply: "My life is up to heaven now!" Before boarding a ship in Tianjin, being uncertain about his family's fate, Liang Sicheng sent several academic papers written in English about discovering ancient architecture, enclosed with Lin Huiyin's letters to their American friend Wilma Fairbank, asking her to try her best to help publish the papers, and attached a note: "We plan to sail to Qingdao, pass through Jinan from there to any place, preferably Changsha, where we will change trains or ships no more than five times while avoiding air strikes as much as possible on the way. Hopefully, once the war is won, we will end our escape journey." Unexpectedly, after arriving in Changsha, they then turned to Kunming and finally settled in a secluded place they had never heard of before—Li Zhuang village in Nanxi, Sichuan province, where they lived in seclusion.[4]

So unbearably barren and harsh were the living conditions in Li Zhuang that it was difficult to carry out any academic research. As previously planned, Lin Huiyin mainly intended to collate the records and other ancient building materials collected during her fieldwork from Foguang Temple in Wutai Mountain, Shanxi Province a few years previously, in the hope of writing a book on the History of China's Ancient Architecture. However, the relapse of her tuberculosis, accompanied with low fever from time to time, caused the writing process to be painfully slow. Nevertheless, she did manage to complete a paper of high academic value, entitled "References of Modern Housing", which was published in the *Journal of China Construction Society* (Vol. 7 II), despite all the ailments she endured.[5]

Chen Yinke, the master of traditional Chinese culture, also went through a variety of adversities in his escape. He once packed and transported a batch of precious books, annotated in his painstakingly written regular tiny script, to Yunnan province. However, upon opening the package, he found only a few bricks in the box, with no books at all! He was totally shocked by the horrible scene and fainted on the ground. After recovering from a seemingly serious illness, he was not to be defeated by the tough conditions of poverty and constantly running air-raid warnings; but rather, he dragged his sick body, relying on his one nearly blind eye to prepare lessons, write handouts and lecture for the Department of History at the History and Language Research Institute, the Southwest United University, and the Institute of Liberal Arts of Yenching University. Moreover, he even completed his immortal masterpiece—*Outline of the Origin of the System of the Sui and Tang Dynasties*, which established his status as a world-class scholar.[6]

Dong Zuobin, a distinguished scholar of oracle bone science, lived in the Chestnut Memorial Archway Alley after going to Li Zhuang following the escaping crowd. Under extremely grimy conditions, Dr. Dong continued his hard research that had been carrying out over the past ten years or so, and finally completed his monumental work *Calendar of the Yin Dynasty*, a landmark in the history of oracle bone studies, which was published by Li Zhuang Town's Stone Press. After reading it, Chen Yinke praised: "This book can definitely be described as the number one academic work during the eight years of Anti-Japanese War." [7]

The ultimate goal set by Fu Sinian, Dean of the History and Language Research Institute of the Central Research Institute, who also fled to Li Zhuang, was to preserve and cultivate "seeds" of academic research in order to further revitalize it as a national career in the future. The famous poet Xu Zhimo said, Chinese young scholars at that time were almost all filled with the ideal aspirations of "rejuvenating our nation by way of promoting new cultures and applying modern science" .[8]

Li Ji, 27, had earned his PhD from Harvard University, the first Chinese to receive such an honor in the USA. However, he immediately packed up and bid farewell to the picturesque banks of the Charles River and returned to his troubled motherland as a "returned scholar" , crossing the vast ocean with violent waves. Years later, he said, "At that time, Chinese students studying abroad all returned home upon their graduation. When choosing careers, they rarely considered how much money they could make to support their families. It was in that atmosphere that I chose my favorite subject—anthropology—as my career." Afterwards, he went to various places for fieldwork, living in the wilderness to excavate and collect dozens of boxes of unearthed artifacts, which were all well preserved at the Tsinghua Academy of Chinese Studies, laying the foundation for modern Chinese archaeology.[9]

After Tong Dizhou obtained his doctorate in science (biology) in Belgium, his supervisor Professor Darke asked him to wait another year and write a thesis so that he could receive another special doctorate. However, he politely declined since he was so eager to return to his motherland to serve. Soon after his return, sadly he joined the exodus. In Li Zhuang, there were only a few pieces of rudimentary equipment, no electricity, only vegetable oil lamps. In the light from the snowy days or sunlight, he conducted some experiments under a tatty microscope. He took his students to rice paddies to capture frogs, using their eggs as the source materials for his embryo experiments. Dr. Tong then wrote several high-quality papers that were later published, attracting the attention of biological circles at home and abroad. The famous British biochemist Joseph Needham also came to Li Zhuang during that time. Surprised by Dr. Tong's achievement, he asked him: "Did you use this kind of equipment to accomplish such difficult experiments on such primitive land? It's incredible!" [10]

Before the relocation of National Tongji University to Li Zhuang, a disease known as "foot numbness plague" was prevalent in the southern Sichuan region. Once infected with the disease, the feeling of numbness started from the feet of the patients, accompanied by vomiting and diarrhea, then spread throughout the patient's body. Once numbness extended over the chest, death followed immediately. Professor Tang Zhe from the Medical College of the same University, after consulting with other doctors and repeatedly conducting various experiments and analyses on animals, found that the cause was the chronic poisoning by barium chloride contained in edible salt, and consequently a radical cure was formulated. The people in Li Zhuang were exultant and passed the good news from mouth to mouth. The research resulted in an academic paper entitled "Research on An Arthromyodynia" , which won the first prize for "National Applied Science Invention 1943" awarded by the Ministry of Education of the National Government. Ever since, it has saved countless people's lives.[11]

Years later, Joseph Needham wrote his world-renowned masterpiece—*Science and Technology in China.* He recalled that he met a group of China's most distinguished scholars in the remote and impoverished areas of China back then; indeed, they won the war both substantively and mentally.[12]

Under the title on the cover of this book, it reads "As the masters have all gone, there are no more masters" . In fact, although the masters have gone, they have not gone far. The cultural and academic seeds they left behind have gone through tremendous hardships and sufferings but have not withered. Instead, they were planted deep into the soil and bore fruits, which have been benefiting us up to now.[13]

注 释

[1] 书名《南渡北归》不宜按字面意思译成 Crossing South and

Returning North，而应根据其实际含义，概述为 Strategic Transferrals。

[2]“有中国即有南开”，不宜按字面意思简单地译成 There is China, there Nankai，此处反译为 China will never give up on Nankai。

[6] 此处的“论稿”不是一般意义上的 draft，它实际上是一部专著，因而译为 Outline。

[8]“新文化，科学救国，振兴民族”，不宜按原文词序译成 new culture, saving the country scientifically, and revitalizing the nation，而应根据其内在含义，作词序调整，即主旨是 rejuvenate the nation，而途径是（通过）“新文化，科学救国”，同时增加必要的动词，因而译为 rejuvenating our nation by way of promoting new cultures and applying modern science。

[12] 此处的“精神上”似乎是 spiritually，但这里更多是指文化、学术、智力、教育等方面，故用了 mentally。

原 文

反省与忏悔

反省与忏悔，都是个人内心活动的一种反思过程。中国人多用“反省”，西方人常说“忏悔”，既有相通之处，也有细微差异。[1]

孔子说，“吾日三省吾身：为人谋而不忠乎？与朋友交而不信乎？传不习乎？”《中庸》讲“君子慎独”，《了凡四训》更是强调“务要日日知非，日日改过。一日不知非，即一日安于自是；一日无过可改，即一日无步可进”。这些是典型的中国式的反省。[2]

在西方，有古希腊神话俄狄浦斯对于杀父娶母的忏悔，有著名的由奥古斯丁、卢梭、托尔斯泰分别写的三大《忏悔录》，有基督教文化定期到教堂对着神父忏悔的习俗，更有诸如德国前总理勃兰特在波兰犹太人纪念碑前下跪谢罪的现代当众忏悔行为。这些是典型的西方式忏悔。[3]

粗略看来，中国式的反省与西方式的忏悔大致有这样一些差别：首先，程度不同，反省一般是指对平时过失，即没有造成重大伤害后果的事情所作的反思，而忏悔是指对造成重大的不可挽回的损失乃至罪责的悔愧。其次，方式不同，反省是一种日常自我身心的修炼，是私密的，大凡不对外人讲，是自己认识、醒悟、纠错的过程，而忏悔则通常要面对神灵、造物主或其代表（如牧师）、受害对象，以求外力的宽恕。再次，重点不同，反省的后果通常是可以弥补的，以便扬长避短，发挥潜能，比以往做得更好，忏悔的意义不在弥补过失，而在洗礼过去的罪孽。[4]

英国著名哲学家、数学家罗素，虽出身贵族，但幼年父母双亡，由祖父母抚养。祖母的一条箴言，成为他一生内心检讨的尺度——“永不可追随众人做坏事”，由此他要求自己不要撒谎，因为撒了一句谎后，为了掩饰，不得不撒更多的谎。法国前总统戴高乐是位著名的“戒烟将军”。1947 年 11 月 28 日，年近花甲的他当众宣布戒烟，此前他每天吸烟 3 盒，但自宣布之日到他逝世的 23 年里，他再没吸一支烟。有人问他成功戒烟的秘诀，他回答：“我从内心深处意识到，保养好自己的身体是对法国的责任，因而绝不对自己的舒适习惯妥协！”这些，若没有时时的反省和高度的自律，是绝难做到的。[5]

有时，“过”与“罪”之间的界限又是模糊的。2013 年 8 月，美国前总统小布什身体不适，住进医院。进行心脏搭桥手术前，他把妻子劳拉叫到身边，拉着手向她坦诚：有件事已在心中辗转反思多年，今天请求妻子原谅，那就是在他担任总统时，曾在一段时期内对国务卿赖斯女士，有着情感上的暧昧。这原是他内心深处的潜意识，世上本无人知晓，包括赖斯女士本人，但小布什是虔诚的基督徒，这种“情感过失”，对于他的主，就是隐藏的罪，也必须面对被伤害的至亲进行忏悔。经上说，忧伤痛悔的心，上帝必不会轻看！这样，原本在常人看来是一般的过错，通过反省升华，深藏在心中的罪便在忏悔中释然了。[6]

人在世上生活、做事，有着七情六欲，受着各种纷扰、诱惑，一定会犯错误，这些并不可怕，因为那只是一时迷失的正常现象。重要的在于及时反思、醒悟，回到正轨。可怕的是得不到及时清洗，藏污纳垢，越积越多，让自己的良知、灵魂淹没在错误与罪恶之中而不能自拔。有研究表明，平时反省的越多，积累成忏悔的机会就越少，因而可随时清理心理负担，提高幸福指数。[7]

其实，中国人自古并非不讲忏悔。面对天灾人祸，商汤忏悔地说："罪当朕躬，弗敢自赦，惟简在上帝之心。其尔万方有罪，在予一人；予一人有罪，无以尔万方。"春秋战国时期，更有大将廉颇向文官蔺相如负荆请罪的著名故事，表现出了君子的豪迈和仁者的勇气。汉武帝曾于征和四年（公元前 89 年）颁布《轮台诏》，这是中国历史上第一份内容翔实、保存完整的罪己诏。[8]

特别是"五四"运动的先驱者们，从一开始就提出了忏悔、自我更新、脱胎换骨的问题。鲁迅的《狂人日记》是中国现代史上反封建的第一声呐喊，也是第一篇忏悔之作；不是个人的忏悔，是整个民族的忏悔。郁达夫可说是第一个忏悔家，他说："'五四'运动最大的成功，第一要算人的发现。从前的人，是为君而存在，为道而存在，为父母而存在，现在的人才晓得为自我而存在了。"他的整个创作过程，就是不断地自我谴责、自我忏悔，灵与肉不断搏斗的过程。从《沉沦》开始，他的每篇小说都是对自己灵魂的无情解剖，对自己行为的痛心疾首的忏悔。同时，瞿秋白的《饿乡纪程》、庐隐的《蓝田的忏悔录》、林徽因的《窗子以外》、丁玲的《暑假中》等，都反映了这种复杂甚至痛苦的忏悔心理过程。[9]

然而，无论反省还是忏悔，要发生在具有一定素质的人身上。其基础是什么？在中国传统文化里，有孟子的“人不可以无耻，无耻之耻，无耻矣”；“耻之于人大矣，为机变之巧者，无所用耻焉。不耻不若人，何若人有？”可见要有最基本的廉耻之心。在西方则认为，“教育本身意味着一棵树摇动另一棵树，一朵云推动另一朵云，一个灵魂唤醒另一个灵魂”，即要具备分清是非的土壤，或称之为“宇宙理性”。[10]

在这一点上，中西方文化又是相通的，因为中西方人毕竟都具人类的属性；而人的理性亦在不断进化之中。因而，在当今纷扰的世界，每个人内心的不断反省与忏悔，应当成为其品质生活的不可或缺的部分。[11]

译 文

Introspection and Repentance

Both introspection and repentance are individuals’ inward activities of self-examination. Chinese people are used to the word “introspect”, while Westerners often say “repent”, but the two terms have both similarities and subtle differences.[1]

Confucius said, “In my daily introspection, I mainly examine myself on three counts: Am I unfaithful to others? Have I failed to make good on my word in my interactions with colleagues and friends? Did I go over what I'd just learnt?" *Doctrine of the Mean* warns "A true gentleman should be self-disciplined specially when he is alone" . *The Four Precepts of Liaofan* emphasizes "Firstly we should review and correct our mistakes on a daily basis. If we do not do so, we will fool ourselves by neglecting our shortcomings and make no progress at all" . These adages are typical of Chinese-style introspection.[2]

The West has the ancient Greek mythology of Oedipus's confession of killing his father and marrying his mother, plus the famous three *Confessions* written by Augustine, Rousseau and Tolstoy respectively. Living in mainstream Christian culture, people customarily go to church to confess to their priests. Fairly recently, a past German Chancellor, Wilhelm Brandt, knelt down to apologize in front of the Polish Jewish Monument. These are not uncommon ways for Westerners to put their repentance into practice.[3]

Generally speaking, there are some differences between the Chinese style of introspection and that of Western repentance. Firstly, the degree of seriousness is different. Introspection usually refers to reflection on ordinary mistakes which have not caused significant harm, while repentance is more dedicated to remorse or even guilt for triggering major irreparable losses. Secondly, the ways of practicing them are different. Introspection is a kind of daily physical and mental self-cultivation, a truly private practice of reflecting, awaking and correcting oneself, while repentance normally confronts some sort of deity, creators or their representatives (such as priests), or the victims in order to seek forgiveness externally. Thirdly, the focuses are different. As a result of introspection, lessons can be learnt, losses compensated, weakness strengthened, so as to further develop the potential for a better prospect, while repentance does not make any amendments, but pursues redemption through salvation.[4]

Bertrand Russell (1872-1970), the well-known British philosopher and mathematician, although born into the nobility, was raised by his grandparents after his parents passed away. One of his grandmother's proverbs became the benchmark of his self-examination—"Never follow others to do wrong things", for that matter never tell lies either, since one lie always triggers more lies to cover it up. Nicknamed the "general of quitting smoking", former French President Charles de Gaulle publicly announced his decision to quit smoking on November 28, 1947 when he was almost 60. Previously, he had smoked three packets a day, but after the announcement he touched none of them until 23 years later when he died. When asked the secret of his success, he answered: "In the depths of my heart I realize that looking after my health is my duty to France, so I should never compromise with my comfortable habits!" Clearly, it was extremely difficult to achieve without constant introspection and a high degree of self-discipline.[5]

Sometimes, the boundary between a "fault" and "sin" is not

clear-cut. In August 2013, former US President George W. Bush felt unwell and was admitted to hospital. Before undergoing heart bypass surgery, he called his wife Laura to his side and held her hands to confess, which he had been contemplating for years, to seek his wife's forgiveness. During his presidency, he had an "emotional affair" with then Secretary of State Condoleezza Rice for a period of time. It was rooted in his subconsciousness, no one in the world, including Ms. Rice, had ever known about it. However, as a devout Christian, George W. Bush treated this extramarital "affectional fault" as a hidden sin against his God, for which he must repent to his loved one who might have been hurt. As the scripture says, God will not belittle anyone who has a sorrowful and repentant heart. In this way, his heart struggled with a common fault in the eyes of ordinary people, which had been sublimated through repentance and his sense of guilt was relieved in salvation.[6]

Living in the world and engaging in worldly affairs, ordinary people, endowed with instinctive emotions and desires, confronted with all sorts of attractions, are bound to make some mistakes, which is a normal sign of "temporary derailment" , nothing terrible. The crucial thing is to be able to reflect, review oneself and get back on track in a timely manner. Otherwise, faults and sins will be accumulated, polluting the soul and downgrading the conscience, to the point where one can hardly extricate oneself from the mire. Research has suggested that the more you introspect yourself, the fewer chances you have to repent, and as mental burdens have been appropriately removed, your happiness index will be higher.[7]

In fact, the Chinese people have not been unrepentant since ancient times. Facing some natural and man-made disasters, for example, Emperor Tang of the Shang Dynasty (1600 BC-1046 BC) confessed: "I have committed sins and I dare not to absolve myself, since Heaven observes them so clearly out there. I am the root cause of all these faults, for which I dare not blame you guys." During the Spring-Autumn and the Warring States period (770 BC-221 BC), there was a popular story about General Lian Po pleading guilty by carrying the rod on his back to the civil servant Lin Xiangru, revealing the bravery of a gentleman and the courage of a benevolent heart. Emperor Wu of the Han Dynasty (206 BC-220 AD) released the "Luntai Edict" in the fourth year of Zhenghe (89 BC), which was the first detailed and well-preserved Sin Edict ("decree of self-punishment") in China's history.[8]

In particular, the pioneers of the May 4th Movement from the very beginning raised the issue of repentance, self-renewal and rebirth. Lu Xun's *The Diary of a Madman* was the first cry of anti-feudalism and the first work of repentance in modern China. Its repentance, however, was not personal as such, but rather national as a whole. Yu Dafu, another prominent figure of the time, could be called the first confessor of modern China. He believed that "The greatest discovery of the May 4th Movement is human nature. Previously, the Chinese people lived for their emperors, parents or the *Dao*, now they've realized that they must live for themselves as human beings" . Consequently, his entire creative process, beginning with *Sinking*, dedicated to merciless self-dissection, self-reproach and self-repentance, as well as the constant struggle between spirit and flesh. At the same time, Qu Qiubai's *Journey to the Hungry Town*, Lu Yin's *The Confession of Lantian*, Lin Huiyin's *Outside the Window*, Ding Ling's *Summer Vacation*, and so on, all reflect this kind of complex and even painful psychological process of repentance.[9]

Nevertheless, either introspection or repentance, has to happen to a person with certain qualities. What are these? In traditional Chinese culture, they are seen in Mencius's statement that "People cannot live without shame, otherwise he or she can be called a shameless person" ; "Having a sense of shame is crucial. Those who are good at deceiving and cheating, have no place in their hearts to feel shame, nor can they be called human beings" . In the West, it is believed that "Education means one tree shakes another tree, one cloud pushes another cloud, and one soul awakens another soul" . That is, one must have the soil base to grow the value of right and wrong, or to have "cosmic rationality" .[10]

In this connection, Chinese and Western cultures are deeply related, since their peoples after all have human attributes with a constantly evolving rationale. Therefore, living in today's troubled world, constant introspection and repentance should become an integral part of our quality of life.[11]

注 释

[2]“君子慎独”，出自《礼记·中庸》:“莫见乎隐，莫显乎微，故君子慎其独也。”意思是不要在别人见不到听不到的地方放松对自己的要求，也不要因为细小的事情而不拘小节，所以君子要慎独，即使一个人独处、没有人注意时，也要谨言慎行。有的译成 gentleman’s prudence alone、I do the right thing without being asked, even when no one is looking、...being prudent when alone、cautious independence 等，此处译为 A true gentleman should be self-disciplined specially when he is alone，更为细化。

[3]“典型的西方式忏悔”，似可译成 a typical type of Western confession，这里根据具体语境，变通为 ...not uncommon ways for Westerners to put their repentance into practice。

[4]“重点不同”，一般译成 different emphasis、various viewpoints、emphasize differently 等，此处用了 focus，变通为 the focuses are different。

[6]“模糊”，有可对应的 vague、fuzzy、indistinct、obscure、dim 等，此处是就“过”与“罪”之间的界限而言的，故译为 ...is not clear-cut。同时，“情感过失”是个臆造词，似可译成 emotional fault/blame/misstep、sentimental trespass 等，

此处指的是男女之情，但又不是“意淫”（psycholagny、psychosexuality、mental masturbation），故变通为“emotional affair”。

[7]“七情六欲”，“七情”一般是指喜、怒、忧、思、悲、恐、惊，是感情的表现或心理活动；“六欲”指人的眼、耳、鼻、舌、身、意的生理需求或愿望。此处不必分指，而可概述为 instinctive emotions and desires。同时，“一时迷失”，字面意思是 lost in a moment，此处译为“temporary derailment”，是一种具体语境的变通。

[9]“脱胎换骨”，可有多种译法，如 thoroughly to remould oneself、cast off one's old self and take on a new self、create new things out of the old、get rid of one's mutual frame、make a thoroughgoing change、mend one's ways and live almost as a new man、One must amend/correct one's character in a thorough-going manner、turn over a new leaf、undergo a complete or thorough change 等，此处简化为 rebirth。

[10]“无耻之耻，无耻矣”出自《孟子·尽心上》，意思是“不知羞耻的那种耻辱，就是无耻啊！”有的译成 It is a shame indeed when one does not know the sense of shame、shameless shame, shameless、...for the shame of being without shame is shamelessness 等，此处用副词加以简化：otherwise he or she can be called a shameless person。

原 文

我看葡萄牙

上小学的时候，课堂上老师提到“葡萄牙”，我觉得这个国家的名字很有意思，怎么会以“葡萄”命名？且是一个“老牌帝国主义国家”，在遥远的欧洲，曾经航海很厉害，有很多殖民地，但日后衰落了。[1]

后来我有幸到澳门一所大学任教，走进了这座曾被葡国侵占了四百余年的城市。从巴洛克风格的建筑、葡萄牙风味的美食、土生葡人，到身边的葡国同事，使我觉得对于葡萄牙触手可及了，尽管在地理上依旧遥远。于是，我有兴趣更多地了解该国的历史、政治、经济、文化、语言等。那时，澳门刚“回归祖国”不到三年，有很多“中葡论坛”之类的活动，我都积极参加，更拉近了我与葡国的心理距离。[2]

其实“葡萄牙”的名字源于拉丁文，意为“港口”，可见它与海洋的渊源。原来，这是一个有着悠久历史和丰富文化的南欧国家。公元前 218 年，它被纳入罗马帝国，随后在公元 5 世纪被日耳曼人征服，又在公元 8 至 12 世纪被摩尔人统治了 400 余年。直到 1249 年，葡萄牙才驱逐了所有入侵者，基本形成了今天的版图。15 至 16 世纪是葡萄牙的辉煌时期，凭借其强大的航海实力，他们绕过好望角，建立了一个横跨亚洲、非洲和南美洲的帝国，成为当时的世界强国。[3]

其间，我有机会到过马六甲海峡，知道1511年葡萄牙也占领了那里，控制了这一连接印度洋与太平洋的海上通道，将其变成自己进行香料贸易的重要枢纽。那里的人得知我是从澳门来的，感到格外亲切，并一口咬定我会讲葡语，这倒促使我回来后好好补了补语言课。[4]

但有辉煌便有坎坷，因争夺势力范围，葡萄牙曾与西班牙、法国、英国等多次发生战争，耗费了大量资源，还导致了领土的丧失和经济的破坏。特别是1808年，由于拿破仑军队的入侵，为了避免被俘，葡萄牙王室和大部分贵族逃到了其殖民地巴西，并在那里设立了临时首都里约热内卢，这使得巴西成为欧洲国家的第一个海外首都，也是南美唯一讲葡语的国家。难怪这两个国家的关系非同寻常。澳门也有许多经营店铺的巴西人，但葡人与巴西人说的葡语，我一听便能识别出来。[5]

从在澳门的葡国人那里我了解到，如今的葡萄牙已远非其大航海时代了，主要原因是其工业化进程相对滞后，国际竞争力不够。政治上，1974年康乃馨革命虽推翻了独裁政权，带来了民主制度，但现代化改革和经济发展依然面临诸多挑战。早在1986年，葡萄牙便加入欧盟，但在里面是个穷国，每年要从中接受救济，以补贴生活。[6]

2024年6月，我终于来到这个幼时便感到新奇的国家，贴到跟前看一看。先到了著名的罗卡角，因为这里是欧洲大陆的最西端，号称是“大地的尽头，海洋的开端”，感觉到葡国不但在地理位置，而且在实力版图上处于欧洲的边缘地带，但当年却不是；正是这种“边缘优势”使其成为迅速崛起的海洋大国，一度横跨欧、亚、非、南美，不可一世。站在悬崖边，望着无际的滔滔海水，我仿佛看到了葡萄牙昔日的辉煌逐渐被席卷而去。大浪淘沙，风水轮流转，一切都在变迁。[7]

接着，我来到了有“伊甸园”美誉的辛特拉山顶的佩纳宫。这里曾是葡萄牙国王的离宫，金碧辉煌，色彩斑斓，融合了巴洛克式、哥特式、文艺复兴式、摩尔式和曼努埃尔式的建筑风格，对于欧洲的皇室建筑、宫廷生活有着深远的影响，1995 年被联合国教科文组织列为世界遗产。[8]

和这里的普通人接触，发现鲜有极富和极贫的，主要是税收和福利制度起了重要的调节作用。移民到此的中国人，也大都喜欢这里的平淡生活。总体上，我并没有看到一个“老牌帝国主义”，而更像是个“成熟的资本主义”国家。人们不再雄心勃勃，冒险、躁动，似乎也不再稀罕往日的大富大贵，而是甘于日常的平静，甚至“无聊”。其实，这不正是生活的本色吗？[9]

译　文

My Views of Portugal

When “Portugal” was mentioned by my primary school teacher in class, I was curious to know how come a country could be named after “grapes” (since “Portugal” in Chinese is *pu tao ya*, and *pu tao* share the same characters as "grapes"). And I was told that it is an "old imperialist country" , located in faraway Europe, which had been an important maritime power with many colonies in the past but has been in decline for a long time.[1]

Later, I was fortunate enough to be invited to teach at a university in Macao, a city seized by Portugal for more than four hundred years. At the time, I was overwhelmed by things Portuguese, such as the Baroque-style architecture, Portuguese cuisine, locally-born Portuguese, not to mention my Portuguese colleagues. It seemed that Portugal was within reach, despite its geographical distance. This sparked my interest in learning more about the country's history, politics, economy, culture and language. Since Macao had just been "returned to its motherland" for less than three years, there were many activities related to "China-Portuguese Forums" in which I was actively involved, bringing me psychologically closer to Portugal.[2]

The name "Portugal" , in fact, comes from Latin (Portus Cale), meaning "port" , showing its connection with the sea. It turns out that this is a Southern European country with a complicated long history and rich culture. It was incorporated into the Roman Empire in 218 BC, conquered by the Germanic peoples in the 5th Century, and ruled by the Moors from the 8th to the 12th centuries, for over 400 years. It was not until 1249 that Portugal expelled all invaders and roughly formed today's territory. The 15th and 16th centuries witnessed Portugal's glorious period. With its strong maritime power, it rounded the Cape of Good Hope and established an empire spanning Asia, Africa and South America, becoming a world power at the time.[3]

During that period in Macao, I had the opportunity to visit the Strait of Malacca and learned that Portugal also occupied this area in 1511, controlling this maritime passage connecting the Indian and Pacific Oceans, making it an important hub for its spice trade. Knowing I was from Macao, the locals showed me particular affinity and insisted that I spoke Portuguese, which motivated me to brush up on my language skills upon returning.[4]

Portugal's thriving had a glorious history but not without setbacks. It had many wars with Spain, France and England over territorial disputes, consuming vast resources and leading to loss of territories and economic damage. Especially, confronted with Napoleon's invasion in 1808, the Portuguese royal family and most of the nobility fled to their colony in Brazil, establishing a temporary capital in Rio de Janeiro, making Brazil the first overseas capital of an European country and the only Portuguese-speaking-country in South America. Understandably, the two countries have had an unusual relationship ever since. There are also many Brazilians in Macao running their businesses. As for the Portuguese spoken by the peoples of two countries, I can tell the differences as soon as they open their mouths.[5]

I learned from the Portuguese people in Macao that there is no comparison between today's Portugal and its glorious past during the Age of Exploration, mainly due to its sluggish industrialization and impotent international competitiveness. Politically, although the Carnation Revolution in 1974 overthrew its dictatorship and brought in democracy, Portugal's modern reforms and economic development still face many challenges. Portugal joined the European Union as early as 1986, but it remains one of the poorer members, receiving subsidies and aid annually.[6]

In June, 2024, I finally visited the country that intrigued me since childhood, having a first-hand experience. Initially, I went to the famous Cabo da Roca, the westernmost point of the European continent, known as "the edge of the earth and the beginning of the ocean". I had a sense that this country has been marginalized not only geographically but also geopolitically. However, that wasn't the case in the past. It was precisely this kind of "peripherization advantage" that made Portugal a rapidly rising maritime power, building a formidable empire crossing Europe, Asia, Africa, and South America. Standing on the cliff and looking at the vast ocean, I seemingly saw the glory of Portugal being swept away. Yes, "what goes around comes around", everything changes as time goes by.[7]

Consequently, I visited the Pena Palace at the top of Sintra Mountain, known as the "Eden". It was once the summer palace of the Portuguese kings, magnificent and colorful, combining the architectural styles of Baroque, Gothic, Renaissance, Moorish and

Manueline, exerting a profound influence on European royal buildings and court life. In 1995, it was listed as a World Heritage Site by UNESCO.[8]

Interacting with some local people, I found there are rarely extremely rich or poor people, mainly due to the tax and welfare system playing a significant regulatory role. Most Chinese immigrants here also enjoy its peaceful life. Overall, I didn't see an "old imperialist" at all, but rather a "mature capitalist" country. It seems that the people are no longer ambitious, adventurous or restless, nor interested in their worthy past. Instead, they prefer daily tranquility, even "boredom" . Isn't this the true nature of life?[9]

注释

[1]“很有意思”，没有如通常译成 ...very interested in...，而变通为 ...was curious to know...，更体现一种少年的好奇心。

[2]“触手可及”，一般可译成 ...close enough to touch、...near at hand 等；此处通过前后语境 ...was overwhelmed by、...was within reach 体现出来。

[5]“为了避免被俘”，没有特意译出，如译成 to avoid being captured 等，因其意已体现在 ...fled to their colony in Brazil，故省译了。“难怪”一般译语是 no wonder，但此处为了易于句式表达，变通 Understandably。“便能识别出来”，同一“官方语”由不同国家 / 地区人讲出来而产生的语言变异现

象（linguistic variations）普遍存在，如加拿大魁北克语区人与法国人说的法语，阿根廷人与西班牙人说的西班牙语，奥地利人、瑞士人与德国人说的德语等，只要对该种语言有一定了解，都可识别出来。

[6] 这里的“穷国”不是一般的 poor country，而实际情况是（one of）the poor members。

[7] 此处的“不可一世”不是一般意义上的 extremely arrogant、be insufferably arrogant 等，而是融合在了 formidable（empire）之中。

原 文

西班牙看斗牛

以往都是在媒体上看西班牙的斗牛，固然也精彩，但总是想，什么时候能到现场观看，那才真实！机会来了。2024 年 6 月，我们正在葡萄牙旅游时，得知下周四邻国的西班牙有场斗牛表演，于是星夜兼程，赶往此地。[1]

我们来到了马德里的拉斯本塔斯斗牛场。这是西班牙最大的斗牛场，1929 年建成，古迹古风，拥有约 23,000 个座位。斗牛场里熙熙攘攘，几近坐满。抬眼望去，评委们已经就绪，据说皇室家族也来人了。管弦乐队就在我们旁边，不停地奏着各种名曲。[2]

斗牛士们及助手们进场了，骑着马，打着旗，挥手致意。观众们异常兴奋，呼喊着，几乎人人举着手机拍照。简短的入场仪式后，主场斗牛开始了。场中央只留下一年轻小伙，身穿华丽斗牛服，手持斗牛红斗篷（红布）。场边栏杆打开了，一只硕大的黑牛怒气冲冲地狂奔过来，朝着斗篷猛顶；只见斗牛士手臂轻摆，优雅地一侧身，猛牛扑了个空。旁边的导游告诉我，其实牛是色盲，红色只是为了戏剧效果，只要是抖动的东西，牛都要冲撞。斗牛士每抖动一下红布，牛脾气都要发作，不断地来回顶撞，而斗牛士则信心满满，镇定自若，每次都能如行云流水一般，巧妙躲闪而过，这更激怒了公牛，进攻愈加凶猛。经过一通乱撞乱顶之后，公牛站住了，怒目横睁，气喘吁吁，可能心想："该死，我怎么总是扑空呢？"[3]

几个回合后，斗牛士开始出手了。他从迎上来的助手那里接过刺枪，在躲避猛牛的同时，看准时机，将枪刺入牛背。这是风险极高的动作，因既要躲避，又要投刺，弄不好会被牛角尖顶到，这种事以往曾发生过。牛被刺中后，先是一抖，觉到了疼痛，但仍继续顶撞、奔跑。每一枪刺中后，都伴随着观众的欢呼声。[4]

几个刺枪并排插入后，血液冒出，染红了牛背，它的脚步也缓慢下来，但困牛犹斗。斗牛士拿过另一支长矛，刺击牛的肩部，以进一步削弱其力量，但同时也使牛更加怒不可遏。之后，斗牛士又先后将三对彩旗插入了牛的肩部肌肉，展现其极高的精确度和敏感性，自然又赢得了观众的一片喝彩。这牛先是一愣，奇怪自己何时长了翅膀？当然疼痛也加剧了，但它又鼓起怒气，试图报复，然已力不从心，来回晃荡起来。[5]

这时斗牛士换上了红色的披风，高举一把长剑，示意观众，进入了最后击杀阶段，旁边的乐队也高奏凯旋曲。只见斗牛士面对晃晃悠悠冲将过来的公牛，双腿并立，左手背后，看准时机，右手将细细长剑，猛地刺向牛背，观众们都凝神注目，因胜败在此一举……一定是刺中了心脏，牛应声倒地了，观众又欢呼声四起。助手们蜂拥而至，将死牛套上绳索，由几匹高头大马拖了下去。[6]

再一轮开始了，又上来一位年轻帅气的斗牛士，他健步走到场中央，哐的一下，双腿跪在了地上，这是一个冒险动作，因为这使他的防御角度顿时减小了一半，但倘若他成功了，会大大加分。栏杆打开了，但见一愤怒的公牛，咆哮着向跪在那里的斗牛士冲去。说时迟，那时快，只见小伙将红布向身边轻轻一抖，牛扑空了，而他还跪在那里，几乎纹丝没动。那牛转过身来，傻愣着，似乎在琢磨一下到底发生了什么；缓过神后，便又奋力地向挥动着的红斗篷来回冲撞，而斗牛士仍屈膝在地，仅靠着灵活的手臂，左推右挡，硬是让那牛不但没有得逞，而且越来越气急败坏，引得观众阵阵掌声、喝彩。[7]

斗牛士接过了助手递来的刺枪，并未马上出手，而是玩耍一番，做了几个漂亮的动作，才在乐队的奏鸣和观众的欢呼中，把刺枪一一插入了牛背。接着，有人举起了白纸、白手绢，这是呼吁评委应给斗牛士以奖励，渐渐地观众席上成了一片白色的海洋，而评委席也作出了回应，以证明该斗牛士会受到相应的嘉奖，形式可能是奖品、奖分等。最后，一如既往，当长剑刺入后，那牛便只有躺着被拉出去的结果了。[8]

接下来一轮中，这牛一出场，就与前面的不大一样，它不是跑着，而是有节奏地蹦着走，还东张西望，似乎不是来参加一场生死对决，而是被邀来娱乐的。面对斗牛士挥舞的红布，它也不瘟不火，不是奋力去顶，而是欲碰又止，有时还走到场边，去“开小差”，需由助手哄赶回来。这可惹恼了观众，他们喊着并有节奏地拍起了三长一短的掌声，这是要求换牛。怎么换呢？是赶出去，牵出去，拉出去，还是抬出去？正在疑惑之中，只见栏杆打开，拥进了一群花里胡哨的母牛。它们围着公牛打转，“牛姿百态”，发出各种声音（或许还有气味），令它神魂颠倒，很快就被俘虏了，于是追随着母牛群跑出了场外，引得观众一片笑声、掌声。我以为，这牛有福了，可逃过一死；但导游告诉我，不是的，这牛回到场外就会被宰杀，因为它已失去“战斗价值”，只是一堆食物了。[9]

斗牛继续到深夜，尽管每一轮的程序、步骤大致相同，但因斗牛士不同的个性处理及牛的秉性差异，每次的表现又是千差万别的。[10]

在最后环节，斗牛士及他们的助手都悉数出场了。主裁判手托一个银盘，上面放着两只牛耳朵，那是从刚拖出去的牛头上割下的。果然，裁判把这作为奖品授予了刚才跪地斗牛的勇士。他双手接过牛耳，高高举起，向观众展示，并环场一周，接受观众的欢呼和掌声。其他参与者，亦纷纷鞠躬致谢。[11]

观众们也起身了，现场的奏乐仍不绝于耳，今晚的斗牛就要这样结束了。导游转身对我说：“今天你很幸运，见到了一些难得的斗牛场面。”[12]

对于西班牙的斗牛，近来也是颇有争议的。有人认为，斗牛对动物过于残忍、血腥，质疑这种传统是否应继续存在，因而西班牙的部分地区和城市已经通过法律禁止斗牛，如加泰罗尼亚地区、加那利群岛、巴塞罗那等，但毕竟还只是少数。[13]

那么，西班牙斗牛的性质到底是什么？上面说到是“表演”，其实不大准确；哪有以生死攸关对决作为单纯表演的？其实，斗牛的起源可以追溯到古罗马时期的角斗士比赛，而现代西班牙斗牛的形式主要发展于18世纪，与宗教性质的节日庆典、仪式相融合。不过，我还宁愿把它看作是西班牙的一种文化传统，是其旅游业的一张靓丽的名片。无论如何，面对狂暴、凶野的公牛，斗牛士们所表现出的那种大智大勇、优雅从容和非凡技艺，总能激发出我内心深处的一种英雄情节。[14]

译 文

Watching Bullfighting in Spain

Having watched bullfighting in Spain on the media so many times, which was very exciting, I always had the impulse to watch it live. It would be cool! We finally got the chance. In June of 2024 while travelling in Portugal, we were told that there would be a bullfight in neighboring Spain the next Thursday, so we hurriedly made our way there. [1]

Arriving at Las Ventas in Madrid, the largest bullring in Spain, carrying the ancient legacy but built only in 1929, I found the 23,000 seats were nearly full. With judges ready upstairs, it was said that members of the royal family were also present. The band beside us was playing various popular tunes constantly. [2]

The bullfighters and their assistants entered, riding horses, waving flags and greeting the audience. The crowd was extremely excited, shouting and taking pictures/videos with their phones. After a brief opening ceremony, the main bullfight began. A young man stood in the center of the arena, wearing a magnificent bullfighting costume and holding a red cape (muleta). As the gate opened, a large black bull charged in angrily. The bullfighter elegantly sidestepped as the bull rushed at the cape. The tour guide beside me explained that bulls are actually colorblind and the red color is only for dramatic effect, but the bull will charge at anything that moves. With each movement of the cape, the bull got angrier and charged more fiercely. The bullfighter, however, still confident and calm, dodged each attack gracefully, further infuriating the bull. After several reckless dashes, the bull stood still, panting, extremely angry, perhaps thinking, "Shit, why do I keep missing?" [3]

After a few rounds, the bullfighter started his attack. He took a lance from his assistant, aiming carefully while dodging the bull's attacks, and thrust it into the bull's back. This is a highly risky move as it requires both evasion and precision, or the bull may gore the bullfighter as has previously happened. The bull shuddered in pain but continued to charge and run. Each targeted thrust of the bullfighter aroused cheers from the audience. [4]

After several lances were inserted side by side, blood gushed out, staining the bull's back. As its steps started to slow down, the trapped bull still struggled to fight. The bullfighter then took up another long lance, stabbing the bull's shoulders to further weaken its strength, making the bull even more furious. Followed this, the bullfighter inserted three pairs of colorful flags into the bull's shoulder muscles, demonstrating his high level of precision and flexibility, naturally winning a round of applause from the audience. Initially, the bull was stunned, wondering when it had grown wings? Being further suffered and irritated, the bull tried to retaliate, though it was already exhausted, swaying back and forth.[5]

At the following moment, the bullfighter changed his red cape, raised a long sword high, signaling to the audience that it was entering the final stage of killing. The band started to play a triumphant march. Facing the staggering bull charging towards him, the bullfighter stood straight with his left hand behind his back, catching the right moment, as the outcome depended on this single strike, and audience all watched intently. He thrust the long slender sword into the bull's back. It must have pieced its heart, as the bull fell to the ground at once. Immediately, the audience erupted in huge cheers. Then, the assistants swarmed in, tied the dead bull with ropes, and had it dragged away by a few tall horses.[6]

Another round began, and a young, handsome bullfighter stepped into the center of the ring. Suddenly, he knelt down on both knees. This was a risky move, as it greatly reduced his defensive angle, but would earn him greater rewards if successful. The gate opened, and an angry bull, roaring, charged at the kneeling bullfighter. In the blink of an eye, the young man lightly shook the red cloth beside him, causing the bull to miss, while he still remained kneeling almost motionless.

The bull turned around, confused, seemingly trying to figure out what had just happened. After regaining its composure, it charged fiercely at the waving red cape again and again. The bullfighter, however, still kneeling, used his flexible arms to push and block, deftly dodging, making the bull increasingly frustrated and eliciting rounds of applause and cheers from the audience. [7]

The bullfighter took the lance handed to him by his assistant, but did not strike immediately; instead, he played with it, performing several stylish moves. Only then, accompanied by the band's music and the audience's cheers, did he insert the lances one by one into the bull's back. At that time, some people raised white papers or white handkerchiefs, calling for the judges to reward the bullfighter. Gradually, the audience became a sea of white, and the judges responded, indicating that the bullfighter would receive corresponding rewards, which could be a prize or points. Finally, as always, after the long sword was thrust in, the bull had no choice but to be dragged out as a dead body. [8]

In the next round, the bull that appeared was quite different from the previous ones. Instead of running, it bounced rhythmically and looked around as if it had been invited for entertainment rather than a life-and-death duel. Facing with the bullfighter's waving red cloth, it didn't charge aggressively but hesitated, sometimes even wandering to the edge of the ring, requiring the assistants to herd it back. This annoyed the audience, who began shouting and chapping metrically, demanding a change of bull. The problem was how could they do that? Would they chase it out? Drag it out? Lead it out? Or carry it out? While these questions lingered, to my surprise, the gate opened, and a group of colorful cows rushed in, circling around the bull, displaying various postures, and making all sorts of sounds (perhaps with scents too), mesmerizing the bull. Soon, it was captivated and followed the herd of cows out of the ring, causing the audience to laugh and applaud. I thought this bull was lucky enough to escape death, but the guide told me that it wasn't the case; the bull would be slaughtered outside the ring since it had lost its "fighting value" and what was left was just a piece of meat.[9]

The bullfighting continued into the night. Although each round followed roughly the same procedures and steps, the unique handling by different bullfighters and the varying temperaments of bulls made each performance distinct.[10]

In the final segment, all the bullfighters and their assistants appeared on the field. The main judge carried a silver tray with two bull ears on it, cut from the head of the bull that had just been dragged away. As expected, the judge awarded these as prizes to the brave "matador" (bullfighter) who had fought the bull just on his knees. The receiver accepted the bull ears with both hands, raised them high to show the audience, and made a lap around the arena, appreciating the cheers and applause from the spectators. The other contestants also bowed in respect.[11]

The audience then stood up, as the music at the scene continued to play. Tonight's bullfighting was about to come to an end this way. The guide turned to me and said, "Today you are very lucky to have witnessed some rare and exceptional bullfighting scenes." [12]

Spanish bullfighting has become quite controversial in recent years. Some believe that bullfighting is too cruel and bloody to animals, and question whether this tradition should continue. As a result, some regions and cities in Spain have passed laws banning bullfighting, such as Catalonia, the Canary Islands, and Barcelona, although these areas are still in the minority. [13]

After all, what exactly is the nature of Spanish bullfighting? "Performance" , as described above, seems not quite accurate, for what kind of performance involves a life-and-death struggle? In fact, the origins of bullfighting can be traced back to the gladiatorial contests of ancient Rome, and the modern form of Spanish bullfighting mainly developed in the 18th century, blending with religious festivals and rituals. However, I still prefer to see it as a cultural tradition of Spain, a dazzling aspect of its tourism industry. No matter what, in the face of the fierce and wild bulls, the wisdom, bravery, grace, composure and extraordinary skills displayed by the bullfighters always evoke a sense of heroism deep within me. [14]

注　释

［1］“总是想”，一般似可译成 always thinking、constantly thinking、always wondering、perpetually thinking、continually thinking 等，但此处用了更强力的 impulse，该词本义为 a driving or motivating force，如 The impulse behind the movement was a desire for social change.（这一行动背后的动机是对社会变革的向往。）

“那才真实！”按字面意思，似应译成 That's the real thing! / That's the real deal! / That's truly real! / That's authentic! / That's genuine! 但此处的真实含义是，“那就太棒了！”故译为 It would be cool!

这里的“表演”没有译成 performance，具体原因见原文第［14］中的解释。

［3］“猛撞”、“顶撞”、“冲撞”等可对应的词语很多，比如 ram、charge、clash、butt、hit hard、bump、collide、confront 等，可根据不同语境，选择相应的词进行翻译。

“行云流水”，形容自然、流畅，常见的英译文，如 like flowing clouds and water、smooth and flowing、effortless and natural、graceful and fluid、with ease and grace 等，用以形容各种动作、风格、表现等，此处精简为一个词 gracefully，以表现斗牛士的镇定与优雅。

[5] “力不从心”，按字面意思可译为 one’s strength does not match one’s ambition、the spirit is willing, but the flesh is weak、unable to do as much as one wishes、beyond one’s capability、feeling powerless 等，此处浓缩为 exhausted 一词。

[7] “说时迟，那时快”，似乎还可译为 no sooner said than done (highlights that something happens almost immediately after it’s mentioned or requested)、in a flash (emphasizes something happening very quickly, almost like a flash of light)、in an instant (conveys that something occurs immediately, without delay)、before you could say Jack Robinson (a colloquial way of saying something happens so quickly that you barely have time to react) 等；此处用了 In the blink of an eye，以形容 the event occurs so fast that it’s almost imperceptible, much like how quickly your eyes blink. It’s often used to describe dramatic or surprising changes that happen almost instantly.

[11] 此处的“参与者”没有译成通常的 participants，而是在场的 contestants，以更准确。

[14] “靓丽的名片”，字面意思为 eye-catching business card、elegant business card、stylish business card、attractive business card、chic business card 等，此处译为 a dazzling aspect (of its tourism industry)，是一种引申翻译。

原 文

儒学对中国古代绘画理论的渗透（1）

儒学对于中国传统绘画理论，虽没有直接、具体的论述，却有着深刻而根本性的影响和奠基作用。[1]

绘事后素

就绘画而言，《论语》中关于色彩、装饰等的论述并不多，但仍可见："子夏问曰：'巧笑倩兮，美目盼兮，素以为绚兮。何谓也？'子曰：'绘事后素。'曰：'礼后乎？'子曰：'起予者商也！始可与言《诗》矣。'"在中国古代，对于不同等级中的不同人的衣装服饰的印染有着严格的规定。例如，君子不以深红色或灰色镶边，不以浅红或紫色做便装。如孔子所说，"恶紫之夺朱也，恶郑声之乱雅乐也，恶利口之覆邦家者"。[2]

这里的关键词语是"绘事后素"，即先有素地，再作彩绘，此可理解为是绘画的基本准则。子夏触类旁通，并又就此提出了"礼后乎？"——以道德行为作为从事艺术的纯正基础，因而大悦其师，受到称赞。[3]

在孔子看来，画者首先应为仁者，然后方可产生有分量的艺术作品，可以说这构成了儒学教化理论的一部分。在其他场合，就“德”与“才”的关系而言，孔子认为，“有德者必有言”，但是逆定理不存在：有才者未必有德。[4]

于是又引申为“文”与“质”的关系，“质胜文则野，文胜质则史；文质彬彬，然后君子”；而君子要有立足之本，本立才能道生，这其中又包括了孝悌。可见其儒学的任何艺术理论，归其根源，都是其教化理论的一部分。进而言之，倘巧言令色而失礼之本，则会以文灭质。因而，无仁何以礼？无礼何以乐？由此，传统儒学逐渐形成其艺术理念：任何艺术作品实则为其人品性情的折射，而仁人是由刚毅、果断、质朴、谨言四种品质构成的。[5]

其实，在孔子看来，一个人的艺术生涯源于其日常的教化生活，“君子食无求饱，居无求安，敏于事而慎于言”。以此标准而言，孔子的大弟子颜回便是这种“就有道而正焉”的君子典范：“贤哉，回也！一箪食，一瓢饮，在陋巷，人不堪其忧，回也不改其乐。”以此，孔子也为中国文人（包括艺人）树立了一个楷模。[6]

同时，一个画家要是一个体贴、理解他人的人，如《论语》所载，学生问道：“克、伐、怨、欲不行焉，可以为仁矣？”答曰：“可以为难矣，仁则吾不知也。”根据儒家的一贯理念，这种素质不可从外部强制而来，而需于内在自觉而生，因为“道之以政，齐之以刑，民免而无耻；道之以德，齐之以礼，有耻且格”。[7]

然而，一切从何而始？答案是“正名”——“必也正名乎”。正如历史证明的，“天下有道，则礼乐征伐自天子出；天下无道，则礼乐征伐自诸侯出”，而绘画之道亦然。[8]

因而，由此形成传统：任何艺术实践均应合乎礼乐道义。[9]

山水比德

在儒家不多的相关绘画的论述中，“乐”的理念颇为突出，影响着后代的中国画坛。就中国画擅长的“山水”而言，孔子说：“知者乐水，仁者乐山。知者动，仁者静。知者乐，仁者寿。”这其实并非是指“智者只是乐于水，而仁者只是钟情于山”；其实质道出了孔子的一贯理念：文人要修养自己首先成为君子。正如《诗经·周颂·般》所颂，“於皇时周，陟其高山。隨山乔岳，允犹翕河。敷天之下，裒时之对，时周之命”，这山河既显周朝开国气象，亦有“德化”色彩。再如，《诗经·鲁颂·閟宫》：“泰山岩岩，鲁邦所詹。奄有龟蒙，遂荒大东。”这里并非单纯写景，而是寓景于情。在西方，由此建立了“移情说”，正如黑格尔所说：“艺术对于人的目的在于让他在外物界寻回自我。”[10]

其实，这又与道家的自然观相吻合，如庄子认为，“与物有宜”，“顺其自然”，“效物而动”，知能所不能等。山水之后其实别有寓意——自然滋养德性，自然是君子性情的一部分。对此，孟子有过更为生动的描述：“原泉混混，不舍昼夜，盈科而后进，放乎四海。有本者如是，是之取尔。苟为无本，七八月之间雨集，沟皆盈；其涸也，可立而待也。故声闻过情，君子耻之。”而观水之术，则更有“比德”的色彩：“孔子登东山而小鲁，登泰山而小天下，故观于海者难为水，游于圣人之门者难为言。观水有术，必观其澜。日月有明，容光必照焉。流水之为物也，不盈科不行；君子之志于道也，不成章不达。”于是，君子之德便以山水绝佳喻之。[11]

“以水喻德”的另一高手是儒家的荀子：“夫水，大遍与诸生而无为也，似德。其流也埤下，裾拘必循其理，似义。其洸洸乎不淈尽，似道。若有决行之，其应佚若声响，其赴百仞之谷不惧，似勇。主量必平，似法。盈不求概，似正。绰约微达，似察。以出以入，以就鲜絜，似善化。其万折也必东，似志。是故君子见大水必观焉。”[12]

同时，“以玉比德”，更有寓意：“夫玉者，君子比德焉。温润而泽，仁也；栗而理，知也；坚刚而不屈，义也；廉而不刿，行也；折而不挠，勇也；暇适并见，情也……《诗》曰：‘言念君子，温其如玉’。此之谓也。”而称颂君子的品格，孔子曾用比喻“岁寒，然后知松柏之后凋也”。到了南北朝时，便有了进一步的比喻。如据史料载，当王公（导）品评太尉（王衍）时，用了“岩岩清峙，壁立千仞”。同时，作为文人的一种品格，他们又都有些高雅的偏好。如，仕人王子猷曾暂居一空室，要求佣人在周围种上竹子，佣人大为不解：“你不过小住一时，何必烦劳此事？”王指着竹子道：“何可一日无此君！”[13]

再如，据《世说新语》记载，东晋简文帝（司马昱）游华林园时，对身边的人说：“情景相通，令人神意相得的地方不必在远处；置身于幽静深邃的林木溪水之间，便会让人产生庄子游戏濠水之上、垂钓濮水之间所具有的情怀，油然感到鸟兽禽鱼，造化万物，自然来和人亲近。”[14]

正是通过这种实践与感悟，“山水比德”的理念逐渐演变成为中国绘画基础理论的一个组成部分。理论上讲，植根于“天人合一”的中国传统哲学理念，使得中国文人很容易找到情与景的天然纽带。由此，逐渐形成了以山水为主题的中国绘画格局，而梅兰竹菊“四君子”的文学化技法，又远不同于西方绘画的“逼真表现”技法。[15]

译 文

The Infiltrated Influence of Confucianism on Traditional Chinese Painting (1)

Confucianism, did not seem to have anything specifically commenting on Chinese painting, the influence is nevertheless fundamental and profound.[1]

Paint on Solid Moral Foundation

Concerning painting, decoration and colors, there are very few comments in *The Analects*. For example, Zi Xia (a disciple of Confucius) consulted Confucius about the meaning of the following verses: “Oh the sweet smile dimpling, the black-white eyes are shining...Are these all like flowers painted on a plain surrounding?” Confucius answered: “Any painting is possible only after the plain ground work has been done." Zi Xia said: "In that case ritual afterwards?" Confucius replied: "Since you have enlightened me up on this verse, now I can begin to discuss *The Book of Poetry* with you." In ancient China, there was a strict procedure of dyeing clothes for people of different ranks in the hierarchical system. For example, in wearing clothes, a gentleman does not use dark red or grey for borders nor light red or violet for casual clothes. Confucius said: "I hate to see replacing vermillion with purple, corrupting Court music with the tunes of Zheng, subverting the state with sharp mouths." [2]

The key words here are "Any painting is possible only after the plain groundwork has been done" , which could be understood as the basic principle for drawing. Zi Xia was able to comprehend what the master preached by analogy—elaborating it with ritual, meaning that a moral act has to be based on a pure ground, which delighted his teacher. [3]

In Confucius' eyes, a painter has to be a moral person before he could produce any substantial artistic work. This actually constitutes part of Confucius' indoctrination theory. On other occasions, concerning the relation between virtue (or moral power) and competence, Confucius believed that "A man who has accumulated moral power (*de*) will certainly also gains loquacity, but someone who has gained loquacity may not have necessarily achieved moral power, pointing out the causality. [4]

In that connection, when natural substance prevails over

embellishment, one would seem uncouth; when embellishment prevails over natural substance, one would become pedantic. Only when these two qualities are duly blended can one turn into a true gentleman. Therefore, it is important for a gentleman to establish himself on a firm basis; when the base is firmly set up, the *Dao* grows. Surely the basis includes filial piety toward one's parents and respect to one's elder brothers. It is thus evident that any artistic theory within Confucianism, when traced to its roots, is part of its educational theory. Furthermore, too much of a pretentious manner may be detrimental to substance: benevolence is rarely found in blandishment. This has some implications for the other qualities of a person: A man who is not benevolent, what can he have to do with rites? A man who doesn't know the rites, what can he have to do with music? In a way, the tradition of Confucianism in this regard had gradually formed the belief that the quality of an artistic work is actually the reflection of the person's nature and quality, and it is the combination of unyieldingness, resoluteness, modesty and cautiousness in expression that constitutes the quality of a benevolent person.[5]

In fact, an artistic life is embedded in his daily noble life—a gentleman seeks neither sated eating nor comfortable dwelling; instead, he is agile in action and cautious in expression. In this respect, one of the most admirable figures was Confucius' great disciple Yan Hui: In his daily practice, he associated himself with the *Dao* and rectified his conduct accordingly. Such a one might indeed be said to be a gentleman: "What a virtuous man Yan Hui was! Living in a mean street on homely fare that others would find intolerable, but to Hui's cheerfulness and aspirations it made no difference at all." To this end, Confucius had set up a paradigm for all literati (including Chinese artists) to follow. [6]

Moreover, if an artist wishes his work to be influential, he himself has to become a considerate person or a helper to others. As recorded in *The Analects*: Zi Si said, "He who has never done others down, bragged about himself and grudged against others may be called benevolent, is that true?" Confucius replied, "What such a one has accomplished is difficult and worthy of praise; but whether he should be called benevolent I am not quite sure." According to Confucianism, however, this cannot be done externally and forcefully, but has to be achieved internally and consciously, since "Regulated by statutes and punishments the people will know how to avoid being caught up but will lack a sense of shame; guided by moral force and keep order among them by rites, they will not only keep their self-respect but also discipline themselves accordingly" . [7]

And where has all this to be started? The answer is from rectifying the name: "The sure thing to do is to rectify legitimate names." As history has revealed: "When the *Dao* prevails under Heaven all orders concerning rites, music and military affairs are issued by the Emperor. When the *Dao* elapses, all these matters will be decided by dukes or princes." And there is no exception when it comes to Chinese painting.[8]

Clearly, from this point of view, any artistic practice has to be carried out in accordance with the rituals, righteousness and *Dao*.[9]

Virtue is Analogized by Natural Scenes

Among very few Confucian comments on painting, one of the prominent thoughts was *le* or enjoyment, which has had lasting influence on Chinese painting of successive dynasties. In viewing natural scenes, which had the favored topic of Chinese painting, for instance, Confucius said: "The wise delights in water while the benevolent in mountains; the wise are active while the benevolent are still; the wise enjoy life while the benevolent attain longevity." This is not to say that a wise man takes delight in water while a benevolent one in mountains, but in essence it was a generalization that Confucius required literatus to cultivate themselves in order to become true gentlemen. The idea originated from *The Book of Poetry* compiled by Confucius. For example, in the "Hymns of Zhou" (the King's Progress), it sings: "Oh great is the state of Zhou/I climb up mountains high/To view their rise and fall/The two rivers rushingly flow/Gods are worshipped/we bow under the vast sky/All is determined by the virtue of high" . These landscapes are manifested with ambience of founding a state as well as moralized by its virtue. Also, in "Hymn to Marquis of Lu" : "Lofty is Mount Tai/Looked up at from the Lu State/ Mounts Gui and Meng stand high/Eastward wave and wave" . Clearly, it is here not simply about describing the scenery but rather infusing the scenery with emotions and sentiments. To this end, Western aestheticians have established the theory of empathize, as Hegel said "The purpose of art is to inspire people to find 'the self' from their external surroundings" .[10]

This is also very much in line with the natural view of Taoism, such as Zhuang Zi believed that he who knows the work of nature lives in accordance with nature; He who knows the work of man will nourish what is unknown to his knowledge with that which is known. The intention behind the scene is: The virtue of a character has to be nurtured by nature; or nature is an integral part of a gentleman's quality. In this respect, Mencius had a vivid prescription: "The spring of water gushes out day and night. It fills up holes and overflows, flowing on to the four major seas. Such is the case with anything of abundance, which is valued by Confucius. But suppose that anything without a source would be like rainwater. In the seventh and eighth months there is copious rainfall overflowing all the ditches and gutters, and yet they may all dry up for just a while if you stand by. So a gentleman is ashamed of a reputation not fully merited." The aspirations were most gaudily expressed when watching waters: "When ascended the Eastern Mountain, Confucius thought the State of Lu had shrunk. When stood on Mount Tai, he felt all beneath the heavens had been belittled. So, it is difficult for someone who has sighted the sea to think anything of other waters. By the same token, it is hard for someone who has learned truth with sages to think anything of other words. In contemplating water we ought to take a sophisticated approach—appreciating its foaming in waves. Similarly, the brilliancy and light of the sun and moon are admitted and felt even through the tiniest chinks. Flowing water is such a thing which will proceed until it fills up all the hollows in its course. A gentleman who has set his mind on the *Dao* cannot succeed without achieving a certain degree of attainment." In this way a gentleman's virtue is perfectly analogized by the natural scenes.[11]

Another prominent figure of Confucianism was Xun Zi (313 BC-238 BC), who also had brilliant elucidation concerning "water-appreciation" : "Oh, water! It bestows itself everywhere to all the living things without any interference, in a way it resembles virtue; it flows to fill the low ground zigzag, in a way it resembles morality; it rushes unceasingly and inexhaustibly, in a way it resembles the *Dao*; if there is anything blocking its course, its response would be like a reverberating echo by traveling through chasms that rods deep fearlessly, in a way it resembles courage; in filling out an empty place, it is surely to level itself, in a way it resembles justice; when it fulfills something completely it requires no leveling stick, in a way it resembles rectitude; gently but firmly it penetrates into the subtlest matters, in a way it resembles sensibility; everything is washed and purified in its current, in a way it resembles the transforming power of benevolence; passing through myriad turns and twists it steadfastly flows to the east, in a way it resembles the willpower. It is precisely for these reasons that a gentleman contemplates a lot when watching a great stream." [12]

Using jade as a metaphor, Confucius further explained: "Jade is something analogizing a gentleman's inner power—sophisticated and shining, magnifies benevolence; regular and refined, magnifies knowledge; hard and strong, magnifies morality; sharp and yet beneficial, magnifies appropriateness; flexible and yet stubborn, magnifies courage; its blemishes and merits are both visible, magnifies its genuineness. As an *Ode* of *The Book of Poetry* says: 'In thinking of my gentleman, I cannot but relate him to a refined jade.' This is exactly what I mean". In exalting a gentleman's character, Confucius also made such a figure of speech: Only when the weather turns cold can we witness the pine and cypress are the last to wither and fade. This remark has exerted profound influence on the successive generations in terms of self-cultivation both as a literati and an artist. More specifically, in the Southern and Northern Dynasties (420-589) when people praised another person's integrity, Wang Dao applauded the grand marshal Wang Yan, he characterized him as "a high-towering unsullied peak, standing like a cliff on the spot of thousand *ren* high". Also, as a character of literati, they normally had some noble preferences. Wang Ziyou, a prominent literati, was once temporarily lodging in an empty home, he ordered someone to have bamboos planted. The servant puzzled: "Why you are bothered by this? Don't you just temporarily stay here?" Wang chanted a poem and sighed: "How could I live a single day without these companions?" [13]

Another example, according to *A New Collection of Anecdotes of Famous Personages*: On entering a Flowery Grove Park, Emperor Jian Wen of the Eastern Jin Dynasty said to his attendants: "A comforting spot doesn't have to be far away—near a shady grove or stream, one may naturally acquire the feeling of Zhuang Zi fishing by the Pu River and having fun with water and intimacy with birds, animals, fowls and fish who are unconsciously approaching me." [14]

It was through these practices and comprehension that the approach of "virtue is analogized by natural scenes" had been gradually evolved and shaped as part of the fundamental theories on Chinese painting. Theoretically speaking, deeply rooted in the traditional Chinese philosophical concept of integrating man with nature, it is just natural for Chinese literati to find the common bond between human feelings and natural scenes, which steadily took shape in the Chinese painting tradition dominated by the subjects of nature, such as landscape, mountains, rivers, bamboos and so on. Having become the four major disciplines of plum blossoms, orchid, bamboo and chrysanthemum, Chinese painting is technically literalized expressive rather than re-expressive as practiced in western painting.[15]

注释

[2]“起予者商也！始可与言《诗》矣”，出自《论语·八佾》。孔子说《诗》，一向讲究比兴，就是要超越诗的字面意义作延伸理解，所以对子夏的话很是欣赏。礼不离本，这一段孔子和子夏的对话说明文后于质，指礼的本质就是仁。这句话的意思是，“你真是能启发我的人，现在可以同你讨论《诗经》了”，故译为 Since you have enlightened me up on this verse, now I can begin to discuss *The Book of Poetry* with you。另外，“恶紫之夺朱也，恶郑声之乱雅乐也，恶利口之覆邦家者”，出自《论语·阳货》，其意为“憎恶紫色夺去红色的光彩和地位，憎恶郑国的乐曲扰乱典雅正统的乐曲，憎恶用巧言善辩颠覆国家的人”，因而译为 I hate to see replacing vermillion with purple, corrupting Court music with the tunes of Zheng, subverting the state with sharp mouths。

[4]“有德者必有言”，出自《论语·学而》，后句为“有言者不必有德”，其意为“有德行的人一定有善言，有善言的人却不一定有德行”，该引文译为 A man who has accumulated moral power (*de*) will certainly also gains loquacity，其中特别对“德”和“言”作了强调和变通处理；loquacity 的本义为 the quality of being wordy and talkative。

[5]“质胜文则野，文胜质则史；文质彬彬，然后君子”，出自《论语·雍也》，有的译成 When a man's natural, honest

plainness, exceeds his ornamental accomplishments, he is a mere rustic; on the other hand, when his ornamental accomplishments exceed his natural, honest plainness, he is a mere scribe (or fop); but when substantial plainness, and polite accomplishments, are properly blended, they form the superior man. 此处加以变通，译为：In that connection, when natural substance prevails over embellishment, one would seem uncouth; when embellishment prevails over natural substance, one would become pedantic. Only when these two qualities are duly blended can one turn into a true gentleman. 以更符合其艺术作品鉴赏语境。

另外，“无仁何以礼？无礼何以乐？”出自《论语·八佾》，若按其字面意思译成 If a man has no humaneness what can his propriety be like? If a man has no humaneness what can his music be like? 未必准确。其意实为“做人如果没有仁德，怎么对待礼仪制度呢？做人若不懂礼仪制度，怎么对待音乐呢？”故应译为：A man who is not benevolent, what can he have to do with rites? A man who doesn’t know the rites, what can he have to do with music?

[6]“敏于事而慎于言”出自《论语·学而》，似可译成 quick in work and cautious in speech、A gentleman would rather be quick in action than talk a lot、A true gentleman should act with haste and talk with cautiousness 等，此处结合具体语境，变通为 a gentleman... instead, he is agile in action and cautious in expression。

[7]“道之以政，齐之以刑，民免而无耻；道之以德，齐之以礼，有耻且格”，出自《论语·为政》，可有多种译法，如：If you govern the people legalistically and control them by punishment, they will avoid crime, but have no personal sense of shame. If you govern them by means of virtue and control them with propriety, they will gain their own sense of shame, and thus correct themselves./If in government you depend upon laws, and maintain order by enforcing those laws by punishments, you can also keep the people away from wrong-doing, but they will lose the sense of shame for wrong-doing. If, on the other hand, in government you depend upon the moral sentiment, and maintain order by encouraging education and good manners, the people will have a sense of shame for wrong-doing and, moreover, will emulate what is good./If the people are governed by laws, and order is kept by punishment, they would be obedient but not conscientious. If they are led by virtue and order is kept by the rites, they would be conscientious and act in agreement with what is right. 等，此处译为 Regulated by statutes and punishments the people will know how to avoid being caught up but will lack a sense of shame; guided by moral force and keep order among them by rites, they will not only keep their self-respect but also discipline themselves accordingly，其中特别对“耻”（a sense of shame、self-respect）和“格”（discipline themselves accordingly）作了异样处理。

[8]“天下无道，则礼乐征伐自诸侯出”，出自《论语·季氏》，其意为“国家政治昏暗的时候，制作礼乐和出兵打仗等事宜由诸侯决定”，一般可译成 When bad government prevails in the empire, ceremonies, music, and punitive military expeditions proceed from the princes 等，此处译为 When the *Dao* elapses, all these matters will be decided by dukes or princes，以更贴近原文，并与后面的 And there is no exception when it comes to Chinese painting 更加衔接。

[10]“山水比德”，指“以山水比喻德性”，形容仁者和智者，意指“仁义的人宽容而不易冲动，性情好静，就像大山一样稳重、安宁，故译为 Virtue is analogized by natural scenes。

[12]“是故君子见大水必观焉”出自《荀子·宥坐》，其中的“观”为仔细观察、思考，故此处用了 contemplates a lot（when watching a great stream）。

原 文

儒学对中国古代绘画理论的渗透（2）

以意逆志

在“山水比德”的基础上，产生了中国绘画批评，而这主要源于孟子。作为儒学的重要经典著作，《孟子》主要由其本人及其弟子所编纂，在儒学发展史中承前启后，在中西文化交流中亦不可替代。《孟子》的主题思想是建立在人性善理论基础上的“仁政”，而要做到这一点便首先要从我做起，即“万物皆备于我”。由“我”而强调“思”——“心之官则思”，此种理念对各种学科都产生了广泛的影响。[1]

就文学艺术及其批评而言，孟子推崇“知人论世”观，如“颂其诗，读其书，不知其人，可乎？是以论其世也，是尚友也”。所以，解释诗词时，不要以文字而误解其词语，亦不可因词语而曲解其意，而应以辞会意。此处孟子探究的是“形式”（语言）与“内容”（意思）的关系，而其不仅限于文学，还适用于其他艺术形式。[2]

孟子以《诗经》来阐述其意，就“普天之下，莫非王土；率土之滨，莫非王臣”而言，孟子问：如果舜做了天子，瞽叟却不是臣民，哪有这样的道理？所以，要搞清楚语境、对象、原意，才能准确理解其诗意。就历史发展而言，“以意逆志”对于后世的艺术批评产生了深远的影响。[3]

胸中与眸子

如上所述，在孟子看来，万物皆源于人们与生俱来的“性本善”，因而最为重要的便是自我修养，或曰“养浩然之气”。然而，其具体为何物？“难言也。其为气也，至大至刚，以直养而无害，则塞于天地之间。其为气也，配义与道；无是，馁也”。[4]

当被问之何为“善”与“信”的时候，孟子答道：“充实之谓美，充实而有光辉之谓大，大而化之之谓圣，圣而不可知之之谓神。”“君子所性，仁义礼智根于心，其生色也睟然，见于面，盎于背，施于四体，四体不言而喻。”[5]

广义而言，自古文人多磨难，从来痛苦出杰作。对此，最有名的，算是司马迁在《报任安书》中的一段：“盖西伯拘而演《周易》；仲尼厄而作《春秋》；屈原放逐，乃赋《离骚》；左丘失明，厥有《国语》；孙子膑脚，《兵法》修列；不韦迁蜀，世传《吕览》；韩非囚秦，《说难》《孤愤》。《诗》三百篇，大抵贤圣发愤之所为作也。此人皆意有所郁结，不得通其道，故述往事，思来者。”[6]

此外，《孟子·尽心》说：“人之有德慧术知者，恒存乎疢疾；独孤臣孽子，其操心也危，其虑患也深，故达。”《孟子·告子下》说：“动心忍性，增益其所不能。……困于心，衡于虑，而后作；……然后知生于忧患而死于安乐也。”赵岐注：“而后作为奇计异策、愤激之说也。……故知能生于忧患。”[7]

桓谭在《新论·求辅》中亦言：“贾谊不左迁失志，则文采不发；……扬雄不贫，则不能作《玄》言。”赵岐在《〈孟子〉章句·题辞》中说：“余困吝之中，精神遐漂，靡所济集，聊欲系于翰墨，得以乱思遗老也。”钟嵘的《诗品·汉都尉李陵》说：“生命不谐，声颓身丧，使陵不遭辛苦，其文亦何至此！”[8]

即是说，经历磨难之后，真君子应全力实现其使命：他应住在最广的宅院——“仁”里，占据最正确的位置——“礼”中，行走在最宽广的路——“义”上。得志时，便携百姓同行，失意便独守自我之道，“富贵不能淫，贫贱不能移，威武不能屈，此之谓大丈夫”。[9]

然而，大丈夫还需具有某些超乎生命的可贵品质：“生亦我所欲也，义亦我所欲也；二者不可得兼，舍生而取义者也。生亦我所欲，所欲有甚于生者，故不为苟得也；死亦我所恶，所恶有甚于死者，故患有所不辟也。”而评判一个人的品格，又需综合来考察，就此孟子提出了“胸中与眸子”的概念：观察一个人，再没有比凝视他的眼睛更好的了；因为眼睛不能掩饰一个人内心的丑恶。心正，则眼明；心不正，则眸混沌。所以，听其言，观其眸，其性情无掩。[10]

世人可能有所不知，该理念最早是针对中国绘画提出的，后多用于揭示人物品格与其作品的关系——视其为素养的外在体现，由此对中国绘画，特别是人物画产生了深远的影响。[11]

译 文

The Infiltrated Influence of Confucianism on Traditional Chinese Painting (2)

The Form is Shaped by the Thought

Based on the idea of "virtue is analogized by natural scenes", Chinese painting criticism started to develop, which was initiated mainly by Mencius. As an important component in the classics of the Confucian School, *Mencius*, compiled by Mencius himself and his disciples Wan Zhang and Gongsun Chou among others, serves as a link between the past and future of Confucianism, playing an irreplaceable role in further developing Confucius' ideology and the cultural exchange between the east and the west. The main thought of *Mencius* is to carry out a "benevolent government", and theoretical foundation of such government is the benevolent human nature ("instinct of goodness") endowed by Heaven. To realize the heavenly mission everything has to start from the self— "Everything is here in me" as he put it. Consequently, he paid much attention to the function of thinking by claiming that "The brain is the very organ where thinking takes place". This kind of emphasis had extensive effects on other areas of learning.[1]

Concerning literature and art, in Mencius' view, any critique of artistic work has to be grounded by knowing the author and time he lived: When studying their books and reading their poems, is it possible not to know the person? This has to ascend the authors' historical background and making friends with them. In this regard, when interpreting the odes, one should not distort the sense of phrases with any characters, nor should one twist the real meaning of them with any phrases. The right way therefore should be to read their minds through the language in order to gain the proper apprehension. Here, Mencius explored the issue of relations between form (language) and content (meaning), which applied not only to literature but also other types of art.[2]

Mencius illustrated the idea using a poem in *The Book of Poetry*: "The land under the sun/Is all emperor's domain/The people far and near/Are all the royal heirs." He said, since Shun was the emperor already, what was the blind old man if not his subject? So in what context did he raise the question? To whom? What purpose? Only when all these questions were cleared could we have the right idea of the poem. Historically, the concept of "the form is shaped by the thought" had an everlasting impact on the criticism of artistic works of successive generations.[3]

The Coherence of Mind and Eyes

As mentioned above, according to Mencius, everything is

determined by the benevolent human nature endowed by Heaven, therefore it is paramount to exercise "self-cultivation" or "nourishing the passion-nature" , which is difficult to put in words—"it is extremely great and strong nourished by rectitude, righteousness between heaven and earth; without it man is in the state of starvation" .[4]

When asked what is meant by being "good" and "sincere" ? Mencius answered: "To be imbued within authentically is called 'beauty' ; to be fulfilled and manifested is called 'brilliance' ; to be transformed grandly is called 'sage' . When such sageness is beyond our comprehension is called 'deity' ." "Benevolence, righteousness, propriety and wisdom are deeply rooted in a gentleman's nature, and manifested mildly in his countenance, radiated to his back and limbs, conveying message without the use of any language." [5]

In viewing Chinese history that since ancient times, the literati have been a kind of people doomed to draw their inspirations from sorrow and calamity to create their masterpieces. As the well-known historian Sima Qian commented: "When King Wen of the Zhou Dynasty was arrested, he deduced the classic *The Book of Changes*; Confucius wrote *The Spring and Autumn Annals* while he was experiencing adversity; Qu Yuan produced his monumental long poem *On Encountering Sorrow* during his exile. When Zuoqiu Ming lost his sight and Sun Tzu had his feet chopped off, they edited their writings and stratagems. After Lü Buwei was forced to live in Shu, then the valuable *Lü's Spring and Autumn Annals* was fortunately handed down to posterity. Similarly, when Hanfeizi was imprisoned in Qin, *On Difficulty* and *On Resentment*—two precious books—were written by him. *The Book of Poetry* was also produced roughly in the same way, where the writers' hearts were smoldering in the doldrums and had no way out: they therefore conveyed everything in words narrating the past and contemplating the future." [6]

Along the lines of these comments, Mencius believed that "Adversity and suffering are often the cause for men to acquire virtue, wisdom, intelligence and ability. Alienated people and descendents of concubines, since they behave themselves with the greatest caution and are constantly aware of the dangers, survive and prosper while others are in trouble" . And again, "By sending them affliction, Heaven strips their mental lassitude, perfects their abilities through various tough measures... It is only when they are frustrated and contemplative that they start achieving something... And thus we know life survives and thrives in calamity and perishes in ease and pleasure." As Zhao Qi put it in his explanatory note: "It is only under such conditions that a man conceives extraordinary plans and strategies, or generates emotional eloquence... Hence it is that we survive in hardship." [7]

Huan Tan put his views in *New Judgments*: "If Jia Yi had not been degraded and disheartened, his literary talent would never have manifested itself... If Yang Xiong had not been destitute, he would never have composed *The Mystery*." As Zhao Qi said in his preface to *Mencius*: "In my adversity and impoverishment, my spirit indulged itself in endless reveries and I could not bring it back to have peace of mind. I finally decided to fetter my mind to brush and ink, so as to employ my fantasy to nullify the approach of old age." In his *Ranking of Poets*, Zhong Rong comments on the Han figure Li Ling: "His life and fate were out of harmony with one another, so that his reputation tarnished and his body was left in a foreign land. If Li Ling had not suffered such agony, how could his writing have ever achieved its excellence?" [8]

That is to say, once a man has survived the hardship, however, he should fulfill his mission wholeheartedly. A true gentleman should dwell in the spacious place of the world (benevolence), occupy the right position of the world (justice), and walk down the broadest way of the world (righteousness). When he achieves his purpose, he will go along the way with the people; when he fails to achieve his purpose, he will practice the *Dao* alone. He cannot be dissipated by wealth and honors, nor re-orientated by poverty and obscurity, nor made to bend by power and force—all these characteristics constitute the great man.[9]

However, some noble quality must have been infused into a true gentleman, which is grander than life: "Life is what I desire, and righteousness is also what I long for; if in an occasion where I cannot have both, I will certainly leave life and go for righteousness. I like life indeed, but there is something which I like more than life, I thus will not seek to obtain it in any ignoble ways. I dislike death, but there is something which I dislike even more than death, so I would sometimes not eschew disaster." Concerning the characteristics of a person, they have to be viewed as a whole. In this regard, Mencius initiated the idea of "the coherence of mind and eyes" . That's to say, the best way to observe a man is to look at the pupils of his eyes, which cannot hide his ill-feelings. If within the heart all be right his pupils are bright; if not, they are dull. Thus, listen to his words and watch his pupils, no one can conceal his character.[10]

Few people may know that this idea was primarily concerned with painting, however since it had revealed the rational relations between a person's quality and his "products"—could all be viewed as his manifestation, it exerted profound influence on the tradition of Chinese painting, particularly the figure paintings.[11]

注 释

[1]"以意逆志"，出自《孟子·万章上》，全句为，"故说《诗》者，不以文害辞，不以辞害志；以意逆志，是为得之"，指用自己的心思去揣度别人的意图，包含了孟子对艺术欣赏的深刻理解：要全面分析诗的整个篇章和正确理解诗所表达的思想情感。此处根据中国绘画语境，变通为 The form is shaped by the thought。

[2]“颂其诗，读其书，不知其人，可乎？是以论其世也，是尚友也”出自《孟子·万章下》，其意为“吟咏他们的诗，读他们的书，不知道他们到底是什么人，可以吗？所以要了解他们所处的历史时代，与他们交朋友”。似乎可以译成 When you sing their poems, read their books, but you don't know who they really are, can that be possible? So it's important to understand their historical era and make friends with them./ Is it alright to chant their poems, read their books, but not identify who they really are? Therefore, learn about their historical backdrop and become companion to them. 等，此处稍将语序调整，变通为 When studying their books and reading their poems, is it possible not to know the person? This has to ascend the authors' historical background and making friends with them。

另外，“以辞会意”出自《孟子·万章上》，其字面意思为 to convey meaning through words，其实可以译得更加充实：to read their minds through the language in order to gain the proper apprehension。

[4] 此处的“胸中”不是一般意思上的 bosom 或 heart，而是指一种认知，故选用了 mind。

另外，“养浩然之气”似还可译成 fostering one's great noble spirits，此处变通为 nourishing the passion-nature。

[5]“四体不言而喻”，出自《孟子·尽心上》，简单而言，可译成 It speaks for itself，但此处不妨译得翔实些：conveying message without the use of any language。

[7]“生于忧患”似还可译成 born of distress、life springs from sorrow and calamity、hardship will lead to prosperity 等，此处简化为 survive in hardship。

[9]“富贵不能淫，贫贱不能移，威武不能屈，此之谓大丈夫”，出自《孟子·滕文公下》，按照字面意思，似可译成 Neither riches nor honors can corrupt him; neither poverty nor humbleness can make him swerve from principle; and neither threats nor forces can subdue him—all these make a person a true gentleman. 此处变通为：He cannot be dissipated by wealth and honors, nor re-orientated by poverty and obscurity, nor made to bend by power and force—all these characteristics constitute the great man，以更符合具体语序。

[10]“死亦我所恶，所恶有甚于死者，故患有所不辟也”，出自《孟子·告子上》，其意为“死亡是我所厌恶的，我所厌恶的有比死亡更厉害的东西，所以有的灾祸我不躲避”，故译为 so I would sometimes not eschew disaster。

原 文

儒学对中国古代绘画理论的渗透（3）

阴阳和谐

在中国传统文化里，因万物源于阴阳对立面的组合，故艺术品的质量在很大意义上取决于阴阳和谐的程度。“阴”和“阳”的概念最早由《易经》这本凝聚了独具中国传统智慧（特别是“易学”）的书加以详述；该书揭示了作用于世间的基本原则，对后世乃至当今中国人生活的方方面面产生了深远影响。[1]

人类如何理解自然变化规律，自早期历史开始这便是困扰中国人的问题。他们逐渐意识到，应当理性地观察天地之变化（领会天意），而不是迷信地供奉以趋利避害。如文献所载，圣贤们默默地以卦占卜以求得奇迹，即“极数知来之谓占，通变之谓事，阴阳不测之谓神”。[2]

同时，用天数和地数（如二、三）来分别代表奇数和偶数，这些数字演变成了六条线，“六画而成卦；分阴分阳，迭用柔刚，故《易》六位而成章”，“刚柔相推，变在其中矣；系辞焉而命之，动在其中矣”。[3]

就其形式而言，不同的组合（杂卦）预示着不同的事物，如《乾》刚，《坤》柔，《比》乐，《师》忧；《临》《观》之义，或予或求。《屯》见而不失其居，《蒙》杂而著。[4]

《周易》认为，如地之厚重，文人的品性亦应博大无边，与万物规律合拍。应用到日常生活，则观形议象，效法乾坤，如此可赐予天命。[5]

同时，中国文人开始关注词（形式）与意（内容）的关系，对于万物的认识，无论是老子的“道”，还是孔子的“礼”，都须合乎自然变化的规律，与阴阳合拍。然而，二者的不相称，似乎又是永恒的，如孔子所言，“书不尽言，言不尽意”。[6]

孔子这种对于形式与内容关系的思考，对于后世作者与其作品的关系，有着长久的启示。对于这些变化的透彻理解，涉及形象塑造、角度设计、主观判断、变幻移情、盈涨消衰等，而阴阳八卦的转换，以及乾卦的多种组合，呼风唤雨、形态节气等，都可反映在一个人的作品中。[7]

如《周易》所说，“夫大人者，与天地合其德，与日月合其明，与四时合其序，与鬼神合起吉凶；先天而天弗违，后天而奉天时。天且弗违，而况于人乎？况于鬼神乎？”可见，只有深层把握阴阳变幻，才能创作出有分量的作品。关于艺术创作，如刘勰在《文心雕龙·物色》中所言：“春秋代序，阴阳惨舒，物色之动，心亦摇焉。盖阳气萌而玄驹步，阴律凝而丹鸟羞，微虫犹或入感，四时之动物深矣。若夫珪璋挺其惠心，英华秀其清气，物色相召，人谁获安？”[8]

所以，阴阳的驱动与和谐是艺术创作的基础。在中国绘画史上，典型的例子，如《世说新语》所记载，东晋时期的大画家顾恺之把其好友谢幼舆画在岩石之中，当问起他为何如此时，他说，谢的阴阳情怀全在丘壑之中，超越他人，自有天趣，故当如此着笔。在其他场合，顾恺之画人像时，有时几年都不点上眼睛的瞳孔，人们问其原因，他说，“四肢的美丑，本于画的奥妙所在无甚紧要，而人物的平衡支点、传神之处，全在眼睛”。他为后人留下了许多精品。[9]

总之，不同于西方摄影艺术式的现实主义绘画（如德拉克洛瓦的《自由领导人民》和《希俄岛的屠杀》，籍里柯的《梅杜萨之筏》等那样震撼人心的作品），中国绘画渗透着儒家根深蒂固的阴阳和谐理念，既情动于中而“外张”，又节制收敛而“内顺”，整体平衡，体现着中国文人的情操、性格和趣味。[10]

译 文

The Infiltrated Influence of Confucianism on Traditional Chinese Painting (3)

Harmonizing *Yin* and *Yang*

Since everything in traditional Chinese culture is constituted of two opposites—*yin* and *yang*, the quality of an artistic work is therefore to a great extent determined by the degree of harmonizing *yin* and *yang*. The concepts of *yin* and *yang* were initially elaborated in *The Book of Changes* which accumulated inestimable wisdom of Chinese tradition, particularly the “changeology” that is uniquely Chinese. The book reveals some fundamental principles that are believed to have been operating in the world, and thus has profound influence on almost every aspect of the Chinese way of living even today.[1]

How could the human mind embrace the natural law of change? This was an issue hung up in people's mind in the very early stage of China's history. The Chinese thus realized that it was necessary to be rational in observing the changes of heaven and earth (following the minds of heaven and earth), and not to be superstitious with sacrifice and divination in order to pursue good fortune and avoid misfortune. As it is recorded, the sages silently prayed to the bright and miraculous nature by making yarrow stalks for divination. To count all numbers with yarrow stalks in predicting the future is called "divination" ; to comprehend changes of all things of creation is called "states under heaven" ; to envisage the uncertainty of *yin* and *yang* is called "subtle spirit" .[2]

Meanwhile, they used heavenly and earthly numbers (e.g. two and three) to signify odd and even numbers, and these numbers further evolved into six lines. The six lines were then subdivided into three pairs of *yin* and *yang* positions and distributed with alternation of yielding and firm lines, formulating the completed pattern of changeology. When yielding and firm lines vary coordinately, the philosophy of change is functional; when the hexagram and linear judgments are attached to explain good fortune and misfortune, the law of changes became manifested.[3]

In terms of formality, different combinations (mixed hexagrams) denote different things. For example, the Qian (乾) hexagram symbolizes firmness and Kun (坤) hexagram yieldingness. The Bi (比) hexagram signifies joy, and Shi (师) hexagram worry. The implications of the Lin (临) and the Guan (观) hexagrams are to provide and pursue respectively. While the Tun (屯) hexagram stands for birth of life without losing the proper places, the Meng (蒙) hexagram represents the mixed bright and dark state of obvious childlike innocence.[4]

As it is stated in *The Book of Changes* that since earth is thick and obedient, a literati accumulates his virtue and embraces all things of creation in a boundless way, which are in turn reflected in typical patterns of thinking analogical to the natural law. In applying it to daily life, a true gentleman, in his usual time ponders over the images and dwells on the hexagram and linear judgments before taking action. In this way, he will be blessed by heaven and good fortune.[5]

In the meantime, the Chinese literati began to pay attention to the relation between word (form) and meaning (content)—whether it was a name for the ontology of the universe as Lao Zi called it the *Dao*, or was the name perceived by Confucius as ritual, it had to be reasonable and correct in the sense of following the natural law of changes, or the properly balanced *yin* and *yang*. However, the mismatch between the two had always been there as Confucius realized: "Writing cannot record an utterance in full just like an utterance cannot convey a person's thought in full." [6]

What Confucius contemplated about the relation between word and meaning had everlasting implications for successive generations in terms of studying the relation between the author and his works. The thorough understanding of all these changes involves the invention of images, design of hexagrams, attachment of judgments, alteration and transformation, encouragement and elaboration. Mutual communion, alternation between yielding *yin* and firm *yang* had evolved into the eight trigrams, and various combinations of two trigrams form the six-four hexagrams. It is just like thunder rumbles, wind breezes, rain moistens, the sun, the moon, seasons... waving in cycles, and those patterns, features and shapes may all be manifested in man's works.[7]

As *The Book of Changes* says, "After an arduous period of cultivation, a true gentleman should have virtue as enormous as heaven and earth, and wisdom as brilliant as the sun and moon. He works in a fine order as the alteration of the seasons and reveals destiny miraculously as ghosts and gods do. So tacitly agreed with one another, the action he takes is by no means contradictory to the heavenly will whether in advance or after the event. Since heaven does not do anything against him, how can man do? And how can ghosts and gods do?" Only firmly based on this ground can a literati produce something meaningful since the correlation between his practice and the law of *yin-yang* has been established. Concerning artistic creation, as the famous critic Liu Xie (465-520) remarked: "Springs and autumns alter in succession with gloomy *yin* and cheerful comforting *yang*. As the sensuous colors of physicals are stirred up to move, so the mind is shaken. When the *yang* force vegetates, the black ant rushes out; when the *yin* force aggregates, the mantis cherishes. It affects the responses of even the tiniest insects as the four seasons agitate everything profoundly. Then there is a piece of jade that evokes the humane mind, and the grandeur of flowers that flicks the pure and fresh air. As all the sensuous colors of physicals arouse one another, how amid all this can man keep unaffected?" [8]

Therefore, the alteration and harmonization of *yin* and *yang* both internally and externally constitute the foundation for artistic creation. A typical example was the well-known painter Gu Kaizhi (344-405), who once painted his friend Xie Youyu among crags and rocks, as *A New Collection of Anecdotes of Famous Personages* had recorded. When someone asked him why he drew the figure like that, he said, in my view Xie's balance of *yin* and *yang* and enormous interest had totally been in these gullies and gorges, which exceeded anybody else, so it's better for me to put him in that background. Also, in some occasions, Gu painted a portrait without dotting the pupils of the eyes for several years. When asked the reason, he replied that the beauty or ugliness of the four limbs is basically irrelevant to the subtlety of a painting; the vital part of a person's balance lies precisely in these dots which convey lifelike expressions. In that way, his many masterpieces as cultural heritages have been left today.[9]

In short, unlike western paintings, widely recognized by their photographic realism, such as Eugène Delacroix's *Liberty Leading the People* and *The Massacre at Chios*, Théodore Géricault's *Raft of the Medusa* and so on, which are thrilling and heart-shaking indeed, Chinese painting as a whole, being embellished or even flamboyant externally but reserved and restraint internally in a balanced way, mainly conveys the literatus' sentiment, character and taste shaped by the philosophy of *yin* and *yang*, which is after all deeply rooted in the tradition of Confucianism.[10]

注 释

[1]“组合”的对应词有 combination、assembly、group 等，此处结合前面的“阴阳对立面”，译为 is constituted of (two opposites—*yin* and *yang*)。

[2]“极数知来之谓占，通变之谓事，阴阳不测之谓神”，出自《周易 · 系辞上传》，有的译成 Calculating to predict is called Divination; access to the secrets of change is called Acumen; not knowing the reason of Shade and Shine is called Mystery. 实有误解。该段的意思为：极尽数术的推演，知道将来的变化就是“占”；通达变化之道就是“事”；能运用阴阳之道，解神奇奥妙、变化莫测者，就是“神”，即一种理解力。故

此，译为 To count all numbers with yarrow stalks in predicting the future is called “divination”; to comprehend changes of all things of creation is called “states under heaven”; to envisage the uncertainty of *yin* and *yang* is called “subtle spirit”，强调的是种悟性。

[3]“六画而成卦；分阴分阳，迭用柔刚，故《易》六位而成章”，出自《周易·说卦》，意为“六画卦体中分有阴位与阳位，柔与刚在阴位阳位上来回交替变化；如此，《易经》六十四个卦体都有六个不同的爻位形成了各自不同的特性和章法”，故译为 The six lines were then subdivided into three pairs of *yin* and *yang* positions and distributed with alternation of yielding and firm lines, formulating the completed pattern of changeology。

另外，“……动在其中矣”，出自《周易·系辞下传》，指天下各种活动便都在其（《易经》）中了，但此处不必刻意译成 in this way, all kinds of activities are included in *The Book of Change*，可以变通为 the law of changes became manifested，以求译出其实质。

[4]“《屯》见而不失其居，《蒙》杂而著”，出自《周易·杂卦传》，意为“屯卦是万物开始出现，各不丧失其位置，蒙卦是万物杂处而显著”，此处将其意思作了些变通：While the Tun（屯）hexagram stands for birth of life without losing the proper places, the Meng（蒙）hexagram represents the mixed bright and dark state of obvious childlike innocence.

[6]“书不尽言，言不尽意”，出自《周易·系辞上传》，该句不可就字面意思译成 The book does not say everything it says, nor all its meanings in the language，而宜变通为 Writing cannot record an utterance in full just like an utterance cannot convey a person’s thought in full.，以译出其实质。

[8]“天且弗违，而况于人乎？况于鬼神乎？”出自《周易·乾卦》，其意为：“天尚且不违背他，何况人呢？何况鬼神呢？”故变通为：Since heaven does not do anything against him, how can man do? And how can ghosts and gods do?

原文

我愿在睡梦中逝去

我愿在睡梦中逝去，
没有挣扎、痛苦、累赘、叹息；
在和谐中悄然无声，
人与自然最完美的统一。

人生本是一段奔波的旅途，
看遍路旁风景，
尝够酸甜苦辣，
走到尽头之时就该知足！

译 文

I Wish to Depart from the World in My Sleep

I wish to depart from the world in my sleep,
No burdensome struggle, pain, or weep;
Everything harmonizes in silence,
Nature's fruits I eternally reap.

Life is a journey,
Perfected by sceneries, joys and sorrows all the way with thee;
Never ever reluctant,
Everything has its destiny.

深度解析篇

原 文

探究审美认知的神经机制

人类自古追求美，人类的审美文化源远流长。它经历了各种阶段，如今进入了新的研究领域。[1]

其源头，可溯及古代神话。中国的有仓颉造字、伏羲画卦、嫦娥奔月等，西方以古希腊神话为代表，如“伊利亚特”、“奥德赛”、“神谱”等。从现代审美角度看，中国神话故事注重的是德性美、行为美和社会美，而古希腊神话故事，更多地表现为艺术美、生命美和情感美。[2]

中国的传统审美文化，如同其传统哲学一样，也是建立在“天人合一”的理念之上的，主要体现为心物交感、传神达意、知行合一的人格涵养之美，言行仪表、烹饪餐饮、园林建筑等的实用之美，山水花草、星移斗转、万物逢时的象征之美，但却从未触及审美行为的情感机制和认知层级，更不用说大脑神经活动。[3]

西方的审美文化，基于其艺术和理性的基因，到了 18 世纪中叶，已呈现出自下而上的思致升级过程，特别是鲍姆嘉通《美学》的问世，标志了美学这一独立学科的建立。鲍氏认为，人的认识活动有“明晰的认识”和“朦胧的认识”两种形态，对其研究而言，前者是逻辑学的任务，后者则是美学的任务。[4]

比较中西传统审美文化，尽管二者有某些根本性质的不同，但就中国的“天人合一”论与西方的“主客一体化”思想而言，二者又有某些契合之处，对于探究人类审美的认识规律、建立人文与科学相统一的美学认识论有独特的启示。只是，西方美学中的科学因素逐渐起到主导作用，以至最终走向了具有自然科学性质的学科。[5]

18世纪后叶，美学在有关人类知性、智性想象和理性意识建构方面有了突破性的发展，其中康德、黑格尔等作为美学思想家的贡献功不可没。例如，在《纯粹理性批判》中，康德以严谨的逻辑论证了人类认知活动从感性、知性到理性的必然路径，为美学体系的深化和完整构建提供了思想框架。黑格尔则又从诸多方面，直接或间接地提升了美学研究的主体品格、主观意识和人类审美认知的创造性特质。然而，应当说，直到19世纪中叶，美学研究在世界范围，还只处于审美认知活动的低级阶段，尚未触及认知活动核心动力和审美情感评价系统的深层结构。[6]

20世纪中下叶，审美研究随着人类心脑本体论的审美认知而转向，特别是20世纪80年代脑科学的蓬勃发展，为美学形成真正意义上的认知机制奠定了坚实的基础。[7]

2014年以来，《自然》等著名科学杂志发表了一系列对于美学的跨学科性研究，取得了重大成果，标志着“神经美学”的正式诞生。这是一门新兴的涉及认知神经科学的交叉性学科，探究的是理解审美经验的生物学基础。由此，人类对于美学的研究进入了探究审美认知神经机制的崭新阶段。[8]

概括而言，这种探究主要在三个领域进行：其一，通过对有关审美行为的神经电生理学实验进行观测，为人们提供了用于观察人的审美情感反应、审美知觉判断、审美记忆加工和审美意象输出的精准的电脑指标；其二，有关审美情感、审美想象和审美意识的神经成像研究，为人们提供了在审美情感活动、审美想象活动和审美表达活动等方面的结构性特征、功能性指标及其信息变化模式；其三，有关审美活动中大脑神经化学物质变化的实证研究成果，为人们深入、具体、细致地标定人类审美的正负情感、情感反应强度、映射审美表达活动的分子神经生物学反应模式等，提供了精准的定量数据。[9]

目前为止，神经美学在探索艺术与审美创造的大脑机制方面，取得了开拓性的成果，为美学研究开辟了新途径，有利于提升美学研究的客观化品格。其部分理论，得到了认知神经科学及神经影像学最新实证研究的间接印证，在前额叶背外侧正中区负责加工审美对象、前额叶腹内侧正中区负责加工审美情感、眶额皮层负责加工审美观念等诸方面，体现出宝贵的认知价值。[10]

诚然，审美认知神经机制的探究，涉及人脑与机体的多层级的神经化学反应、脑电活动与生理变化等等，内容异常复杂。特别是要在传统智慧的基础上运用现代科技成果，构制出具有中国特色的审美认知心脑模型，还有很长的路要走。[11]

译 文

Exploration into the Neural Mechanism of Aesthetic Cognition

While human beings have always been in pursuit of beauty since ancient times, aesthetic culture has also gone through various phases, and has now entered a new field of research.[1]

Its origin can be traced back to ancient mythologies: in ancient China, "Invention of Characters by Cang Jie", "Fuxi's drawing the trigrams", "the Goddess Chang's fly to the moon" and so on, while in the West, ancient Greek mythologies, such as the "Iliad", "Odyssey" and "Genealogy" among others. Viewed from the perspective of modern aesthetics, Chinese mythologies manifest more the beauty of virtue, behavior and community, whereas ancient Creek mythologies reflect more the beauty of art, life and emotions.[2]

Like its traditional philosophy, Chinese traditional aesthetic culture is also based on the theory that "humanity is an integral part of nature", embodying the beauty of personal cultivation through empathy, vividness and execution, its functionality in courtesy, cuisine and landscape, and the symbolism of mountains, waters, flowers, grass, changing of the seasons and the myriad of things that thrive at the right time. Nevertheless, it never touched upon issues like the emotional mechanism of aesthetic behavior and cognitive tiers, let alone neurological activities in the brain.[3]

Rooted in its artistic and rational genes, the mentality of Western aesthetic culture had been continuously upgraded up to the 18th Century, highlighted by the publication of Baumgarten's *Aesthetics*, which marked its birth as an independent discipline. According to Baumgarten, there are two forms of human cognition—one transparent and the other vague. In terms of exploration, the former is the task of logic while the latter requires attention of aesthetics.[4]

In comparing Chinese and Western traditional aesthetic cultures, despite fundamental differences, there are certain similarities or overlaps between the Chinese theory of "man as an integral part of nature" and the Western concept of "integration of subject and object" , which shed unique light into probing the laws of human aesthetic cognition and forming its epistemology based on the combination of humanities and science. However, the scientific factors in Western aesthetics have gradually played a dominant role, eventually moving it towards a subject of a scientific nature.[5]

In the late 18th Century, aesthetics made a breakthrough in areas of intellect, imagination and rationality. Among aesthetic thinkers, Kant and Hegel made significant contributions. For example, in *Critique of Pure Reason*, Kant demonstrated with rigorous logic the inevitable path of human cognitive activities from sensibility, through intellectuality to rationality. In this way, it provides an intellectual framework for the deepening and complete construction of an aesthetic system. He was followed by Hegel, who directly or indirectly promoted their subjective character, consciousness and aesthetic cognitive creativity in research from various aspects. However, it should be pointed out that until the middle of the 19th Century, aesthetic research in the world was still at the level where aesthetics' core cognitive motives and the deep structure of emotional evaluation remained yet to be explored.[6]

In the latter half of the 20th Century, aesthetic research witnessed a turn to the ontology of heart and brain. The vigorous development of brain science in the 1980s, in particular, laid a solid foundation for the establishment of the cognitive mechanism of aesthetics in a true sense.[7]

Since 2014, a series of interdisciplinary research papers on aesthetics have been published in several prestigious scientific journals, such as *Nature*. With these significant research achievements, "Neuroaesthetics", a new interdisciplinary subject, emerged, involving cognitive neuroscience and exploring the biological basis for understanding aesthetic experience. With this development, the study of aesthetics has entered a brand new stage of exploring the neural mechanism of aesthetic cognition.[8]

Generally speaking, the explorations are being carried out in the following three fields. First, the experimental observation of neuroelectrophysiology on aesthetic behaviors offers accurate computing indicators for perceiving people's aesthetic emotional responses, perception judgment, memory processing and imagery outputting. Second, neuroimaging research on aesthetic emotion, imagination and consciousness is providing the structural characteristics, functional indicators and informational change patterns in aesthetic emotions, imaginations and expressions. Third, the empirical results of neurochemical changes in the brain produce accurate quantitative data for people to deeply, concretely and carefully calibrate their positive and negative aesthetic emotions, emotional response intensity, and molecular neurobiological response patterns that map their aesthetic expressions.[9]

Neuroaesthetics has so far made pioneering achievements in exploring the brain mechanism for artistic and aesthetic creation, opened up a new frontier for aesthetics and improved the objectivity of research. Some of its theories have been indirectly confirmed by the latest empirical research in cognitive neuroscience and iconography. People's previous cognitive values are mainly reflected in the dorsolateral medial prefrontal area (responsible for processing aesthetic objects), the ventromedial prefrontal area (responsible for processing aesthetic emotions), and the orbitofrontal cortex (responsible for processing aesthetic concepts).[10]

Surely, given its involvement with multi-level neurochemical reactions between the human brain and body organism, brain electrical activities, physiological transformations and so on, the exploration of the neural mechanism of aesthetic cognition can be extremely complicated. In particular, there is still a long way to go when it comes to constructing a characteristically Chinese mental model of aesthetic cognition by applying modern scientific and technological achievements on the basis of traditional wisdoms.[11]

解 析

翻译：在人文与科技间着笔

该文涉及美学研究的一个新领域——“神经美学”，即传统人文领域的美学与现代医学中神经学的结合，其中的概念和内容自然多属跨学科的。对于翻译，既提出了挑战，又提供了可探究的新课题。

一、“硬概念”的疏通

所谓“硬概念”（hard concepts），在此主要有两种含义，一是指本身具有丰厚的历史、人文内涵，二是指由人文与科技间跨学科生成的新概念。

[1] 中的“审美”（美学）一词源于希腊语 Aisthetikcs，基本含义是“用感官去感知”，最早由德国美学家鲍姆嘉通于 1750 年在其《美学》（*Ästhetik*）一书中提出（[4]），他认为 Ästhetik

的意思是“感性之学”或“感知—情感之学”，其研究对象是“完美的感性认识”。他将人的心理活动分为情、知、意三个方面，认为美学是研究人的情感和艺术活动的一门科学，因为人类的情感活动不是独立的行为，而是相当于人之认识活动的感性阶段（Baumgarten, 2010: 29）。

如［8］中所述，西方美学经过各个历史阶段的发展，最终出现了“神经美学”。对于该词的翻译，采用了前缀 neuro- 与 aesthetics 相结合的方式。神经是人的中枢，本应与人的所有智力活动密切相关。然而，之前 neuro- 多与自然学科相结合，如 neuro-anatomy（神经解剖学）、neuro-oncology（神经肿瘤学）、neuro-ophthalmology（神经眼科学）等，后随着跨学科的涌现，亦偶有与文科结合的现象，如 neuro-linguistic programming（神经语言程序学）等。但随着“神经现象”的扩展，又相继出现了有关术语。例如，在西方，当神经知识日益渗透到人们日常生活、社会实践及智力讨论中时（neuroscience knowledge partakes in our daily lives, social practices and intellectual discourses），又出现了“神经文化”（neuroculture）一词（Illes, 2013: 163）；而当脑科学和认知科学的教育用途服务于广泛社会功能时（educational applications of the brain and cognitive sciences serve a wide range of social functions），人们又创造出了“神经教育者”（neuroducator）一词，该角色责任明确地致力于弥合神经科学与教育之间的差距（a person explicitly devoted to bridging the gaps between neuroscience and education responsibly）（Illes, 2013: 809）。

同时，[9]中的“神经电生理学”，可由neuro-、electro、physiology合成为neuroelectrophysiology，“分子神经生物学反应模式”，则可将其中的成分同位相加，为molecular neurobiological response patterns，而短语“大脑神经化学物质变化”，又可将“大脑”译成状语in the brain，形成neurochemical changes in the brain。此外，一学术专著中有如此论题——人工美的审美创造特征（丁峻，2018: 13），其中的“美”不宜译成beauty，而应变换词性，将其扩展为beautification，其意是making something more beautiful，故该话题可译为Creative Features of Aesthetic Value in Artificial Beautification。

以上是关于交叉美学学科的一些术语，而文化厚重类的，如[5]中的“‘天人合一’论与西方的‘主客一体化’”，前者有多种译法，如：the harmony between the heaven and human、integration of nature and human、combination of heaven and man、a combination of nature and humanity、correspondence between heaven and human、unity of man and nature、self as universe、nature and man are a whole one等，而后者的译文可有：subject-object all-in-one approach、subject and object are integrated as one等，考虑到前后的关联性，不妨分别译为man is an integral part of nature和integration of subject and object。

其实，对于类似理念的翻译，还可有许多变通，如《庄子·齐物论》中的“天地与我并生，而万物与我为一”，可谓“天人合一”的源头，不妨译为Heaven and earth were born with me, and myriad things have thus become one with me. 而当代哲学家金岳霖对此的诠释是:“最多、最广义的‘天人合一’，就是主体融入客体，或客体融入主体，坚持根本同一，泯除一切显著差别，从而达到个人与宇宙不二的状态。”这段话翻译时可作更大尺度的变通，如：In the most general sense, “harmonizing man and nature” means that the subject and object are mutually merged as one, eliminating all substantial differences, so as to reach a state of unity between individuals and the universe. 特别是将其中的“主体融入客体，或客体融入主体，坚持根本同一”浓缩为 the subject and object are mutually merged as one，使译文更加简练。

中国著名美学家李泽厚提出了“人类学本体论美学”，似可译成 The Ontological Aesthetics of Anthropology，但分析起来，Ontology 和 Anthropology 的实质分别是 the nature of existence、the study of the human race, especially of its origins, development, customs and beliefs，结合作者的释意“审美之本质内容、美学之根本对象只存在于人类自身之中”（李泽厚，2002: 3），很容易使美学陷入主观唯心主义之中，而将自然之美和艺术之美等排斥在外了。另一位美学家蒋孔阳在《美学新论》中创立了一个新学派——“新实践–创造美学”（蒋孔阳，2005: 160），英文是 New Practice-Creative Aesthetics，但其中的 New Practice 会让英语读者费解，因为相对的 Old Practice 是什么呢？二者之间的根本区别有哪些？其实，在美学研究领域，通常将人类实践活动划分为“物质性实践”（physical practice）、“科学性实践”（scientific practice）、“认识性实践”（cognitive practice）、“审美性实践”（aesthetic practice）等几种形态，因而，中国美学家在提出相应概念时，不妨参照一下西方美学界的流行概念。

二、整体意义上的等值

这类人文与科技跨学科的文章，其中不但多“硬概念”，而且多复杂句子，需作诸多分解、变通和调整，但就翻译而言，应始终注重其对原文的整体等值效果。

［10］中，“目前为止，神经美学在探索艺术与审美创造的大脑机制方面，取得了开拓性的成果，为美学研究开辟了新途径，有利于提升美学研究的客观化品格”，其中的“开辟了新途径”一般译成 has opened up a new way for...，但鉴于美学在不断开拓新领域，特别是近年形成了“精神美学”等新学科，不如用 a new frontier for aesthetics...，而“有利于提升……”似可用从句 which is conducive to enhancing... 来译，但考虑到语境前后的连贯性，此处以紧凑为宜，故可译为 ... improved（the objectivity of the research）。另外，“在前额叶背外侧正中区负责加工审美对象、前额叶腹内侧正中区负责加工审美情感、眶额皮层负责加工审美观念等诸方面，体现出宝贵的认知价值”，其中下画线部分若都采用从句 which is responsible for...，不但使句子冗长，而且很难通顺，故将这一部分放入括弧中：People's previous cognitive values are mainly reflected in the dorsolateral medial prefrontal area (responsible for processing aesthetic objects), the ventromedial prefrontal area (responsible for processing aesthetic emotions), and the orbitofrontal cortex (responsible for processing aesthetic concepts)，以作为其前置词的补充说明，使得文章主干清晰、明了，而并未扭曲其意。

对于［11］，“……审美认知神经机制的探究，涉及人脑与机体的多层级的神经化学反应、脑电活动与生理变化等等，内容异常复杂；特别是如何在传统智慧的基础上运用现代科技成果，构制出具有中国特色的审美认知心脑模型，还有很长的路要走”，若按原文句式翻译，很难摆脱“翻译腔”，故需动较大“手术”。首先，将“涉及人脑与机体的多层级的神经化学反应、脑电活动与生理变化等等”作状语，置前处理：given its involvement with multi-level neurochemical reactions between the human brain and body organism, brain electrical activities, physiological transformations and so on，然后将主语 the exploration of the neural mechanism of aesthetic cognition（审美认知神经机制的探究）引出，将“内容异常复杂”（extremely complicated）译作表语，前面补充 can be；最后一句“还有很长的路要走”，为了强调，将其提前，置于句首：there is still a long way to go...，而以 when 带出从句 it comes to constructing...；“要在传统智慧的基础上运用现代科技成果”，可理解为手段，译成状语 by applying modern scientific and technological achievements on the basis of traditional wisdoms，以求整体“信”而“达”的效果。

就“神经美学”的相关论述而言，亦可采取类似的翻译策略。例如，“（认知神经美学研究）可形成全新的审美认知的心脑范式，包括建立兼容互补与灵活切换的人脑审美认知的自由式低耗能范式与模式化高耗能范式之对立统一性框架、形成审美与艺术活动的“二度创作”认知原理及其心脑机制等，克服现行审美认知研究侧重实验数据平均化加工和基于高耗能高代谢水平判断大脑认知功能状态等认识论与方法论偏向，有效提升审美认知理论的解释力和预见性品格”（丁峻，2018: 25）。其中有许多人文与科技相结合的新概念和长句子，需“分而治之”、“综合处理”。具体而言，“全新的审美认知的心脑范式”，可为 a new paradigm of “heart-and-brain” aesthetic cognition、“二度创作”，未必是 secondary creation，而可为 by-product creation、“审美认知理论（的解释力和）预见性品格”，也不必是 character of...，而不妨用 predictability of aesthetic cognitive theory 等；就句式而言，若在一句中包括“……二度创作”，会使句子冗长，难脱翻译腔，故不妨另起一句，可以稍加重复 Such a new paradigm should... ；特别是“克服……偏向”，由于定语成分过多，宜用分句 which... 表明其内容，同时鉴于此处长句丛生，更宜将其放入括弧之中；因而，该段不妨译为：Cognitive-Neuroaesthetical research can form a new paradigm of “heart-and-brain” aesthetic cognition, including establishing a framework for a complementary unity between the free-form, low-energy-consumption paradigm and the patterned high-energy-consumption paradigm of human brain aesthetic cognition compatible with complementarity and flexible switching. Such a new paradigm should develop the cognitive principle of “by-product creation” and the mechanisms of the mind and brain that motivate aesthetic and artistic activities, in order to overcome that epistemological and methodological bias of the current aesthetic cognition research (which emphasizes the average processing of experimental data and the judgment of the cognitive function of the brain based on high energy consumption and high metabolic level), so as to effectively enhance the explanatory power and predictability of aesthetic cognitive theory.

再如，“有道是‘外观有限，内涵无穷’。人类的审美行为也是如此，其间所引发的超级复杂的精神嬗变及脑体进化事件，当然会远远超过外显的感性事象与物性事体。说来也算巧合，神经美学难道不正是由美学和神经科学这一对特殊的主客体系统发生相互作用而化合新生的学科交叉体与知识综合体吗？”（丁峻，2018: 31）其中，“外观有限，内涵无穷”，不宜按字面意思直译成 limited in appearance and unlimited in content，而应以英文形合特点加上相关连词、代词等，将其贯穿起来，可译为：while appearances are limited, their connotations are infinite；“说来也算巧合”，似乎是 it is a coincidence...，但结合后面的问句“难道不正是……？”可理解为“并非巧合”（It is not by coincidence that...），以示强调，而“新生的学科交叉体与知识综合体”，看似是两个新概念，实则为同位语，因而整段不妨调整为：As the saying goes, “while appearances are limited, their connotations are infinite”. The same is true of the aesthetic behavior of human beings, in which the super-complex spiritual evolution and the fruits of the evolved brain, will certainly far surpass explicit, perceptual and physical things. It is not by coincidence that aesthetics and neuroscience interact and combine into a special subject-object system, a new interdisciplinary field.

尽管由于人文与科技融合的特点，译文在字面上与原文看似不大对称，但经过种种变通与调整之后，仍可在整体上达到大致等值的效果。

三、重叠成分的处理

由于中英两种文字的成分、结构的不同，特别是在跨学科的语境下，在转述中有时需进行浓缩或删减。

具体而言，[3]中，有“……的人格涵养之美”、“……的实用之美”、“……象征之美”，不必将其对应为 the beauty of personal cultivation、the beauty of functionality、the beauty of symbolism，而可将后面两个 beauty 省略。[4]中的“‘明晰的认识’和‘朦胧的认识’两种形态”，不宜译成 the transparent cognition and the vague cognition，而不妨译为（there are two forms of human cognition）—one transparent and the other vague。

[6]中的“人类知性”是 human intellectuality？“智性想象”是 intellectual imagination？“理性意识”是 rational awareness？“主观意识”是 subjective consciousness？显然，这类词组中前面的成分对于后面的成分来讲，是不言自明的，应删去，而只分别保留 intellect、imagination、rationality 和 consciousness 即可。

同样，[9]中“审美情感活动、审美想象活动和审美表达活动”，亦可浓缩为 aesthetic emotion, imagination and consciousness；“实证研究成果”不必是 the empirical research results，而

可将其中的 research 省去。

［10］中的“客观化品格”不必用 objective character，而代之以 objectivity。

其实，学科间的划分，从根本上来讲，是人为的；而随着社会实践的发展，学科间的融合、跨学科的层出不穷，又是一种必然趋势。作为译者，需不断增强这方面的意识，力求在人文与科技交界的译海中游刃有余。

参考文献

① 丁峻等．当代神经美学研究［M］．北京：科学出版社，2018.

② 金岳霖著；金岳霖学术基金会学术委员会编．金岳霖学术论文选［M］．北京：中国社会科学出版社，1990.

③ 蒋孔阳．蒋孔阳全集（第 3 卷）［M］．合肥：安徽教育出版社，2005.

④ 李泽厚．美学四讲［M］．天津：天津社会科学院出版社，2002.

⑤ Baumgarten A. G. *Aesthetica Scripsit* [M]. Gutenberg: Nabu Press, 2010.

⑥ Illes, Judy. *The Oxford Handbook of Neuroethics* [M]. New York: Oxford University Press, 2013.

原 文

作为特殊形态的法律外交

“外交”，长期以来是个颇为复杂的概念，中外学者容易将其与对外政策等相混淆；而近年出现的“法律外交”新概念，更是一种特殊的外交形态。[1]

在本质上，外交是指一个国家为实现其对外政策所从事的处理国际关系的活动。因而，外交是国家之间进行和平交往的方式，分为多个种类、不同层次。[2]

自古以来，中华民族有着丰富的法律文化资源，如儒家的“出礼入刑”、“德主刑辅”、“仁爱、和谐、诚信、中庸”、“君子和而不同”、“和为贵”；道家的崇尚自然，主张清静无为，追求神灵、天道；佛家的自主调整、以德报怨等等。同时，我国亦有着数千年的外交实践和丰富的外交思想，如知己知彼、纵横捭阖、远交近攻、睦邻以礼等，独具特色。而早在春秋战国时期，中华法制思想便初具雏形，至隋唐有了完备体系，后逐渐形成以中国为中心，包括日本、越南等亚洲国家在内的中华法系，在其对外关系中起到重要作用。[3]

鸦片战争之后，清王朝统治者意识到闭关锁国的危害，开始主张参照西方大陆法系、英美法系来变法图存。特别是改革开放以来，中国全面推行依法治国，逐步形成自己独特的大国外交风格，改革完善全球治理体系，日益走近世界舞台的中央。[4]

纵观国际关系发展史，其文明的进步，主要体现在从武力到外交、从实力外交到法律外交的演变过程。丛林法则逐渐退出国际秩序，靠的是建立在现代文明基础上的法治意识和法律手段。[5]

随着法律对于政治、经济、军事、文化、环境等广泛领域的渗透，法律外交成为必然趋势，这是一种与政治外交、经济外交、军事外交、文化外交、环境外交等并行不悖而又有所区别的特殊外交。[6]

概括而言，“法律外交”指以法律为内容、机制和媒介的外交活动，把法治理念贯穿在外交活动之中，善于将某些外交问题转化为法律问题，以合法的程序和行为处理外交事务，从而更有效地化解外交纠纷，开辟外交局面，服务国家战略。[7]

法律外交包括“涉法”和“涉外”两个方面，即围绕法律和外交两个轴线构建起相互联动的法律外交体系。[8]

法律外交是新时代背景下诞生的新兴交叉学科，国家对外工作的需要是法律外交学科发展的不竭动力。贯彻落实习近平法治思想，就要坚持问题导向，集中多学科力量、跨学科专家智慧创新研究，把握学科发展规律，推动法律外交理论与实践的高度结合。[9]

全球化开启了法律外交的新时代。对这一特殊外交形态的深刻认识和有利把握，是我们有效展开大国外交的崭新维度和坚实基础。[10]

译 文

Legal Diplomacy: A Special Role to Play

"Diplomacy" is a concept which has long been complicated and confused with foreign policies by scholars at home and abroad. "Legal diplomacy", an issue which emerged in recent years, is certainly a special type of diplomacy.[1]

Essentially, diplomacy refers to the international relations that a country engages in in order to implement its foreign policies. Diplomacy, with its tremendous diversity, is therefore a method of peaceful exchanges between nations.[2]

Since ancient times, the Chinese nation has had rich legal cultural resources. Renowned doctrines, such as Confucian "punishment based on rituals", "morality given priority over penalty", "the decency of integrating kindheartedness, harmony, integrity and moderation", "a gentleman gets along with others, but does not necessarily agree with them", "the supremacy of harmony"; Taoist advocations that nature should be upheld and actions follow its spirit and natural law; Buddhists' self-adjustment and rendering good for evil and so on. Meanwhile, with a history of thousands of years of diplomatic practices, the Chinese are characteristically rich in diplomatic concepts, such as knowing both ourselves and our adversaries, manoeuvring among various political groupings, keeping friendly relations with distant states and confronting those nearby, remaining on friendly terms with the neighbors by way of following rituals and so on. The Chinese legal system began to take shape as early as the Spring-Autumn and the Warring States periods (770 BC-221 BC), was systematized during the Sui and Tang Dynasties (581-907) and gradually formed a more comprehensive Chinese legal system centering on China and embracing Japan, Vietnam and some other Asian countries, which played an important role in China's foreign relations.[3]

After the first Opium War (1840-1842), the rulers of the Qing Dynasty (1636-1911) realized the danger of shutting down the country and began to advocate political reform to survive by referencing Western civil law and common law systems. Especially since the "reform and opening up", China has gradually stepped onto the center of the world stage through implementing law-based government and participating in reforming and improving the global management system, with its unique diplomatic style as a major country.[4]

Taking a sweeping view of the development of international relations, its civil progress has mainly been reflected in the evolution from using force to engaging in diplomacy, from power diplomacy to legal diplomacy. The law of the jungle has been gradually replaced by legal means in the world stage with the awakening of modern civilized legal awareness.[5]

With the widespread application of laws to politics, culture, economy, military, environment and other broad fields, legal diplomacy has become an inevitable trend in practice, playing its role harmoniously with but differently from political, cultural, economic, military and environmental diplomacy.[6]

Generally speaking, this so-called "legal diplomacy" refers mainly to diplomatic activities guided by the idea of rule of law, involving legal substance, mechanisms, media and the intention to turn certain diplomatic issues into legal ones. In conducting foreign affairs, proper legal procedures and methods play an active role in resolving diplomatic disputes, opening up new prospects and serving national strategies.[7]

Dealing with both fields, legal diplomacy formulates an interactive legal diplomatic system centering on the two axes of law and diplomacy.[8]

As a fresh interdisciplinary subject, "legal diplomacy" is emerging against the background of the new era where the high demands on our foreign relations are an inexhaustible driving force for its development. In implementing Xi Jinping Thought on the Rule of Law, we must follow the law of disciplinary growth by concentrating multidisciplinary forces and interdisciplinary expertise on innovative research based on the problem-oriented approach. In such a way, legal diplomacy theory and practice will be further integrated.[9]

Globalization has opened a new era of legal diplomacy, which lays a foundation for us to effectively carry out all-round major-country diplomacy in a particular form from a new dimension, provided that we have a thorough knowledge of its essence and manoeuvre skillfully.[10]

解 析

法学新语境下的有效转述

——首届中国法律外交翻译大赛点评

"法律外交"是在经济全球化、世界多极化、全球治理法治化大背景下形成的一个日益引人注目的新概念，极具理论价值和实践意义。以此为主题所进行的首届法律外交翻译大赛，吸引了来自法学院、翻译学院、外语院校师生，法学界人士，法律工作者和广大法律翻译爱好者的兴趣和参与。经过初评、复评、终评，选出了不同等级的获奖者，举行了发奖仪式，大赛圆满落幕。

作为本届大赛的设计者和评委，现就大赛译文中的一些颇具典型性的问题进行分析、点评，以作为日后大赛的借鉴。

一、词语的推敲

对于一种法学新背景下的语言现象和行文表述，其英译必然会遇到许多新的问题。

就题目“作为特殊形态的法律外交”而言，参赛者一般译成 A Special Form of Legal Diplomacy、Legal Diplomacy as a Unique Diplomatic Form、Legal Diplomacy as a Special Form of Diplomacy、Legal Diplomacy as a Unique Diplomatic Form 等，看来都惯于将“形态”与 form 相关联。但分析起来，form 的本义是 one of several or many different ways in which something is seen, experienced, or produced，如“他们憎恶任何形式的暴力。”（They hate violence in any form.）；“这种病毒可能有几种不同的形式。”（This virus can take several different forms.）等。然而，就法律外交在国际关系中所发挥的日益重要的作用而言，不妨用 play a role或role to paly。类似的用法，如“环境因素是种特殊形态。”（Various environmental factors may have a special role to play.）；“文化背景是否也会具有特定的影响？”（Does cultural background play a special role?）等。同时，为突出主题词，可将其译为：Legal Diplomacy: A Special Role to Play。

然而，又不必拘泥于“固定对应”，而要根据具体语境有所变通，如［1］中的“一种特殊的外交形态”，则不妨为 a special type of diplomacy。同时，“颇为复杂的概念”，参赛者大都将“复杂”译成形容词，如 has long been a rather complicated concept。但就中外的外交实践而言，这一概念在不同的语境中的确被人为地复杂化了，并时常与国际关系、对外政策等相混淆，故不妨结合上下文译为 ...which has long been complicated and confused with foreign policies，更为生动、简练。

［3］中有着较为密集的古文引用词语，参赛译文异彩纷呈。较为典型的，如“出礼入刑”，一般译成 Punishing acts against norms./Penalty shall be imposed on all violations of propriety./Anything in contravention of rites shall be subject to penalty. 等，然而究其原义：“礼之所去，刑之所取；失礼则入刑，相为表里”（《汉书·陈宠传》），即是一种先礼后刑的关系，故可用 punishment based on rituals。类似的，“德主刑辅”，直译似乎是 primary virtue and accessory punishment/Morality is the primary, punishment is secondary./morality as the first and punishment as the supplement，但在行文上可稍加变通，如 morality given priority over penalty。对于“仁爱、和谐、诚信、中庸”，大都按其字面意思译成四个独立的单词，如 humanity, harmony, sincerity and golden mean/Benevolence, Harmony, Honesty, Moderation/benevolence, harmony, integrity, mean 等，但作为一种法律文化资源，这些价值之间有着内在的联系，故可适当增词，将其整合为 the decency of integrating kindheartedness, harmony, integrity and moderation。同样，“道家的崇尚自然，主张清静无为，追求神灵、天道；佛家的自主调整、以德报怨等等”，显然具有中文“意合”的特点，不宜简单地按其结构转述成英文，如 Taoism advocates nature, quietness and inaction, pursues gods and heaven;

Buddhism makes independent adjustments, repays grievances with virtue and so on. / Taoism's worship of nature, advocating quietness and inaction, the pursuit of the gods, the way of heaven; Buddhist's autonomous adjustment, repaying injury with kindness. / In Taoism, it advocates naturalness, non-action and tranquility, an action should follow its spirit and natural law; also in Buddhism, "self-adjustment", "rendering good to evil" 等，而应尽可能发挥英文"形合"的特点，使其更加连贯，如 Taoist advocations that nature should be upheld and actions follow its spirit and natural law; Buddhists' self-adjustment and rendering good for evil and so on. 另外，"中华民族有着丰富的法律文化资源"，其中的"有着"一般用 has had 亦可，而许多用了 possessed（rich legal culture resources）则显然搭配不当。此外，中国的朝代，在英译文中还应标示出年代，如"春秋战国时期"、"隋唐"，以及［4］中的"清王朝"、"鸦片战争"，可分别译为 the Spring-Autumn and the Warring States periods (770 BC-221 BC)、the Sui and Tang Dynasties (581-907)、the Qing Dynasty (1636-1911)、the first Opium War (1840-1842)，这一点在许多参赛译文中被忽略。

特别是，［4］中的"清王朝统治者"，竟有相当多的参赛者译成了 the Qing dynasty governors ；应当说，governor 是个相对现代的概念，其本义为 in most cases, a public official with the power to govern the executive branch of a non-sovereign or sub-national level of government, ranking under the head of state. In federations, governor may be the title of the politician who governs a constituent state and may be either appointed or elected. The power of the individual governor can vary dramatically between political systems, with some governors having only nominal, largely ceremonial power, while others have complete power over the entire government; In some systems of government, a governor is a person who is in charge of the political administration of a state, colony, or region，而此处的“统治者”甚至不宜用 dominator，最恰当的应为 ruler。

同段中，“逐步形成自己独特的大国外交风格”中的“大国”，有的用了 big power，但 power 的本义为 a state having international influence, esp. based on military strength，带有以军事实力威胁他国的强权内涵，不符合中国倡导的相互尊重、合作共赢的“新型大国关系”的概念，故宜用中性的 major country。

［6］中，“随着法律对于政治、经济、军事、文化、环境等广泛领域的渗透”，其中对“渗透”的翻译，参赛者用得最多的是 penetration，显然是受字典解释的影响，其次是 With the infiltration of、With the influence of law into、As the law has found its way into a wide range of 等；其实，该词在此的含义，是指法律在这些领域的日益广泛应用，即 With the widespread application of laws to...，遗憾的是，这样译的参赛译文甚少。

此外，［9］中的“习近平法治思想”大都被译成 Xi Jinping's Thought on the Rule of Law；然而，鉴于这是一个专用词语，如同“毛泽东思想”（Mao Zedong Thought）一样，有固定的译法，故宜译为 Xi Jinping Thought on the Rule of Law。

实际译文中的词语选择远超词典所列。为寻求最确切的“那一个”，还须紧贴语境，千变万化不逾矩。

二、词序的调整

由于中英语言结构的内在区别，中译英一般需作相应大幅度的调整，特别是在一种新的法学语境下，又有某些新的语言现象。

就结构转述而言，[4]中的“①特别是改革开放以来，②中国全面推行依法治国，③逐步形成自己独特的大国外交风格，④改革完善全球治理体系，⑤日益走近世界舞台的中央”，绝大多数参赛译文都遵循了原文的结构，译为：① Especially, since reform and opening up, ② China has comprehensively pursued the rule of law, ③ gradually developed its own unique style of major-country diplomacy, ④ reformed and improved the global governance system, ⑤ and moved closer to the center of the world stage./ ① Especially since the reform and opening, ② China has comprehensively administered a country according to law, ③ gradually formed its own unique great-power diplomatic, ④ reformed and improved the global governance system, ⑤ and increasingly approached to the center of the world stage./ ① Especially since the Reform and Opening up, ② China has fully implemented the rule of law, ③ gradually formed its own unique style of big power diplomacy, ④ improved the global governance system, ⑤ and increasingly approached the center of the world stage. 等，因而显得颇为中文腔（Chinglish）。有些译

文只是在状语位置上稍作调整，如：Notably, ② China has been fully advancing the law-based governance ① since it began to reform and open up. ③ Its distinct diplomatic style as a major power has been phased in. ④ Premised on this breeding ground, China reforms and bolsters the global governance system and ⑤ approaches ever closer to the globe's center. / ② The People's Republic of China, ① especially since its reform and opening-up, has been pushing forward the rule of law across the board, ③ forming its own unique style of major country diplomacy, ④ and participating in reforming and developing the global governance system. ⑤ It is now getting much closer to the center of the world stage. 等等。

分析起来，原文中的最后一句"日益走近世界舞台的中央"，是前面铺垫之后的结论性文字，因而在英文中是重点，需要强调、突出，不可与它在原文里的分量、位置相等同。类似的，如"如果想在有生之年做一点什么事，学一点什么学问，充实自己，帮助别人，使生命成为有意义，不虚此生，那么就不可浪费光阴"，如果遵循原结构译为 if you want to do..., learn..., improve..., help... more meaningful, fruitful,... time must not be wasted. 这样似乎忠实，但不符合地道的英语表达习惯。相反，如果将结论句提前译为：Time must not be wasted if you want to do your bit in your remaining years or acquire some useful knowledge to improve yourself and help others, so that your life may turn out to be significant and fruitful.，译文就会更有层次，重点突出。在这一点上，《邓小平文选》的一段翻译堪称典例："中国的事情能不能办好，社会主义和改革开放能不能坚持，经济能不能快一点发展起来，国家能不能长治久安，从一定意义说，关键在人。”翻译时，应对原文的结构作前后大幅度的调整，可译为：In a sense, personnel form the key to the issue of whether we can do well in China's domestic matters, whether socialism, reform and opening up can be adhered to, and whether the economy can grow faster and the country enjoy long-term peace and stability.

因而，就该段的翻译而言，亦可将结论性文字提置前面，即在状语之后：Especially since the “reform and opening up”, China has gradually stepped onto the center of the world stage，而为表述如何形成这个结果，可在后置部位加以说明，如通过（through）“中国全面推行依法治国”，在这个意义上，“改革完善全球治理体系”也在同一层次，而“逐步形成自己独特的大国外交风格”则可在这一过程中处理成方式状语 with...。这样一来，译文的结构则须作出较大调整：① Especially since the “reform and opening up”，⑤ China has gradually stepped onto the center of the world stage ② through implementing law-based government and ④ participating in reforming and improving the global management system, ③ with its unique diplomatic style as a major country.，以求重点和层次的更加明了。

相关的，[9] 的结构大致如此：“①法律外交是新时代背景下诞生的②新兴交叉学科，③国家对外工作的需要是法律外交学科发展的不竭动力。④贯彻落实习近平法治思想，⑤就要坚持问题导向，⑥集中多学科力量、跨学科专家智慧创新研究，⑦把握学科发展规律，⑧推动法律外交理论与实践的高度结合。”纵览参赛译文，基本上延续了这一结构，如：① Legal diplomacy is ② a rising interdisciplinary subject that emerged in the new age ③ in keen response to the practical necessities of national foreign policy. ④ The implementation of the Xi Jinping Thought on the rule of law also calls for a solid combination of legal diplomacy theories with practice, ⑤ which requests a question-directed mind, ⑥ innovative studies by interdisciplinary experts with the convergence of multidisciplinary resources, and ⑦ mastery of the development trend in related disciplinaries and ⑧ promote a high combination of practice and theory of legal diplomacy. / ① Legal diplomacy is ② a new-born cross-discipline subject in new background. ③ The needs of the country’s foreign work relentlessly motivate the development of this discipline. ④ To implement President Xi’s law spirit, ⑤ we must adhere to the problem-oriented approach, ⑥ concentrate multidisciplinary forces and interdisciplinary experts to innovate and research, ⑦ grasp the development, and ⑧ promote a high degree of integration of legal diplomacy theory and practice. / ① Legal diplomacy is ② an emerging interdisciplinary under the background of new era. ③ The need of the country’s external work is the inexhaustible motive force for the development of the subject of law and diplomacy. ④ To implement Xi Jinping’s thought on the rule of law, ⑤ we need to remain to the problem-oriented approach, ⑥ pool the wisdom and innovation of multi-disciplinary forces and experts.

⑦ To grasp the discipline development rules and ⑧ promote the high combination of theory and practice of legal diplomacy. 等等。

然而，分析起来，原文中“新兴交叉学科”固然是宾语，但在译文里，可作状语处理，且为了强调，可提前至句首，如 As a fresh interdisciplinary subject，而“新时代背景下”可作状语的另一部分融入接续句子中，即 against the background of the new era，其益处在于容易以介词引出后面的从句，即 where...。对于“③国家对外工作的需要是法律外交学科发展的不竭动力”，大多参赛译文都用了独立句子完成：The needs of the country's foreign work relentlessly motivate the development of this discipline，但用从句来表达，就自然、通顺很多：where the high demands on our foreign relations are an inexhaustible driving force for its development. 从依法治国理念与法律学科的发展规律而言，与“④贯彻落实习近平法治思想”最为紧密相关的是“⑦把握学科发展规律”，而“⑤就要坚持问题导向，⑥集中多学科力量、跨学科专家智慧创新研究”，在译文中可理解为达到上述目的的手段，可作状语处理，用 by concentrating... 引出。“⑧推动法律外交理论与实践的高度结合”在原文中是前面陈述的自然延续，但在译文里，可另起一句，如用 Only in this way can we...、In such as way...、Following this path,... 等，作一小节性归纳。

因而，翻译这段话时，需要从结构上作一较大调整：② As a fresh interdisciplinary subject, ①“legal diplomacy” is emerging against the background of the new era where ③ the high demands on our foreign relations are an inexhaustible driving force for its development. ④ In implementing Xi Jinping Thought on the Rule of Law, ⑦ we must follow the law of disciplinary growth ⑥ by concentrating multidisciplinary forces and interdisciplinary expertise on innovative research ⑤ based on the problem-oriented approach. ⑧ In such a way, legal diplomacy theory and practice will be further integrated.

文无定序。译文中的句子结构是为转述原文主旨服务的，并无固定模式。

三、整体的等值

对某些颇富特色表述的英译，需兼顾法学、文化和语言的考量，作出某些特殊的处理。但这种处理的最佳效果，不是零打碎敲，而应具有整体意识。

在［2］中，“多个种类、不同层次”，一般都习惯地译成 which can be divided into several types and different levels、can be divided into multiple types and different levels、differentiating into varied forms and levels、It can be divided into many kinds and different levels、divided into diverse types and gradations 等，固然都不错，但有时也可译得更具概括性。这一类例子在汉译英中有很多，特别是汉语中富有铺排特性的表述，英译时更需变通，如：“自古而今，马在中华民族文化中都是美好寓意的代表，如‘马到成功、万马奔腾、兵强马壮’等”，若单引号中的成语都按其字义表述出来，译为 to win success immediately upon the arrival of the horses; ten thousand horses gallop forward; strong soldiers and sturdy horses，则未必能转达出其内在含义，倒不如以 it usually means instant success and powerful strength 加以概述。

结合以上分析，参考译文用了 with its tremendous diversity，插在主语（Diplomacy）与表语（is therefore a method of...）之间，以求精练。

［8］中，“法律外交包括‘涉法’和‘涉外’两个方面”，大多参赛译文都作了分别表述，如 Legal diplomacy includes law-related and foreign-related、Legal diplomacy includes two aspects: law and foreign affairs、Legal diplomacy includes two aspects of “law” and “foreign affairs” 等。就上面的语境看，这两方面所指已颇为明确，故可直接用 Dealing with both fields,...；至于“围绕法律和外交两个轴线构建起相互联动的法律外交体系”，则不妨条分缕析地说明，从而形成一种详略互补：Dealing with both fields, legal diplomacy formulates an interactive legal diplomatic system centering on the two axes of law and diplomacy.

［5］“纵观国际关系发展史，其①文明的进步，主要体现在从武力到外交、从实力外交到法律外交的演变过程。丛林法则②逐渐退出国际秩序，靠的是建立在③现代文明基础上的法治意识和法律手段。”其中以数字标示部分，参赛译文大都作了不同的处理，例如：Judging from the history of international relations, ① the progress of the civilization mainly finds expression in the transformation from force to diplomacy, from power diplomacy to legal diplomacy. The law of the jungle ② gradually withdrawing from the international order depends on ③ the awareness of the rule of law and legal means based on modern civilization. / Throughout the history of international relations, ① the progress of its civilization is mainly reflected in evolution from force to diplomacy, and from power diplomacy to legal diplomacy. ②The gradual withdrawal of the law of the jungle from the international order depends on ③ the legal consciousness and legal measures built on modern civilization. / Throughout the development history of international relations, ① the progress of its civilization mainly reflects in the evolutionary process, ranging from force to diplomacy and from power diplomacy to legal diplomacy. ②The gradual withdrawal of law of jungle from the international order relies on ③ legal consciousness and legal means built on the basis of modern civilization. 等。分析起来，①"文明的进步"，一般可以译为 the progress of civilization，但此处不是讲一般意义上的 civilization，而是指国与国之间的关系，尤其是指法律外交的趋势发展，同时兼顾具体语境的表述，可译为 its civil progress（has been reflected...）；②"逐渐退出"，参赛者大都按其字面意思译成了 gradually withdrawing from 或 The gradual withdrawal of 等，其实这里的主要含义是指，在处理国际事务时，法律的手段更多地取代了非法律的手段，因而用 replaced 更为恰当；③"现代文明基础上的法治意识和法律手段"，很容易译成 legal consciousness and legal means built on the basis of modern civilization，其实此处的 built on the basis of 用 based on 即可，同时方式状语还可根据此处语境调整为 with the awakening of... ；

而“现代文明”与“法治意识”可结合为 modern civilized legal awareness；至于“法律手段”（legal means），因前面已经提到，此处可不必重复。因而，该段可变通为：Taking a sweeping view of the development of international relations, its civil progress has mainly been reflected in the evolution from using force to engaging in diplomacy, from power diplomacy to legal diplomacy. The law of the jungle has been gradually replaced by legal means in the world stage with the awakening of modern civilized legal awareness.

相应的，[10]“全球化开启了法律外交的新时代。对这一①特殊外交形态的②深刻认识和有利把握，是我们有效展开③大国外交的④崭新维度和⑤坚实基础”，下面是一些典型的参赛译文：Globalization has ushered in a new era of legal diplomacy. ② A deep understanding of and a favorable grasp of this ① special form of diplomacy is ④ a new dimension and ⑤ a solid foundation for our effective conduct of ③ big-country diplomacy. / Globalization has started the era of legal diplomacy. ② A profound understanding and proper utilization of ① this special form of diplomacy are a ④ brand-new dimension and ⑤ solid foundation for us to effectively carry out ③ big power diplomacy. / Globalization has launched a new era of legal diplomacy.② An insightful understanding and a positive perception of ① this special form of diploma are ④ a brand-new dimension and ⑤ solid foundation for us to effectively carry out ③ major country diplomacy. 其中，②“深刻认识和有利把握”，一般被译成 A deep understanding of and a favorable grasp of、A profound understanding and proper utilization of、An insightful understanding and a positive perception of，似乎都有一定理由，但鉴于是对“法律外交”这一新型法学本质的理解，不妨使用 essence，同时“把握”可译为动词，体现其实践的一面，如 have a thorough knowledge of its essence and manoeuvre skillfully；③“大国外交的”，直译似乎是 big-country/big-power diplomacy，但 major-country 在此是更具学术性的表述，例如：“大国关系攸关世界和平和人类福祉。”（Major-country relations bear on world peace and well-being of the mankind.）；“财政危机的压力，将迫使每个大国重新审视自己与美国之间的关系。”（Every major country will be driven by the constraints of the fiscal crisis to re-examine its relationship to America.）；In recent years, the security architecture and major-country interactions in the Asia Pacific have attracted wide attention.（近年来，亚太地区的安全架构和大国互动备受各方关注。）等。同时，在相互之间的衔接上，也应作相应调整，整段可译为：Globalization has opened a new era of legal diplomacy, which ⑤ lays a foundation for us to effectively carry out all-round ③ major-country ① diplomacy in a particular form from ④ a new dimension, provided that ② we have a thorough knowledge of its essence and manoeuvre skillfully.

总之，所谓译文与原文的含义等值，并非指具体词语的一一对应，而是指最终成果的对等。就本文而言，在进行法律外交翻译时，要具有法律外交意识，注重疏通中英文内涵，从而最大限度地做到整体等值。

原 文

法律外交与政治文明

法律外交是国际政治发展的必然趋势，是中国由法律大国向法治强国迈进的必由之路，同时也是人类社会文明演化的客观反映。[1]

人类社会从漫长的弱肉强食的“丛林法则”中痛定思痛，逐渐发展、完善了相互妥协的“文明法则”，进而从暴力政治走向协商政治，从野蛮社会进入文明社会，其中规则和法律起了决定性作用。[2]

正如法国思想家卢梭所说，“即使是最强者也绝不会强得足以永远做主人，除非他把自己的强力转化为权利，把服从转化为义务”。即一种持续稳定的政治秩序，一定要建立在合理、公正的权力与义务关系之上。[3]

就本质而言，传统政治活动围绕权力而展开，即是“权力政治”。随着政治文明的发展，人们逐渐学会了如何有效地调整权力与权利的关系，转移到以权利为核心，使权力服从权利，权力保障权利，权利制衡权力，即形成“权利政治”。[4]

在国际政治方面，则是将相关法治理念、法律原则应用到外交活动之中，善于将外交问题转化为法律问题，以合法的行为和程序化解外交纠纷，处理外交事务，从而建立、创造最符合本国利益的国际关系与国际环境。[5]

随着全球化的日益深入，世界正经历着百年未有之大变局。通过将国际关系各领域的问题法律化，国际社会业已从强权政治时代步入了多元共存的新时代。外交领域只有顺应此种变化，与时俱进，将政治、经济、文化、军事、环境等问题作为法律议题展开外交活动，才能事半功倍，取得理想效果。[6]

尊崇法律、践行法治已经成为当代世界的主流意识、主导文化和最大共识，得人心、顺民意，是形成良好国际秩序与和谐世界的基本前提和根本保障。[7]

同时，不同的法律体系、法域、法律制度也在一定程度上产生趋同化。这种世界各大法系的彼此融合，为各国政界、法学界的相互理解、促进合作创造了条件，为法律外交提供了无限的机遇，亦不断丰富着其内容与形式。[8]

可见，在当今国际舞台上，法律外交与政治文明之间相辅相成，互为因果。[9]

作为联合国安理会常任理事国，中国在国际事务中发挥着越来越重要的建设性作用。因而，全方位地展开以法律为基础、内容和形式的外交活动，对于讲好中国法治故事，开展法治外交，塑造法治中国形象，意义重大，影响深远。[10]

译 文

Legal Diplomacy and Political Civilization

As an inevitable trend in the development of international politics and the civilization of human society, legal diplomacy is the only route for China to transform itself from a major country with adequate laws to one under the rule of law.[1]

Human society has painfully evolved by constantly improving the mutually compromised "law of civilization" out of the "law of the jungle" through agonizing reflection, moving from barbarism into a civilized society underpinned by rules and laws.[2]

As Rousseau, the French thinker, said, "Even the strongest man can never be sure his power will guarantee his mastership forever, unless he is able to transform his strength into right, obedience into duty" . That is, a sustained and stable political order has to be based on reasonable and just relations linking power to obligation.[3]

Essentially, traditional political activities have centered around competition for power, namely in the "politics of power" . With the development of political civilization, people have gradually learned how to effectively adjust the relationship between power and rights, shifting to rights as the core, making power subordinate to rights, protecting rights as a balance to power, resulting in the "politics of rights" .[4]

In terms of international politics, legal diplomacy is meant to apply relevant concepts of the rule of law and legal principles, transform diplomatic issues into legal issues, resolve diplomatic disputes and deal with its matters through legal actions and procedures, so as to establish and create international relations in an environment that best serves national interests.[5]

As globalization increasingly deepens, the world is undergoing major changes unseen in a century. By legalizing the problems in various fields of international relations, the international community has stepped into a new era of pluralistic coexistence from the era of power-dominated politics. Furthermore, only by complying with such changes, keeping pace with the times, and taking political, economic, cultural, military and environmental issues as legal issues, can diplomatic activities be carried out in a more effective way and achieve satisfactory results.[6]

In the contemporary world, respecting the law and practicing the rule of law have become the mainstream consciousness, dominant culture and greatest consensus, following the people's will and winning popular support, which are the basic prerequisites and guarantee for formatting a sound international order and a harmonious world.[7]

In the meantime, different jurisprudences, jurisdictions and legal systems somehow tend to converge on certain common grounds. The integration of different genealogies of law in the world has created favorable conditions and unlimited opportunities for mutual understanding and cooperation between peoples in the political and legal circles of all countries, and the contents and forms of legal diplomacy have also been constantly diversified and enriched.[8]

In a way, legal diplomacy and political civilization complement and even play a causal role to one another in today's international arena.[9]

As a permanent member of the UN Security Council, China is playing an increasingly important and constructive role in international affairs. Therefore, it is of great significance to carry out all-round law-based diplomatic activities, both substantive and procedural, so as to narrate well the legend of China and boost its international image as a major country that is ruled by law diplomatically.[10]

解　析

斟酌·变通·调整

——第二届法律外交翻译大赛点评

在 2021 年首届法律外交翻译大赛基础上，此次大赛共有六百余人参赛，全国多所高校师生、法律工作者及法律翻译爱好者都积极参与。经过初评、复评和终评，由专家评委评定出了一等奖 2 名，二等奖 8 名，三等奖 15 名，优秀奖 60 名。优秀组织单位 1 个，最佳组织单位 5 个。

一、词语的斟酌

翻译，一般从对词语的分析、考量开始；对于该届大赛的分析，亦不妨由此入手。

就题目而言，"法律外交与政治文明"，有的译成 Legal Diplomacy and Politics Civilization，但 politics 指政治、政治学，是个名词，而 political 的本义是 connected with the state, government or public affairs，是形容词，故宜译为 political civilization。

[1] 中，"法律外交……是中国由法律大国向法治强国迈进的必由之路"，其中的"迈进"，多数参赛译文译成 to advance、change、stride forward、onwards 等，但这些都只译出了"迈进"的表面意思。transform 的本义是 to change something or someone completely and substantially in appearance or nature，即是更实质性的变化，如：It was an event that would transform my life.（那是能够彻底改变我一生的事件。）；He actually wants to reconstruct the state and transform society.（其实，他想重建国家、改造社会。）等，所以，宜用 transform。

"大国"，多译成 big country、great power、leading power 等，通常是不错的；但分析起来，big country 多指地理、人口概念上的，而 power 又稍显"霸气"，故我国在对外宣传上，现多用

major country，如："作为一个世界大国，中国始终从战略高度和长远角度看待中美关系。"（As a major country in the world, China always views its relations with the U.S. from a strategic and long-term perspective.）；"这体现了我们处理大国关系的新思维，也体现了中国对国际社会的责任和担当。"（It shows a new approach on the part of China to handle major country relations; Also, it shows China's sense of responsibility for the international community.）；"中国作为域外大国第一个加入《东南亚友好合作条约》，第一个与东盟建立面向和平与繁荣的战略伙伴关系。"（China is the first major country outside the region to accede to the *Treaty of Amity and Cooperation in Southeast Asia* and to forge a strategic partnership for peace and prosperity with ASEAN.）等。

［2］中，"痛定思痛"固然可以译成 recall a painful/bitter experience，但亦可不将"思"明译出来，而是用形容词，融化于过程之中，如 painfully evolved by constantly...；"野蛮社会"、"文明社会"，参赛译文大都译成了 the society of barbarism、the society of civilization，但其实不必过于刻板，而可作些变化，如 from barbarism into a civilized society 等。

［4］中的"权力政治"、"权利政治"，许多参赛者译成power politics、right politics，实则为the "politics of power"、the "politics of rights"，且应像原文一样加上引号。

［6］中的"事半功倍，取得理想效果"，参赛者一般都能将二者结合起来翻译，如 ...then twice as much can be accomplished with half the effort and the ideal results are achieved./... as legal issues in diplomatic activities can we achieve the desired results with half the effort./Diplomacy can only achieve the desired results with half the effort if it responds to. 等。其实，“事半”可不必如画线部分译得那么“实”，而可根据语境，译出其主旨，如 can diplomatic activities be carried out in a more effective way and achieve satisfactory results 等。

翻译中，若固守一贯解释，可能会选用某些看似“对称”的词，但推敲后，却发现其未必“等值”。所以，选词时须反复斟酌，在具体的译文语境中找到最确切的“那一个”。

二、表述的变通

在词语基础上，某些语义的表述在翻译过程中也需作相应的变通。

[1] 中，“法律外交是国际政治发展的必然趋势，……同时也是人类社会文明演化的客观反映”，其中的“客观反映”一般被译成 ...but also serves as an objective reflection to the evolution of human society，但英译文以“形合”、简约为上，于是有的译文作了些变通，以避免重复，将整段译成 Legal diplomacy is an inevitable trend of international political development and is the only way for China to advance from a big country with laws into one under the rule of law. Meanwhile, it reflects the evolution of human civilization objectively.，但仍显赘余。分析起来，“必然趋势”（inevitable trend）已有了“客观”之意，而“演化”与“发展”

同义（亦可译成 evolution），因而不妨将其整合为一句：an inevitable trend in the development of international politics and the civilization of human society。之后的“法律大国”和“法治强国”没有固定译法，故可有不同的发挥。有共识的是，“法制”译成 rule by law，“法治”译成 rule of law，因而“由法律大国向法治强国迈进”的译文就有了 from a “Big country of rule by law” to a “Great country of rule of law”、a “Major country applying law” to a “Great country under the rule of law” 等尝试。应当说，这些译法都有相当的合理性。参考译文在前句基础上，将其接续译成 legal diplomacy is the only route for China to transform itself from a major country with adequate laws to one under the rule of law，这主要是以 a major country with adequate laws 和 one under the rule of law 区分了前者与后者，使译文更加简明、精练。

［2］中，“人类社会……其中规则和法律起了决定性作用”，参赛译文一般都将最后一句分译成 Human society... In this process, the rules and laws have played a decisive role./...in which rules and laws played a decisive role./In this process, the existence of rules and laws played a crucial role. 等。这些译文固然是忠实的，但可否再“形合”一些，比如用 underpin 支撑起整句？该词的本义是 to form part of, strengthen, or replace the foundation of something's structure，于是参考译文将其变通为 Human society has painfully evolved...moving from barbarism into a civilized society underpinned by rules and laws. 其内在逻辑是：基础性地支撑其结构，不正是 played a decisive/crucial role 吗？故其意是不言自明的。

［3］中，“一种持续稳定的政治秩序，一定要建立在合理、公正的权力与义务关系之上”，一般都自然而然地将画线部分译成：...a sustainable and stable political order must be grounded on a reasonable and just relationship between rights and duties./It means that a continuous and stable political order must be based on just and equitable relationship between rights and obligations. 但深究其意，此处讲的并不是二者的平等关系，而是强调权力必须与其义务相关联（注意：“权力”不是 rights 而是 power），故参考译文为 That is, a sustained and stable political order has to be based on reasonable and just relations linking power to obligation.，以点明要旨。

［4］中，“人们逐渐学会了如何有效地调整权力与权利的关系，转移到以权利为核心，使权力服从权利，权力保障权利，权利制衡权力……”其中画线部分需重点关注。此处的“使……服从”不是 to enforce power to concede，而是 make power subordinate to rights，即是一种从属关系；“权利制衡权力”不能译成 power counterbalances power，此处应以“保障权利”为核心，即 protect rights as a balance to power，整句为：...people have gradually learned how to effectively adjust the relationship between power and rights, shifting to rights as the core, making power subordinate to rights, protecting rights as a balance to power,...。

［5］中，“……以合法的行为和程序化解外交纠纷，处理外交事务，从而建立、创造最符合本国利益的国际关系与国际环境”，其中画线部分译文问题最多，较为典型的译文

如：...applying due conducts and processes in the resolution of diplomatic disputes and the management of diplomatic affairs, by virtue of which the international relations and environments that are in the utmost national interests can be created and established. 分析起来，此处的“行为”不是一般的 conduct，而是 legal action，“程序”也不是 process，而是 legal procedure；而此处的 national interests 不是要被 created，而是要 serve；而需要 create 的倒是 international relations。因而，该句应重新理解、变通为 ...resolve diplomatic disputes and deal with its matters through legal actions and procedures, so as to establish and create international relations in an environment that best serves national interests.

合理的变通是在准确、深刻理解原文基础之上的“语言重组”。意是本，言是末，得意可忘言。

三、句式的调整

在许多情况下，词语的斟酌和表述的变通，须与句式的调整相结合。

［1］中，“法律外交是国际政治发展的必然趋势，是中国由法律大国向法治强国迈进的必由之路”，参赛者一般都按原文词序译成：Legal diplomacy is an inevitable trend in the development of international politics. It is the only way for China to move from a country with laws to a country under the rule of law. / Legal diplomacy is an inevitable trend of international political development and is the only way for China to advance from a big country with laws into one under the rule of law./Legal diplomacy is an inevitable trend in the devclopment of international politics. It is the only way for China to move from a major rule-by-law country to a great rule-of-law power. 等。其实，不妨“退让一步”，将状语提前，即 As an inevitable trend in the development of...，使行文更加舒缓，这也是英文的惯用表述方式。

［2］中，“人类社会从漫长的弱肉强食的‘丛林法则’中痛定思痛”，有的译成 Having reflected on the long history of the “law of the jungle...”，若能与下文恰当结合，是可取的，但通常参赛译文中缺乏有机衔接；而“进而从暴力政治走向协商政治，从野蛮社会进入文明社会，其中规则和法律起了决定性作用”，参赛者一般都按原文语序译成 ...and gradually developed and perfected the “law of civilization” of mutual compromise, and then moved from violent politics to consultative politics.../...the world has made efforts to improve laws of civilization which involves two-way compromise and has moved from violent politics to consultative politics.../Human society gradually developed and improved the “law of civilization” featured with mutual compromise, then shifted from the violence politics to the consultative politics. 等等，意思固然都不错，但为突出重点，表述畅顺，参考译文为 Human society has painfully evolved by constantly improving the mutually compromised “law of civilization” out of the “law of the jungle” through agonizing reflection...，其中“痛定思痛”融合在 painfully evolved 和

agonizing reflection 中；对于“协商政治”，参考译文将通常意义上的名词组 mutual compromise、consultative politics 译为形容词 mutually compromised，来修饰“law of civilization”；同时，打破了 from...to... 的句式，用了 ...out of...through... 的表述方式，以错落有致。

［4］中，“就本质而言，传统政治活动围绕权力而展开，即是‘权力政治’”，有的参赛译文似乎有意作了语序调整，如 In essence, traditional political activities, namely the politics of power, focus on the power，但并不顺达，且语法欠妥；类似的译法还有：In essence, traditional political activities follow a power-centric approach, in other words, “power politics”./In essence, traditional political activities revolve around power—as “power politics”./In essence, traditional political activities revolve around power, i.e. “power politics”./As for its essence, traditional political activities are carried out embracing power, which means power politics. 等等，都可谓有益尝试，但似乎还可进一步细化，如：Essentially, traditional political activities have centered around competition for power, namely in the “politics of power”.，其中的 competition for 属增译，以进一步点明传统政治活动的实质。

［6］中，“外交领域只有顺应此种变化，与时俱进，将政治、经济、文化、军事、环境等问题作为法律议题展开外交活动，才能事半功倍，取得理想效果”，其中的“外交领域”在原文中是主语，但在译文里可变换位置和语法成分，如在译文 Only by adapting this sort of change, advancing with times and conducting diplomatic activities which takes problems concerning politics, economy, culture, military affairs, environment and so on as legal issues can human achieve twice the result with half the effort and gain an ideal effect eventually. 中，它是宾语；在译文 Only by responding to such changes and keeping pace with the times by regarding political, economic, cultural, military and environmental issues as legal issues in diplomatic activities, can it achieve the desired results with half the efforts. 中，它是状语；在参考译文 ...only by complying with such changes, keeping pace with the times, and taking political, economic, cultural, military and environmental issues as legal issues, can diplomatic activities be carried out in a more effective way and achieve satisfactory results. 中，diplomatic activities 仍作主语，但为被动语态，以更恰表述。

[7] 中，"尊崇法律、践行法治已经成为当代世界的主流意识、主导文化和最大共识……"，其中"当代世界的"似乎是定语，大部分参赛者都译为 The respect for law and the practice of ruling by law have become the mainstream consciousness, the dominant culture and the most significant consensus of the contemporary world. 但分析起来，此处应理解为"在当今世界"，故可处理为状语，可置前或置后，如 Upholding law and fulfilling the rule of law have become the mainstream, dominated culture and largest consensus in the contemporary world. / In the contemporary world, respecting the law and practicing the rule of law have become the mainstream consciousness, dominant culture and greatest

consensus. 等。类似的，［9］中，“可见，在当今国际舞台上，法律外交与政治文明之间相辅相成，互为因果”，画线部分亦宜置后译出，如 In a way, legal diplomacy and political civilization complement and even play a causal role to one another in today's international arena.，以使层次更加清晰。

［10］中，“全方位地展开以法律为基础、内容和形式的外交活动，对于讲好中国法治故事、展开法治外交、塑造法治中国形象，意义重大，影响深远”，其中的“意义重大”，在多数译文中都作了明显的语序调整，如“...China has carried out all-round diplomatic activities based on law in both content and form, which has great significance and far-reaching impact on telling the story of its rule of law, carrying out rule of law diplomacy, and shaping the image of China under the rule of law.” / ...Carrying out diplomatic activities where the laws act as base, content and form in all direction is of great significance and far-reaching influence for telling the story of the rule of laws in China, carrying out the diplomacy of the rules of laws and shaping the image of China ruled by law. / China's all-round diplomatic activities based on law, its own contents and forms, are of great meaningfulness and have far-reaching impact on telling China's story about rule of law, carrying out diplomacy of rule of law and shaping China's image of rule of law. 然而，还不够，应将此意进一步提前，至句首，译为 Therefore, it is of great significance to carry out all-round law-based diplomatic activities, both substantive and procedural, so as to narrate well the legend of China and boost its international image as a major country that is ruled by law diplomatically.，从而突出重点，统领全句。

此外，值得指出的一个问题是，相当数量的译文明显有使用翻译软件的痕迹；不是不可以使用，但要做必要的加工与编辑，否则不但不会得到理想的成绩，反而失去了参加翻译比赛的意义。

总之，此次翻译大赛在数量与质量上都比上一届有所提高；希望通过不断分析、总结，后续的比赛会有新的进步。

原 文

法律外交在国际争端中的价值

国与国之间，由于国家利益、主张、权利，乃至对客观事实认定的不同，发生国际争端并不稀奇，问题在于如何解决。[1]

解决国际争端的方式有两种：战争与和平。在丛林法则时代，国际争端多以战争方式解决；二次世界大战、特别是联合国成立之后，则主要遵循国际法，和平解决。《联合国宪章》明确规定，不得以武力或武力威胁方式解决国际争端。在此之中，法律外交体现出极其重要的价值观外交。[2]

法律外交的核心是法治——信仰法治，崇尚法治，以法律思维和法律手段展开外交。在国际交往中，主要体现在尊重国家主权和领土完整、互不侵犯、互不干涉内政、平等互利、和平共处。法律外交处理国际争端的主旨，不是基于意识形态，而是在国际法框架内对于法治价值的追求。[3]

法律外交与国际法的理论和实践高度重合：国际法的基本原则是法律外交理论体系的重要内容，而国际立法、国际司法及其执法活动，则是法律外交实践体系的重要内容。法律外交既包括在日常外交中运用国际法，也包括在外交实践中对国际法的制定与完善，从而推动国际社会的更加有序的、良性的发展。[4]

二者的主要区别在于执行主体方面。就国际法而言，国家及某些非政府组织是其主体；而法律外交的主体则是多元化、多样性的，包括外交部委的法律司、立法系统，司法和执法系统，以及研究机构、律师协会、法律专家、学者等。[5]

法律外交与国际法院的职能亦密切相关。对当事国一致同意提交国际法院的法律争端，国际法院根据《联合国宪章》规定以及相关国际条约、公约做出判决，而法律外交则从中积极斡旋，全面配合，起到有力阐释和捍卫的作用。[6]

从实践看，世界上绝大多数国家都声称遵守国际法院的判决，公然对抗的实属罕见。对国际法院判决的所谓“遵守”包含两个要素，即接受法院判决的终局效力和采取合理措施、善意地加以履行的法律义务。换言之，判断当事国是否遵守国际法院的判决，不但要看其口头声明，还要看其实际行动，而如何解释、评判其中的“合理”与“善意”，则给法律外交留下广阔的施展空间。[7]

在国际法中，没有“先发制人”的条款。《联合国宪章》固然有对国家自卫权的规定，但其前提条件是，必须当本国受到武力攻击时才能使用自卫权。因而，在国际争端中，任何先发制人战略都被国际社会公认为是侵略他国的借口，是违法行为，对国际社会和世界和平造成严重威胁。[8]

关于处理国与国关系的智慧，在我国传统文化中亦有着丰富的思想资源。如，中华文化的“礼”，是仁、义、信道德品质的规范化，具有某种“法”的含义；严格恪守“礼”，可调节“物欲”，防止“争夺”。《孙子兵法》中更有“善战而不喜战”、“上兵伐谋”、“不战而屈人之兵”的宝贵思想，这些都可为调节、处理现代国际关系，提供某些借鉴。[9]

回顾新中国外交史，早在 1954 年周恩来总理便提出了“和平共处五项原则”，成为中国处理对外关系的基本准则，这也可说是展开中国法律外交的第一块基石。沿此途径，在当今时代，中国法律外交必将在习近平法治思想、习近平外交思想指引下，在以法治手段化解国际争端、维护世界和平方面，发挥更加令世人瞩目的大国作用。[10]

译 文

The Value of Legal Diplomacy in Settling International Disputes

Since it is not uncommon for international disputes to arise between countries due to conflicts in national interests, claims, rights and even in determining certain facts, the central issue is then how to resolve them.[1]

There are two ways of settling international disputes, namely military and peaceful. In the age of the jungle, international disputes were mostly settled by wars. After World War II, especially with the founding of the United Nations, international conflicts have mainly been resolved peacefully in compliance with international laws.

The *Charter of the United Nations* explicitly stipulates that in the settlement of international disputes, all Members shall refrain from the threat or use of force. In this context, legal diplomacy embodies great values.[2]

The core value of legal diplomacy is the belief in and upholding of the rule of law, conducting diplomacy with legal thinking and means. In international interactions these values are mainly reflected in the principles of respecting national sovereignty and territorial integrity, committing to mutual non-aggression, not interfering in each other's internal affairs, negotiating on the basis of equality and mutual benefit, as well as peaceful coexistence. By the same token, the conduct of legal diplomacy in settling international disputes aims to realize the value of the rule of law within the framework of international law rather than engaging in anything motivated by ideology.[3]

Generally speaking, legal diplomacy and international laws are very much interrelated in terms of their theoretical guidance and actual practice. In fact, the fundamental principles of enacting international laws are an important part of the theoretical system of legal diplomacy, while international legislation, justice and their enforcement constitute the main practice of legal diplomacy, which in turn contributes to the formation and improvement of international legislation, thus ensuring the more orderly and sound development of the international community.[4]

The major difference between international laws and legal diplomacy, however, lies in the subject area of execution. States and certain non-governmental organizations are subject to international laws. On the other hand, the subjects of legal diplomacy are quite diverse, including the legal sectors falling under ministries of foreign affairs, legislative systems, judicial and law enforcement systems, as well as research institutions, bar associations, legal expertise, scholarship and so on.[5]

Meanwhile, legal diplomacy is also closely related to the functioning of the International Court of Justice, which shall, in accordance with the provisions of the *Charter of the United Nations* and relevant international treaties and conventions, render judgements on legal disputes submitted to the Court with the unanimous consent of the parties concerned. During this process, legal diplomacy may play a full and active role of mediation in an all-round manner in elucidating and defending judgements of the Court.[6]

In practice, the vast majority of countries in the world claim to be in compliance with judgments of the International Court of Justice. Blatant confrontation is rare. In this context, the term "in compliance with" implies, first, the acceptance of its final judgements; second, the legal obligation to take reasonable measures to implement them in good faith. In other words, judging the parties concerned on their compliance with the Court's judgements, should not only by their words but by their actions. And how "reasonable" and "good faith" are to be interpreted and judged, leaves great potential for manipulation through legal diplomacy too.[7]

There is no such clause as "pre-emption" whatsoever in international laws. The *Charter of the United Nations* does empower all states the right to self-defense, but this right is conditional on first being attacked by a foreign military force. Therefore, when confronting international disputes, any kind of pre-emptive strategy employed by any country will be regarded by the international community as an illegal pretext for aggression against another sovereign country/region, imposing a serious threat to world peace.[8]

There is also a wealth of intellectual resources in our traditional culture, concerning the wisdom of handling relations between states. The "etiquette" of Chinese culture, for example, is the standardization of the moral qualities of benevolence, righteousness and faith, and integrates certain legal elements. It was believed that by strictly observing appropriate etiquette, people's "physical desire" can be confined and "furious confrontation" avoided. Some invaluable ideas conceived in Sun Tzu's *The Art of War*, such as "being good at but not pleased with war", "the best strategy in warfare is to foil the enemy's strategy" and "subdue the enemy without fighting", may certainly provide securely-based references for regulating and handling modern international relations.[9]

Reviewing the diplomatic history of the People's Republic of China, as early as 1954, Premier Zhou Enlai put forward the "Five

Principles of Peaceful Coexistence”, which have guided its foreign relations ever since and may also be seen as the basic foundation for China’s legal diplomacy. Along these lines, nowadays as a major country in the world, China may play a more prominent role in resolving international disputes and maintaining world peace by means of the rule of law under the guidance of Xi Jinping’s Thought on the Rule of Law and Diplomacy.[10]

解 析

法律语境下的动态对等

——兼评第三届中国法律外交翻译大赛

作为一门新兴交叉学科，法律外交翻译不仅在对外交往，而且在国内法治建设方面也起着重要作用，是培养法律与翻译学科高端复合型翻译人才的重要基地。接续前两届大赛的范例，2023年，在法律英语教学与测试专业委员会、全国翻译专业学位研究生教育指导委员会等的指导下，第三届“和平杯”中国法律外交翻译大赛同样完美收官。作为大赛的终评评委，现拟从动态对等的角度，对大赛译文作一点评。

“动态对等”（Dynamic equivalence）翻译理论是由美国著名翻译理论家奈达（Eugene Nida）于20世纪60年代提出的，其要旨是，翻译所求的不仅是词汇层面上的对等，而且是在不同语境下的全方位的相对等值。

一、法律词语的辨析

就法律词汇层面来讲，同一中文词语在不同语境中，可翻译成不同的英文。本文中的“国家”，就有 country、state、nation 等译法，各自有特定含义和与其他词语的惯用搭配，如我们说 a foreign country，却很少说 a foreign state；同样，［1］中的“国家利益、主张、权利”，不用 countries' 或 states' interest...，而是 national interests...。［2］中“《联合国宪章》明确规定，不得以武力或武力威胁方式解决国际争端”，其中暗指的主语是“所有成员国”，即 all Members。[5] 中的“国家及某些非政府组织是其主体”又应译为 States and certain non-governmental organizations 等。

然而，［7］中“世界上绝大多数国家都声称遵守国际法院的判决”，又宜译为 the vast majority of countries，因为这是联合国的通常表述。似乎，country 和 state 没有严格的区别，但却有其各自的约定俗成。country 的本义是 an area of land that has or used to have its own government and laws，即一般意义上的“国家”概念，而 state 则更加复杂，有特指性，其本义是：A state is considered as an organized political community controlled by one government，即具政治顶层的一统性。由此可知，“国家元首”是 head of state，不是 head of country；“欧盟成员国”是 European Union member states，不是 member countries；“波罗的

海诸国”是 the Baltic States，等等。另外，state 还可指 part of country，如“美国的各州”是 the different states of the US。因而，在法律外交场合更应避免产生歧义。正如［9］中“关于处理国与国关系的智慧”，似乎指的是“国中国”之事，但仍要用 between states，因为它们是不同的政治实体。

另外，［1］中的“权利”不能用 powers 来译。该词的本义是 the ability to control people or things，特别是指 If someone has power, they have a lot of control over people and activities，文中显然不是这个意思；而 rights 的本义是 the qualifications or entitlements endowed by law that nobody can take away，如“你应知道自己的法律权利，以保护自己。”（You should know your legal rights to protect yourself.），更符合文中内涵，故此处应为 rights。同样，［8］中，“《联合国宪章》固然有对国家自卫权的规定”，应为 the right of states to self-defense，而动词可用 empower，意思是 to give someone the power or authority to do something。

文中多次出现的“国际争端”，英译时也有不同选择，参赛译文用得最多的三个词是 conflict、contradiction、dispute，分析起来，它们其实有着相当大的差别。先看前两个词的区别：Conflict is serious disagreement and argument about something important. If two people or groups are in conflict, they have had a serious disagreement or argument and have not yet reached agreement./ Contradiction is a lack of agreement between facts, opinions, actions, etc. 如其中画线部分所示，二者的主要区别在“严重程度”的

不同，前者要严重很多，故多译为“冲突”，如 It seems that the two sides haven’t got to the stage of a full-scale military conflict.（双方似乎还没到达军事冲突的阶段。）Both parties have agreed to a ceasefire for the time being after three months of conflict.（冲突 3 个月后，双方同意暂时停火。）而 contradiction 则没有那么严重，且常译为“争端”，如 Attempting to resolve this contradiction, the two sides have begun a series of negotiations.（为解决这一争端，双方已经展开了一系列的谈判。）After the meeting, the contradiction between the two sides on the issue has apparently been resolved.（会谈后，双方在这一问题上的争端得到了有效的缓解。）

然而，参照《联合国宪章》，在此种语境下，多用 dispute，如 Chapter VI: Pacific Settlement of Disputes（第六章　争端之和平解决）Article 33　1. The parties to any dispute, the continuance of which is likely to endanger the maintenance of international peace and security, shall, first of all, seek a solution by negotiation, enquiry, mediation, conciliation, arbitration, judicial settlement, resort to regional agencies or arrangements, or other peaceful means of their own choice.（第三十三条　一、任何争端之当事国，于争端之继续存在足以危及国际和平与安全之维持时，应尽先以谈判、调查、调停、和解、公断、司法解决、区域机关或区域办法之利用，或各该国自行选择之其他和平方法，求得解决。）分析起来，在某种意义上，dispute 介乎于 conflict 和 contradiction 之间，其基本含义：an argument or a disagreement between two people, groups or countries; discussion about a subject where there is disagreement，即处于可控阶段的分歧、争执；或许，下面这句话能典型地展现出二者的关系：We should manage the dispute to avoid being escalated to conflict.（我们应当管控分歧，避免升级至冲突。）因而，参考译文更多使用了该词。

［3］中的“法律外交的核心是法治……”，对其中的“核心”，参赛者大多译成 the central part、essential part，只有极少数用了 the core value；究其实质，这里指的是“核心价值”，故后者更确切。同段中的“国际交往”，译成 international exchanges 或 international interactions 似乎都可以，但二者有着细微差别：前者更多强调的是物质方面的交换（giving something to somebody or receiving something in return），后者的重点则在互动（mutual or reciprocal action），故后者为佳。

［4］中，“法律外交与国际法的理论和实践高度重合”，其中的“高度重合”大都被译成 highly coincides、is highly overlapped with 、coincides closely，也有的译成are highly in conformity with...，似乎更符合此处的法律语境。这些固然都是合理的、可接受的译文，但是深究其意，此处指的不仅是二者之间的简单“重合”，而更多的是一种内在的关联性，故参考译文用了 ...are very much interrelated in terms of...。至于“良性发展”，则不必按其字面意思译成 benign development，用 sound development 更好。

［8］中，“《联合国宪章》固然有对国家自卫权的规定，但其前提条件是，必须当本国受到武力攻击时才能使用自卫权”，对于后面“条件句”的表述，参赛译文作了多种有益尝试，如 ...but states are supposed to refrain from exercising their right to defense unless they are under armed attacks launched by others. / ... there to be an armed attack on the state before it could exercise the right of self-defense. / ... this right can only be exercised in the event of an armed attack. / ... its precondition is that the right to self-defense be used only when the State is under attack by force. 等，都略显冗赘，而不妨使用一个形容词 conditional，如参考译文：... but this right is conditional on first being attacked by a foreign military force, 便可在相当程度上化繁为简，有举重若轻的效果。

［9］中，“中华文化的‘礼’”，其中的“礼”许多人译成了 propriety，似乎对等，但分析起来，该词的内涵是 moral and social behavior that is considered to be correct and acceptable， 如 Their sense of social propriety is eroded.（他们的社交礼仪意识淡薄了。）I doubt the propriety of doing so.（我怀疑这样做是否适当。）等。相比较而言，Etiquette（a set of customs and rules for polite behavior, especially among a particular class of people or in a particular profession）强调的是一种“规矩”，如“中国是礼仪之邦。”（China is a nation of etiquette.）“他在那种场合的举止显然违反了基本的外交礼仪规则。”（His act in that occasion obviously violates the basic diplomatic rules of etiquette.）等。而原文的具体语境是“礼”“是仁、义、信道德品质的规范化，具有某种‘法’的含义”，因而此处用 etiquette 更为确切。同时，“某些借鉴”，若仅译成 some references，显得不够有分量，因而参考译文不用 some，而是用了 securely-based 作其定语。

可见，翻译中的对等不是静止的，而是在不同语境中的动态平衡。

二、成分增减的考量

如同一般翻译规律，法律汉英翻译亦不可避免要作一些词语上的增减处理。这主要是由两种语言的遣词造句规律迥异所致，处理时需紧扣原意，不可扭曲。

标题“法律外交在国际争端中的价值”，参赛者一般都按字面意思译成 The Value of Legal Diplomacy in International Disputes，看似十分对等，但分析起来，其中有个隐含的动词需要译出来，即 handling、managing、settling 等，故参考译文为：The Value of Legal Diplomacy in Settling International Disputes。同样，［3］“法律外交处理国际争端的主旨，……”，其中的“法律外交”，实则是实施法律外交的行为，因而亦应加动词 conduct（这里要用其名词含义），译为 the conduct of legal diplomacy（in settling international disputes aims to...）。

由于中文“意合”与英文“形合”的特点，在中译英时，需要添加最多的要属连词，其次是副词、介词、冠词等。如“留得青山在，不愁没柴烧。”（<u>So long as</u> green hills remain, there will never be a shortage of firewood.）；“送君千里，终有一别。”（<u>Although</u> you may escort a guest a thousand miles, yet must the parting come at last.）等。同样，［1］中的“国与国之间，由于国家利益、主张、权利，乃至对客观事实认定的不同，发生国

际争端并不稀奇，问题在于如何解决”，暗含一种因果关系，因而英译时不妨加入连词 Since it is not uncommon for international disputes to... ；而［6］中的“法律外交与国际法院的职能亦密切相关”，因与前文是一种并列关系，故可加入 Meanwhile,... 以使行文更加顺畅。

有时为了表意或强调，也需增加某些词语或句子成分，如“翻译理论固然重要，实践尤为重要。”（Translation theory is something but practice is everything. / It is true that translation theory is important, but practice is most important of all.）；“不把中文底子打好，什么也写不成。”（As a matter of fact, without a good foundation of Chinese-writing, no one can hope to be successful in any kind of writing.）；“通过大量阅读让学生掌握英文语感，这是我多年教授英语的最重要的经验。”（The most important experience gained in my teaching over the past years proves its feasibility of letting students have a sense of English through extensive reading.）等。同样，［3］中的“法律外交处理国际争端的主旨，不是基于意识形态，而是在国际法框架内对于法治价值的追求”，因接续的是前面的“在国际交往中，主要体现在……”，故参考译文插入了 By the same token,... 以使行文更加连贯。［4］的首句“法律外交与国际法的理论和实践高度重合”，参考译文在前面加了 Generally speaking，作为一种概述，同时也对应下面的具体语境，如［7］中的“从实践看”（In practice）；［5］中的“而法律外交的主体则是……”，显然是对前面的国际法而言的，故宜以 On the other hand 开句，以使叙述脉络更加清晰。

就［6］中的"法律外交则从中积极斡旋，全面配合，起到有力阐释和捍卫的作用"而言，针对参赛译文的普遍疏漏，参考译文作了添加（下画线部分）：During this process, legal diplomacy may play a full and active role of mediation in an all-round manner in elucidating and defending judgements of the Court，画线部分分别作状语和宾语，特别是在最后，法律外交所"阐释和捍卫"的是"国际法院的判决"，若缺失了，便会损害原文意思的准确性和完整性。

［7］中，"对国际法院判决的所谓'遵守'包含两个要素，即接受法院判决的终局效力和采取合理措施、善意地加以履行的法律义务"，因此处的所谓"遵守"是就具体语境而言的，故加上 In this context 会更加有的放矢；而"两个要素"，为更加清晰、明确，不妨以 first,... second,... 分而述之：In this context, the term "in compliance with" implies, first, the acceptance of its final judgements; second, the legal obligation to take reasonable measures to implement them in good faith. 可说是一种"动态变通"。而［8］中，"在国际法中，没有'先发制人'的条款。《联合国宪章》固然有对国家自卫权的规定，……"，译文中增加了下画线部分：There is no such clause as "pre-emption" whatsoever in international laws. The *Charter of the United Nations* does empower all states the right to self-defense...，体现的是一种语气和强调。

同时，中译英时，亦可将其中可有可无或其意已在其他部分有所体现的词语删去，如"质子带正电，电子带负电，而中子既不带正电，也不带负电。"（A proton has a positive charge and an electron a negative charge, but a neutron has neither.)；“在招聘中，会讲英语者比不会讲英语者更有优势。”（In recruitment, those who can speak English have certain advantages over those who can't.）同样，［5］中的“……而法律外交的主体则是多元化、多样性的”，似不必译成 legal diplomacy are pluralistic and diverse, 而可用 quite diverse 概括“多元化、多样性”之意。［8］中的“……任何先发制人战略都被国际社会公认为是侵略他国的借口，是违法行为，对国际社会和世界和平造成严重威胁”，对于其中两次出现的“国际社会”，亦可合并处理，如 ...any kind of pre-emptive strategy employed by any country will be regarded by the international community as...，imposing a serious threat to world peace；既然对 world peace 造成了威胁，其中自然包括了 international community 的含义，故可不必重复。［9］中的“严格恪守‘礼’，可调节‘物欲’，防止“‘争夺’”，可译为 by strictly observing appropriate etiquette, people's “physical desire” can be confined and “furious confrontation” avoided，即可将第二个 can be 省去。

而且，省略有时又常与变通相结合。如［2］中的“解决国际争端的方式有两种：战争与和平。在丛林法则时代，国际争端多以战争方式解决”，不少参赛译文采取了“相对对等”的方式，如 There are two approaches of settling international disputes, either by military means or peaceful means. During the era of the law of the jungle, disputes were mostly resolved through way of wars.，其中下画线部分有重叠、重复成分，因而有删减、精练的余地；

military means or peaceful means 亦可合并为 military or peaceful means。鉴于 approach、means、way 都有“方式、方法”的含义，故参考译文将其变通、融合为：There are two ways of settling international disputes, namely military and peaceful. In the age of the jungle, international disputes were mostly settled by wars.

总之，增词不增意，或减词不减意，也是一种动态平衡。

三、语序平衡的调整

语序的结构反映的是语言使用者的思维模式，其基本功能是准确、清晰、通畅地表述语意。由于中英文的思维方式和句子结构的显著差异，故在其转换中要不断作出调整。

法律外交翻译亦不例外。如，“他昨天带来的那本《新汉英法学词典》对本次翻译大赛很有帮助。”（It is very useful to consult that *A New Chinese-English Law Dictionary* he bought yesterday for the Translation Contest.），“成员国应在弄清所有相关问题之后，再进行投票。”（Before voting, member countries have to get a clear understanding of all issues concerned.）；“这是目前为止能够想象出来的解决争端的最好办法。”（This is the best solution imaginable for the dispute so far.）。同样，对于［1］中的“国与国之间，由于国家利益、主张、权利，乃至对客观事实认定的不同，发生国际争端并不稀奇，问题在于如何解决”，若如有的参赛者所译：International disputes always exist among countries because of their differences in national interests, assertions, rights and even views on objective facts, which is not surprised but needs to be dealt with properly./Due to national interests, claims, and powers, as well as varying interpretations of objective facts, international disputes are common. The difficulty lies in resolving them./Due to differences in national interests, claims, powers, and even the affirmance on objective facts, it is common that there arise international disputes between states. Thus, the problem lies in how to resolve them. 等，似乎也符合原文，但不大符合英文的表述习惯，故应将 it is not uncommon 前置，形成 ...it is not uncommon for international disputes to arise between countries due to... 的句式。

［3］中的“法律外交处理国际争端的主旨，不是基于意识形态，而是在国际法框架内对于法治价值的追求”，也多被参赛者按原文语序译成：The main purpose of settling international disputes with legal diplomacy is not based on ideology, but the pursuit of the value of the rule of law within the framework of international law./The main thrust of legal diplomacy in resolving international disputes is not based on ideologies, but on the pursuit of the value of the rule of law within the framework of international law./The theme of handling international disputes with legal diplomacy is not based on ideology, but on the quest for the value of the rule of law within an international law framework. 等，而参考译文将语序颠倒，译为：... legal diplomacy in... aims to... rather than... motivated by ideology，以强调其主次关系。

应当说，最需要调整语序结构的，是对于［6］的整段翻译。若完全按原文语序，译成：Legal diplomacy is also closely linked to the functions of the International Court of Justice. With regard to legal disputes submitted to the International Court of Justice by the unanimous consent of the parties concerned, the International Court of Justice has rendered judgments in accordance with the provisions of the *Charter of the United Nations* and relevant international treaties and conventions, while legal diplomacy has actively mediated and cooperated in an all-round way, playing a role in effective interpretation and defense. 其中，不但词序，甚至标点符号都是对等的，然而在实际表述效果上，却未必与原文对等。对此，应充分发挥英文“形合”的特点，如利用从句、倒装，增加副词、介词、状语等，以使译文更加条分缕析、轻重有序。具体而言，参考译文没有跟从原文，将第一句断开，而是在其后加入了从句 which shall, 同时将“当事国一致同意提交……的”这个原文中的定语，处理成介词短语 with the unanimous consent of the parties concerned 作状语，从而将其连成一体，形成完整意思；而从“而法律外交则从中积极斡旋……”开始，另起一句：During this process...，以重点表达 legal diplomacy 在这一过程中亦可发挥其特有的积极作用：Meanwhile, legal diplomacy is also closely related to the functioning of the International Court of Justice, which shall, in accordance with the provisions of the *Charter of the United Nations* and relevant international treaties and conventions, render judgements on legal disputes submitted to the Court with the unanimous consent of the parties concerned. During this process, legal diplomacy may play a full and active role of mediation in an all-round manner in elucidating and defending judgements of the Court. 通过这种大幅度调整，以求在译文中达到某种新的“整体等值”。

［7］中，“判断当事国是否遵守国际法院的判决，不但要看其口头声明，还要看其实际行动”，较为典型的参赛译文：To judge whether a country concerned comply with the decisions of the International Court of Justice, we should look at not just its statement but, more importantly, its action. / Whether or not a state complies with the judgement of the International Court of Justice depends not only on its oral statements, but also on its actual actions. / Judging whether a country complies with the judgments of international courts depends not only on its verbal declarations but also on its actual actions. 等，似乎过于注重词语层面的对等了；其实，不妨作些简化和变通，如：...judging the parties concerned on their compliance with the Court's judgements, should not only by their words but by their actions，以更紧凑、精练。

［8］中，“在国际争端中，任何先发制人战略都被国际社会公认为是侵略他国的借口，是违法行为，对国际社会和世界和平造成严重威胁”，对此，许多参赛译文都漏译了其中的“违法行为”，可能是不易将此概念“融入”该句式，对此，参考译文将其处理成形容词，作定语，即：...illegal pretext for aggression against another sovereign country / region, imposing a serious threat to world peace，形成一种局部协调。

［10］中，“沿此途径，在当今时代，中国法律外交必将在习近平法治思想、习近平外交思想指引下，在以法治手段化解国际争端、维护世界和平方面，发挥更加令世人瞩目的大国作用”，许多参赛译文大都按原文语序译成：In the modern age, under the leadership of Xi Jinping's Thought on the Rule of Law and Xi Jinping's Thought on Diplomacy, China, as a great country, can pursue legal diplomacy and play a more important role in resolving international disputes and maintaining world peace with means of the rule of law./ In contemporary times, China, under the guidance of Xi Jinping Thought on the Rule of Law and Diplomacy, would still be committed to playing a more outstanding role as a major country, resolving international disputes and guarding world peace with the rule of law./Following this path, in the present era, guided by Xi Jinping Thought on the Rule of Law and Diplomacy, China's legal diplomacy will certainly play an even more compelling role as a great power in resolving international disputes and safeguarding world peace by means of the rule of law. 等，似乎都转述出了原意，但在叙述的简明、通顺、地道方面，仍有不少改进空间。为捋清脉络、强调重点，参考译文调整语序为：Along these lines, nowadays as a major country in the world, China may play a more prominent role in resolving international disputes and maintaining world peace by means of the rule of law <u>under the guidance of Xi Jinping's Thought on the Rule of Law and Diplomacy.</u>，以求叙述上

的一种相对平衡、等值，当然未必完美。

总体而言，同之前两届相比，本届法律外交翻译大赛的水平普遍有所提高，“硬伤”比例下降。希望通过不断分析、总结，下一届能有更多的参赛译文达到一个新的高度。

原 文

法律外交与国家崛起

一个国家的崛起，取决于多种因素，但其中重要一项，无疑是法律外交，这已被越来越多的事实所佐证。[1]

法律外交是一种价值观外交，其核心是基于法治价值追求的外交——信仰法治、崇尚法治、具有法治思维，通过理解、参与、运用国际法来展开外交。这不仅有利于该国在国际关系中争取利益，而且能强化其合法性，提高其在国际社会的认可与支持度。[2]

从历史看，以国际法为支撑的法律外交，是所有崛起之国在国际关系中的不二重器。在此过程中，大国固然如是，小国亦然，而且因为其军事、经济、人口等条件的限制，法律外交更是其最佳乃至唯一的选择。[3]

受文明程度和国际法发展水平的制约，在近代之前，国家的崛起一般采取武力征服方式。世界进入近代之后，随着国际交往的增多、国际法体系的不断健全，特别是法律外交的参与，逐步建立起日益文明、合理的全球秩序和国际规则，使得世界和平发展的法治基础得以夯实。[4]

这一过程，有着正反两方面的丰富经验和教训，值得认真汲取。[5]

十五到十六世纪，西班牙和葡萄牙先后改进航海技术，利用数学、地理学、天文学的新知识，广泛进行跨洋贸易，开拓殖民地。特别是两国充分利用了当时国际法规则，如1494年的《托德西利亚斯条约》和1529年的《萨拉戈萨条约》，为其长期在海外争取国家利益奠定了权利和利益的基础。但由于仅仅将其殖民地视为国际法上的无主地，同时忽略了欧洲邻国在海外的利益，因而在这些民族和国家兴起后，注定了这两国失去其领先优势和所属领地的命运。[6]

之后，以工业革命和科学技术为强大实力，英国迅速崛起，建立了一个占世界总面积和人口四分之一的日不落帝国。英国善用法律外交，通过《乌特勒支条约》等国际法规，为其殖民活动确立了法律基础，同时还形成了其将本国法律文化国际化的发展方略，首先提出了“国际法”的概念，并扮演了模范遵守国际法的角色，对世界国际法格局的形成，产生深远意义。[7]

美国的特色崛起，吸取了前车之鉴。早在1823年，美国便提出了不允许欧洲列强干涉美洲事务的“门罗主义”，这一坚决秉持国际法观念和法律外交的立场，涵义至深。二十世纪后，无论是威尔逊总统主张的“十四点”，还是巴黎和会后的华盛顿体系，特别是1945年联合国的创立，国际货币基金组织的形成，世界关税与贸易总协议的制定等，美国的法律外交都从中起了主导作用。[8]

然而，近代德国和日本的崛起与衰落，则为世界留下了值得反思的教训。[9]

十九世纪末，德国已崛起为工业化强国，但它却忽视国际关系的变化和国际法的意义，仍试图以武力方式获取国家利益，因而在第一次世界大战中惨败，成为《凡尔赛和约》的制裁对象。第二次世界大战后的纽伦堡审判，又把战争发动者永远钉在了世界历史耻辱柱上，彰显了国际法的正义与道德力量。[10]

1868 年后，日本经过了明治维新的洗礼，逐步从一个落后的封建制弱国崛起为一个现代化的强国，但它却走上了侵略、掠夺他国之路，违背了当时日趋宽容、理性的国际法精神，以武力不断向外扩张，使中国及相关邻国成为其灾难深重的受害者。然而，国际关系的新格局和国际法的新理念，已经不允许日本采用非和平手段崛起，因而以完败收场。[11]

国际社会正反两方面的实践表明，一个国家的崛起，不仅靠其自身的实力和自然、社会条件，而且还须顺从国际发展趋势，遵循国际法规则，以现代文明理念妥善处理国与国间关系，而所有这些均需通过务实、有效的法律外交加以实现。[12]

译 文

Law-Guided Diplomacy and the Rise of States

The rise of a state depends on various factors. Among them, law-guided diplomacy is undoubtedly one of the essentials, a fact that has been repeatedly proven.[1]

Law-guided diplomacy is rooted in core values, including faith in and respect for the rule of law, a mindset grounded in legal principles, and conducting diplomacy through understanding, engaging with, and applying international law. By adhering to these values, a state can more effectively pursue its interests in international relations, enhance its legitimacy, and garner broader recognition and support from the global community.[2]

History reveals that law-guided diplomacy, supported by international law, has been critical to the ascent of major powers in international relations. This holds true for both large and small nations. For smaller states constrained by limited military, economic, or demographic resources, law-guided diplomacy becomes not just the best option but often the only viable path forward.[3]

In the pre-modern era, due to the underdeveloped nature of civilization and international law, state expansion was typically achieved through military conquest. However, as the world entered modern times—fueled by increased international exchanges and the continual development of international legal frameworks, particularly the emergence of law-guided diplomacy—a more civilized and desirable global order began to take shape, solidifying the foundation for the peaceful global development.[4]

The world has learned many important lessons, both positive and negative, from this process.[5]

In the 15th and 16th centuries, Spain and Portugal successively improved their ways of conducting ocean navigation. By applying new knowledge in mathematics, geography and astronomy, they engaged extensively in transoceanic trade and explored their colonies. In particular, they made full use of the rules of international laws existing at the time, such as the *Treaty of Tordesillas* (1494) and the *Treaty of Zaragoza* (1529), thus making it possible for them to pursue long-term interests overseas. However, since they treated their colonies merely as terra nullius under international laws and ignored the interests of their neighboring European countries, they were doomed to lose their preeminence and occupied territories when these nations and states themselves arose.[6]

Afterwards, Britain, empowered by its industrial revolution and developing scientific technologies, quickly surged and built up an empire "on which the sun never set", covering the 25% of the world's population and area. Skillful in legal diplomacy, Britain took advantage of international rules such as the *Treaty of Utrecht* (1713), legitimizing its colonial activities while strategizing to internationalize its own legal culture. It also originated the concept of "international law" and displayed an exemplary compliance with such international laws, which had far-reaching significance for the format of international laws worldwide.[7]

Drawing on such practices, the United States rose to preeminence. As early as 1823, it adopted the "Monroe Doctrine" which rejected interference by European powers in American continent's affairs. This position, which was based on international law and law-guided diplomacy, had profound implication for later generations. Particularly, in the 20th Century, the United States' law-guided diplomacy played a leading role in a series of landmark events, including the "14 points" advocated by President Wilson, the "Washington System" following the Paris Peace Conference, especially the founding of the United Nations in 1945, and the creation of the International Monetary Fund, and the stipulations in the General Agreement on World Tariffs and Trade and so on.[8]

However, the rise and subsequent falls of Germany and Japan in modern times serve as cautionary tales for the world.[9]

By the end of the 19th century, Germany had emerged as an industrial power. However, it ignored shifts in international relations and law, continuing to seek advantages through force. This led to its catastrophic defeat in World War I and the imposition of humiliating sanctions under the *Treaty of Versailles*. Following World War II, the Nuremberg Trials once again held the architects of war accountable, cementing their place in history's disgrace and affirming the moral authority of international law and justice.[10]

Similarly, Japan, rejuvenated by the Meiji Restoration (1868), gradually transformed itself from a weak, feudal state into a powerful modern nation. However, it pursued a path of aggression, expanding its territory through military force, violating the emerging international legal norms, and causing immense suffering to China and its other neighbors. Japan's failure to follow the trend of inclusive world order and rational international law led to its inevitable defeat, as its "non-peaceful rise" clashed with the principles of international relations and law.[11]

The developments in international society, both positive and negative, have shown that for any country to rise, it cannot rely solely on its own strength or resources. A state must align itself with international trends, adhere to the principles of international law, and engage with other nations in a modern and civil manner. This is only possible through the pragmatic and effective application of law-guided diplomacy.[12]

解　析

法律外交意识下的译语变通

——第四届"和平杯"中国法律外交翻译大赛译文点评

第四届"和平杯"中国法律外交翻译大赛，在指导单位中国外文局翻译院全国翻译专业学位研究生教育指导委员会的大力支持下，由中国政法大学、甘肃政法大学、四川外国语大学和中国仲裁法学研究会法律英语教学与测试专业委员会联合主办，由吉林外国语大学圆满承办。经过严格的匿名初评与终评盲审，在数百名参赛选手中，共评选出获奖选手 44 名，包括一等奖 2 名、二等奖 12 名、三等奖 20 名及优秀奖 10 名。

以下主要围绕"法律外交"的核心概念及由此引发的相关

问题，对本次翻译大赛的译文作一综合点评分析。

一、概念的比较与辨析

不同于一般意义上的外交实践，法律外交有其独具特色的涵义，因而在翻译中须特别注意加以辨析。“法律外交”概念以往通常译成 legal diplomacy，但经过一段翻译实践的考量和检验，现在更多的共识集中在 law-guided diplomacy。分析起来，前者主要指 the practice of conducting diplomacy and managing international relations through legal means, typically using international law as the framework for negotiations and agreements，即利用现有国际法律框架解决国家之间争端的一种外交活动；而后者的本质则是 the diplomacy is guided by legal principles or the rule of law but not necessarily confined to legal processes，即以国际法律框架为原则，但又不刻板地拘泥于某种法律程序，从而为相应的政治、经济及文化等因素在外交中的施展开辟出广阔空间，因而参考译文中采用了 law-guided diplomacy。令人欣喜的是，许多参赛译文也选择了这一术语；当然 legal diplomacy 并非错译，只是在法律翻译中若具有与时俱进意识，则更加难能可贵。

就题目而言，有以下数种比较典型的参赛译文：The Rise of a Country: The Role of Legal Diplomacy/Legal Diplomacy and National Rise/Legal Diplomacy and the Ascent of States/Legal Diplomacy and the Ascendance of Nations/Legal Diplomacy and the Emergence of A Country/Legal-Guided Diplomacy and the Uplift of States/Law-guided Diplomacy and State Surge/Legal Diplomacy and the Boom of A Country/Legal Diplomacy and the Expansion of A State 等。

其中有两个主要概念。

其一，"国家"，参赛译文用了 country、nation、state，三个词语虽然有时可互换使用，但在不同的语境中其具体涵义有所不同。概言之，country: an area of land that has or used to have its own government and laws，指带有明确的边界和政府，强调的是地理概念和国家的整体性；nation: a group of people with the same language, culture and history, who live in a particular area under one government，更强调一个民族或一群人有着共同的文化、历史、语言或种族背景；state: it is considered as an organized political community controlled by one government，即指的是一个政治组织，通常带有主权和政府管理实体，因而在国际法中，state 是对一个国家的正式称呼，故"国家元首"，是 head of state，不是 head of country。因而，在该标题中，宜用 States。

此外，在不同语境还会有其他变体，如《联合国宪章》明确规定，"所有成员国（不得以武力或武力威胁方式解决国际争端）"，其章程译为 All Members... ；"世界上绝大多数国家（都声称遵守国际法院的判决）"，联合国的通常表述是 the vast majority of countries in the world; "欧盟成员国"是 European Union member states，而不是 member countries ；"波罗的海诸国"是 the Baltic States；此外，state 还可指 part of country，如美国的各州（the different states of the US）。在本文［3］中，“崛起之国”，参考译文并未用与“国”相关的词语，而译为 the ascent of major powers，更能体现其性质；同时，“大国固然如是，小国亦然”，又用了 for both large and small nations，以契合语境中的具体涵义。

其二，“崛起”，参赛译文主要用了 rise、ascent、ascendance、growth、boom 等，具体而言，rise: an increase in position, status, or amount; it can refer to a physical elevation, an improvement in status or power, or a growth in quantity or importance，即主要指权力、地位或影响力的增长，故这是参赛译文使用最多、无疑也是最恰当的词语。其余的，ascent: the act of moving upward or rising to a higher position, physically or metaphorically, 表示上升、攀登，亦用于描述社会地位或权力等方面；emergence: the process of coming into view or becoming noticeable after being hidden or unknown; it can also describe the development of something new or important, such as ideas, trends, or phenomena，主要表示从无到有、逐渐显现或形成，多用于指某个新现象、趋势或力量的出现；uplift: the process of raising or elevating something, either literally（as in geological formations）or metaphorically（as in raising spirits or status），通常用于表示精神、情感或社会地位的提升；surge: a sudden and powerful increase or upward movement in something, often in a short period，表示快速而强烈的增长或崛起；boom: a rapid increase in something, typically related to economic growth or sudden demand，强调某种事物的

突然繁荣或快速发展，常与经济、科技或文化相关；expansion: the process of increasing in size, scope, scale or influence， 主要指在规模、体量、影响上的增长。这些词语，虽用在标题上不大适宜，但不等于在下文不同语境中不可应用，如［3］中的"崛起之国"，参考译文为 the ascent of major powers；［4］中，"国家的崛起一般采取武力征服方式"，参考译文为 state expansion was typically achieved through military conquest；［7］中，"英国迅速崛起，建立了一个……帝国"，参考译文为 Britain, ...quickly surged and built up an empire；［10］中，"德国已崛起为工业化强国"，参考译文为 Germany had emerged as an industrial power. 等，故具体概念要具体分析，正如法国哲学家、语言学家米歇尔·福柯（Michel Foucault）所说：*Un même mot dans un nouveau contexte est un nouveau mot*（A same word in new context is a new word）。同时，同义词的使用，也使表述方式更加丰富、精准。

［3］中的"不二重器"，有的按字面意思译成 an indispensable tool，未尝不可，参考译文将其引申为 ...has been critical to...；而"（因为其军事、经济、人口等条件的）限制"，参赛译文中用了 restricted by、limited by、confined by、bound by、hindered by、constrained by 等，但经比较分析后，发现最后一词最为恰当，因 It refers to a situation where certain conditions, rules, or external factors prevent or limit action or freedom；然而，在［4］中，"（受文明程度和国际法发展水平的）制约"，又未必要使用其在词典上的所谓"对等词语"，如 held back by、governed by、impeded by、subject to、circumscribed by 等，而可就其内在涵义，变通为 due to（the underdeveloped nature of civilization...），因为这种字面上的“不等”更能体现其意思上的“等值”。

［10］中的“彰显了（国际法的正义与道德力量）”，参赛译文主要用了 demonstrated、highlighted、manifested、showcased、embodied，这些在词义上都是对应、可取的，而参考译文在其特有的句式中，用了 affirming（the moral authority of international law and justice），也是一种变通的等值。

二、语意的梳理与表述

在辨析词汇的基础上，更应注重整体语意的表达，而这亦离不开对其相应的梳理与变通。

［2］中，“法律外交是一种价值观外交，其核心是基于法治价值追求的外交”，可有两种主要译法，一种将其理解成“作为价值观外交的法律外交”，译成状语，如参赛译文 As a value-based form of diplomacy, the core values.../As a key diplomatic tool, legal diplomacy is grounded in core values/As a valued diplomacy, its core values underpinning... 等，这与原文在表述方式上更为接近；另一种是将其译成一般陈述句式，如参考译文 Law-guided diplomacy is rooted in core values，这有利于接续下文“信仰法治、崇尚法治、具有法治思维，通过理解、参与、运用国际法来展开外交”，不必机械地采用原文的破折号，而用 including faith in and respect for the rule of law, a mindset grounded in legal principles, and conducting diplomacy through understanding, engaging with, and applying international law，使行文更加顺畅、自然。同时，“提高（其在国际社会的认可与支持度）”，未必永远要用 improve、enhance、boost、increase 等常用词，参考译文用了 garner，其本义为 to gather, collect, or acquire something, typically through effort or over time. In essence, it involves accumulating something valuable or necessary，在此处更为贴切。

［3］中，“从历史看”，一般都自然地译成 Historically，但亦可译为 History reveals that...；“在此过程中，大国固然如是，小国亦然，而且因为其军事、经济、人口等条件的限制，法律外交更是其最佳乃至唯一的选择”，比较典型的参赛译文，如 During this process, large countries would naturally turn to legal diplomacy, but it was also the case to small countries. Moreover, subject to military, economic and population conditions, legal diplomacy has become their best or even the only choice. / In this process, it is crucial for both major powers as well as small counterparts. Especially for the latter, legal diplomacy is considered as their best and even sole option due to the limitations in military, economy, population, and other conditions. / As the legal diplomacy works effectively in the rise of great powers, it achieves the same in small countries. Considering various limitations in military affairs, economy and population, small countries prefer the legal diplomacy as the optimal and only choice 等，其中下画线部分，笔者认为是问题要点，如 During this process、In this process 可略去不译，因该意在上下文中已经表明；also the case，语气不够；

small counterparts，用语不准；works effectively、achieves the same、prefer the legal diplomacy as 则表述方式有问题。因而，给出的参考译文为：This holds true for both large and small nations. For smaller states constrained by limited military, economic, or demographic resources, law-guided diplomacy becomes not just the best option but often the only viable path forward. 其中，holds true 可澄清许多模糊表述，而 not just the best option but often the only viable path forward 突出了法律外交对于无论大小国家的特殊重要性质。

［4］中，"世界进入近代之后，随着国际交往的增多、国际法体系的不断健全，特别是法律外交的参与，逐步建立起日益文明、合理的全球秩序和国际规则，使得世界和平发展的法治基础得以夯实"，内容颇为繁杂，需先将其层次梳理清楚，避免漏译成分，如参赛译文：With the increase in international interactions and the continuous improvement of the international legal system, especially with the emergence of legal diplomacy, a civilized and reasonable global order and international rules were gradually established, which had enhanced the foundation for the rule of law in world peace and development. 其中漏译了"世界进入近代之后"（以对应前面的"在近代之前"），而"日益（文明、合理的全球秩序和国际规则）"不宜缩略为 a civilized...，因其有对比之意；同时，在表述上又要避免过于零碎和冗赘，如 With...、especially with...、which had... 可作适当变化和省略。参考译文为：However, as the world entered modern times—fueled by increased international exchanges and the continual development of international legal frameworks, particularly the emergence of law-guided diplomacy—a more civilized and desirable global order began to take shape, solidifying the foundation for the peaceful global development. 其中，However 为必要的增译，以转换语气、连贯行文（类似的，［2］中，在“这不仅有利于该国在国际关系中争取利益”之前，加入 By adhering to these values ；［11］中的“1868 年后，日本经过了明治维新的洗礼”，加入 Similarly, Japan...），同时利用两个破折号，将补充状语成分归纳其中，脉络分明；a more civilized and desirable... 以强调与之前的不同，而动名词 solidifying 使句式更加精练。

［5］中，“有着正反两方面的丰富经验和教训”，若译成 having rich positive and negative lessons to learn，则为中文词序，英文词序是 ...has learned many important lessons, both positive and negative,...。同样，［12］的“国际社会正反两方面的实践表明”，宜译为 The developments in international society, both positive and negative, have shown that...。

对于主语的处理，有时也需作适当调整，以符合特殊语境的表达。如［7］中的“以工业革命和科学技术为强大实力，英国迅速崛起，建立了一个……”，不妨译为 Britain, empowered by its industrial revolution and developing scientific technologies, quickly surged and built up...，以构成与之前西班牙、葡萄牙等国崛起的对比。同样，［11］中的“日本经过了明治维新的洗礼，逐步从一个……”，参考译文为 Japan, rejuvenated by the Meiji Restoration（1868）, gradually transformed itself from...；而［8］中

的“美国的特色崛起，吸取了前车之鉴”，则宜将状语提前，译为 Drawing on such practices, the United States rose to preeminence，以更符合此处的英文表达习惯。

［7］中的“为其殖民活动确立了法律基础，同时还形成了其将本国法律文化国际化的发展方略”，参赛译文一般都顺理成章地译成 ...have laid the legal foundation for its colonial activities, in the same time formulated the strategies to develop its legal culture at the international stage/...employed legal diplomacy, prepared the legal basis for its colonial activities, meanwhile set a strategy for the internationalization of its legal culture/...established the legal groundwork for British colonization, also shaped the developmental strategy for the internationalization of its legal culture 等，意思大都不错；而参考译文为 legitimizing its colonial activities while strategizing to internationalize its own legal culture，其中用了两个动名词，使其表述更加严谨、精练。

［9］中的“为世界留下了值得反思的教训”，若译成 ...have left serious lessons worth reflecting on for the world，无可厚非；参考译文为 serve as cautionary tales for the world，其中 cautionary 的本义是 It typically describes actions, advice, stories, or measures meant to prevent danger, mistakes, or negative outcomes，从而有了 cautionary tale、cautionary sign、cautionary statement、cautionary risk、cautionary principle 等短语，以表其警示性质，在此起强调作用。

［10］中，“……又把战争发动者永远钉在了世界历史耻

辱柱上”，固然可以遵其字面意思译成 ...once again nailed the perpetrators of the war to the pillar of shame in world history，而参考译文 ...once again held the architects of war accountable, cementing their place in history's disgrace，可说是一种变通的意译。

［11］中，“然而，国际关系的新格局和国际法的新理念，已经不允许日本采用非和平手段崛起，因而以完败收场”，对于其中下画线部分的重点词语，参赛者根据自己的理解，给出各种译文，如 However, the new pattern of international relations and the new concept of international law no longer allowed Japan to rise through non-peaceful means, and it ended in complete defeat./ Nevertheless, Japan's aggression ended in miserable defeat, as the new international relations and the new ideas of international law no longer permitted it to rise through non-peaceful means./Nevertheless, the new landscape of international relations and the new concepts of international law no longer allowed Japan to rise through non-peaceful means, leading to its ultimate failure 等，应当说，都没有译错。参考译文为 Japan's failure to follow the trend of inclusive world order and rational international law led to its inevitable defeat, as its "non-peaceful rise" clashed with the principles of international relations and law. 其中，将“新格局”、“新理念”具体化为与法律外交相关的 the trend of inclusive world order and rational international law，而将“不允许”的涵义体现在 failure to follow、clashed with、inevitable defeat 的表述中，却并未用 not allowed、 not permitted、disallowed 等字面对应词语。

三、其他相关问题

其一，漏译。如同以往翻译大赛，此次仍有部分译文漏译标题和内容；其中不乏优质者，但无奈大都在评审早期被淘汰，不免遗憾。

其二，翻译软件。从参赛译文可以看出，有相当比例的人使用了翻译软件，且有若干雷同译文。翻译智能固然在不断演进，但对于其识别的技能也在发展，这不但从文本，甚至从其标点符号中也可看出端倪，因而对全盘照搬软件的译文，其成绩必定会受到影响。并非不可以使用翻译软件，但一定要进行译后编辑和修改处理，否则这类翻译大赛便成了翻译软件大赛，从而对大赛的主办方、参与者和评审者都失去了意义。同时，应当说，到目前为止，还没有哪一款翻译软件可完全代替人工，特别是对于诸如法律外交这类涉及复杂、敏感、微妙，甚至有歧义内容的原文，永远需要译者的真才实学。

其三，格式。译文的呈现方式（presentation），如标题（黑体字）、字体、字号、格式的选择与应用等，似乎还未引起部分参赛者的应有重视，从而影响了对其专业水准的评判。在国外留学或参加过国际大赛的人会知道，不合标准的呈现方式可能导致作品的拒收。因为，在许多情况下，形式其实是内容的一部分。就法律外交翻译大赛而言，优质的译文应当永远与其优质的呈现相匹配。

整体而言，“和平杯”中国法律外交翻译大赛的译文水平，在主要方面是逐届提高的。希望通过及时的分析、总结，下一届能迈上新的台阶。

原 文

典籍中的“通感”

“通感”，这一艺术感知和创作中的特殊现象，为现代学者所重视。其实，在我国古典文献中，亦有许多直接或间接的有关论述。对此，钱锺书先生不但首次将其概念引入中国文化，并作过颇为深入而全面的研究。[1]

早期的相关论述，如公孙龙的坚白论：“目不能坚，手不能白”（《公孙龙子·坚白论》），辅之以庄子的：“譬如耳目鼻口，皆有所明，不能相通”（《庄子·天下》），后又有焦氏的“鼻目易处，不知香臭”（《焦氏易林·随》），以及著名文论家陆机的“臣闻目无尝音之察，耳无照景之神”。[2]

然而，在钱氏看来，“此常世所识也”，而“神秘宗侈陈之高境”则认为：“视听不用耳目”、“神合于无”者，神会而不以官受，如《文子》所言：“故上学以神听，中学以心听，下学以耳听。”[3]

此等高论，悉心探究，其实古已有之。如，“而后眼如耳，耳如鼻，鼻如口，无不同也。心凝形释，骨肉都融”（《列子·黄帝》），晋代张湛对此的注释是：“夫眼耳鼻口，各有攸司。今神凝形废，无待于外，则视听不资眼耳，嗅味不赖鼻口。”

其实，《列子》中的这种实感，不过是发挥了《庄子·人世间》中的“夫徇耳目内通，而外于心知”；“徇”通“洵”，“内通”即“无不同”、“内彻”、“不阂墙壁”。[4]

甚而言之，释典惯言五官通用，如《楞严经》卷四：“由是六根相互为用。阿难，汝岂不知，今此会中，阿那律陀无目而见，跋难陀龙无耳而听，殑伽神女非鼻闻香，骄梵钵提异舍知味，爱若多神无身觉触？”[5]

又卷一〇：“销磨六门，合开成就，见闻通邻，互用清净”；《五灯会元》卷一二，净因继成上堂：“鼻里音声耳里香，眼中咸淡舌玄黄，意能觉触身分别，冰室如春九夏凉”；又卷一三，洞山良价偈：“也大奇，也大奇！无情说法不思议！若将耳听终难会，眼处闻时方得知。”[6]

陆机《连珠》又言：“目无尝音之察，耳无照景之神”，“尝音”之“尝”即“尝食”、“常药”之“尝”，已潜以耳之于音等口之于味；其《拟西北有高楼》明曰：“佳人抚琴瑟，纤手清且闲；芳气随风结，哀响馥若兰”，岂非“非鼻闻香”？[7]

陈与义《简齐集》卷二二《舟抵华容县夜赋》：“三更萤火闹，万里天河横”；黄景仁《两当轩集》卷一九《醉花阴·夏夜》：“隔竹卷珠帘，几个明星，切切如私语”，岂非“眼里闻声”？[8]

至于《琅嬛记》上卷庄氏女的“每弄《梅花曲》，闻者皆云，有暗香”，则更是活生生的通感。所谓道家的“内通”，佛家的“互用”都可在此窥见一斑。[9]

译 文

"Synaesthesia" in Classic Chinese Literature

Synaesthesia, as a concept of the unique phenomenon of art perception and creative writing, first introduced into Chinese culture and studied substantially by Qian Zhongshu (1910-1998), has attracted considerable attention from modern scholars. In fact, the concept has been directly or indirectly mentioned and discussed in classic Chinese literature.[1]

In ancient times, there was a well-known assertion by Gongsun Long (320 BC-250 BC) that "the eye cannot detect hardness and the hand cannot detect whiteness" , complemented by Zhuangzi's (369 BC-286 BC) saying that "It is precisely like the ears, eyes, nose, and mouth, which each has their own sensibilities and discernment that are not interchangeable" . Relevantly, Jiao Yanshou (148 BC-60 BC) also affirmed that "If the nose and eyes are detached from each other, then fragrant and ill smells can hardly be differentiated" . The famous literature critic Lu Ji (261-303) then made a comment: "It is said that eyes are unable to relish sounds, and ears lack the ability to see." [2]

In Qian's view, however, this is merely the limitation of common man and, if a person has reached a heightened stage of mystic appreciation, he will perceive things differently. As such, he can see and hear without using his eyes and ears since the spirit has melted things together with Nothingness. This implies that a higher level of awareness has been attained, which is far beyond the sensory sphere where the highest learning perceives with the spirit, the middle with the mind, and the lowest with sensory organs, as stated in *Wenzi*.[3]

Insightful commentaries like this may also be traced back to ancient Chinese codes and records if one is really interested. Taking *Liezi* as an example, it states that "my eyes, ears, nose and mouth then all seem to be interchangeable and mingled together, differentiating none of them. With this kind of sensation, I have been elevated to a stage where my mind concentrated and my body relaxed; bones and flesh are totally fused" . According to Zhang Zhan, a scholar of East Jin Dynasty (317-420): "With the eyes, ears, nose, and mouth each being in charged in a different sense, the mind is contemplated and the body left out, so that anything external is no longer needed. As a result, sight and hearing are no longer supported by eyes and ears, smell and taste are no longer dependent on the nose and mouth either" . The genuine feeling of Liezi was an actual expansion of the earlier statement in *Zhuangzi* that "Once the inward channels connecting eyes and ears are unblocked, the insightfulness can be transferred directly from the heart. With a thorough appreciation, everything becomes alike, and will no longer be blocked by any partitions in terms of mutual affection" .[4]

Moreover, in Buddhist writings, the interchangeable perceptions of different sensory organs are almost ubiquitous. In *Surangama Sutra*, for example, Buddha says, "After experiencing this event, my six sensory organs can be interchangeably employed. *Ananda*, have you realized that during today's congregation, Aniruddha watched without opening his eyes, Upananda heard without using his ears, the Ganges River goddess scented without using her nose, Gavampati savored using a usual tongue, and Sunyata sensed with an invisible body?" [5]

In chapter 10 of the same text it says: "Leveling the six doorways to make 'open' and 'close' equal; making the seeing and hearing are neighbors so that they can interchangeably employed to achieve calmness." In *The Essence of the Five Lamps*, the *Chan* master Jing Yin Ji Cheng quotes, "While there is sound in the nose and fragrance in the ear, salty and bland flavors can also be found in the eye and blacks and yellows in the tongue; while the mind has the sense of touch, the body can classify things; while the room of ice sometimes may be like spring, in the middle of summer it could be rather cold." In the same work, the monk Liang Jie of Dong Shan recites this gatha: "Fabulous, fabulous! The lectures he conveys with a remarkable calmness that one can never totally comprehend by using merely ears; eyes are an essential requirement as well." [6]

In Lu Ji's assertion quoted earlier ("It is said that eyes are unable to relish sounds, and ears lack the ability to see"), we have another example. *Chang* (relish or savor) is a word normally used to refer to taste and enjoy food or medicine in Chinese. By using it in the way he does, the writing subtly relates the ear's experience of sound to the mouth's experience of food. In another composition, Lu Ji puts it even more plainly: "While a beautiful lady twangs the zither leisurely with her delicate fingers, the fragrant tune composes the breeze that carries it; the lugubrious resonance is as aromatic as orchids." Is this not a case of scenting without using her nose?[7]

Chen Yuyi (1090-1138) wrote a few lines in *On Arriving by Boat at Night at Huarong County*: "In the dead of night, the lighting bugs are noisy and strident as we are watching the Milky Way spreading about myriad miles away." Huang Jingren (1749-1783) also had a song lyric *On a Summer Night*: "When I roll up the jeweled screen behind the bamboo, there are bright stars whispering to one another." Are these not exemplifications of "hearing sounds with the eyes" ?[8]

Lianghuan Ji, a story written by Yi Shizhen in the Yuan Dynasty (1271-1368), describes that "whenever Miss Zhuang plays the zither tune 'Plum Blossoms' the listeners all say that they perceive 'a murky aroma' ", which can surely be deemed as the vivid "synaesthesia" , reflecting more or less of the Taoists' "internal travelling" and the Buddhists' "interchangeable application" .[9]

解　析

深层结构上的贯通

——关于《典籍中的“通感”》的翻译

“通感”（synaesthesia），在心理学上，是指人们的某种感官受到刺激后在另一种不同感觉领域内所产生的体验。特别是在文学艺术创作和欣赏中，指描写一种感觉的语言被用来描写另一种感觉。此种现象早在亚里士多德的《心灵论》中就有所描述，后由著名学者钱锺书介绍到中国。其实，在中国古代典籍中，关于通感性质的论述不但早已有之，而且相当精彩。于是，对其翻译的探究，便别有涵义。

一、特殊感知的转移

对于思维过程的理解，应当说，在西方有着较为前卫的探知。在西方心理学中，将思维活动分为两个阶段：感性认识阶段和理性认识阶段。所谓感性认识，就是人们在实践中通过自己的感官（眼、耳、鼻、舌、身）直接接触客观外界，在头脑中产生感觉、知觉和表象等直观方式的认识。理性认识是对感觉到的材料进行整理、加工和改造的综合过程，属概念、判断和推理阶段的认识。

人们借助于语言将感性认识上升为理性认识，找出不能直接感知的事物的本质和事物之间的内部联系。语言是人们进行思维的主要工具，但不是唯一工具，还有感觉、知觉、记忆、想象等，这些都构成了我们之后称之为“通感”的心理基础。

有的科学家宣称自己在解决难题时，通常不是用词语来思维，而是用所谓的“记号”和“意象”。如爱因斯坦在致数学家雅克·哈达马德的信中写道：“在我的思维机构中，书面或口头的文字似乎不起任何作用。作为思想元素的心理的东西是一些记号和有一定明晰程度的意象，它们可以由我‘随意地’再生和组合。”（克雷奇等，1980：210）

至于文学艺术的创作，则最终离不开感官和想象；艺术的魅力首先来自其感性力量，正如李斯特论肖邦所说：“艺术的多种多样的形式可以说是一种咒语；艺术家想把感觉和热情变成可感、可视、可听，并且在某种意义上是可触的东西，他想传达这些感觉的内在的全部活动，而艺术的各种各样的公式正是供在自己的魔圈中唤起这些感觉和热情所用的。”（富兰兹，1993：203）

所以，在感性认识与理性认识的基础上，感觉、知觉、表象的提升与综合便形成了“感知”，所谓“通感”，实际是一种特殊的感知，并处于一种流动状态。可表述如下：

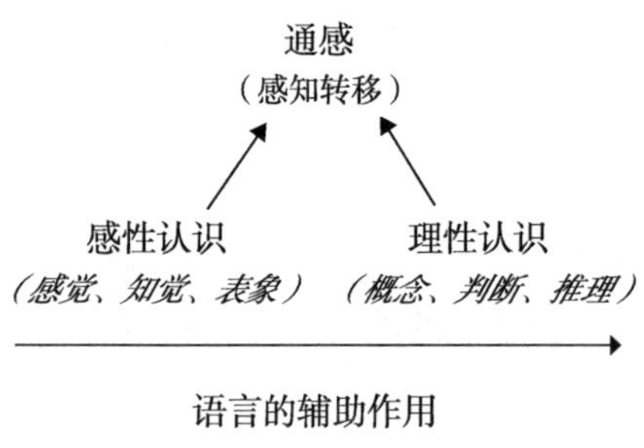

所以，“通感”可以概括为一种在感性与理性认识的基础上，以感觉、表象、概念、判断为元素而形成的特殊感知的转移，它以语言为辅助手段，但不局限于语言范畴。

人们在感知客观事物的过程中，各个感官之间是相互联系的，人们能够以综合感觉的形式获得对事物的总体概念，即某一性质的感觉可以同其他性质的感觉构成某种或同一、或相似、或补充甚至替代的关系。故一个人在认识客观事物的过程中，若愈能沟通各个感官领域之间的关系，其感觉就会愈丰富，表象也就愈多样，判断也便会愈灵敏，而这种作用亦不乏体现在翻译的过程之中。

如前所述，亚里士多德在《心灵论》已经提及，他认为声音有“尖锐”（sharp）和“钝重”（heavy）之分，其比拟从触觉而来（used by analogy from the sense of touch），因为听、触两觉有类似处（Aristotle，1992），那是与触觉比照的结果，“因为听觉与触觉有相似之处”。荷马史诗《伊里亚特》中的那句诗，曾使许多翻译者搔首踟蹰：“像知了坐在森林中一棵树上，倾泻了百合花也似的声音”（Like a cicada that in a forest sit upon a tree and pour forth their lily-like voice）。十八世纪的神秘主义者圣马丁（Saint-Martin）说自己曾“听见发声的花朵，看见发光的音调”（I heard flowers that sounded and saw notes that shone）。英国诗人布莱克（William Blake）曾用“瞎了眼睛的手”（blind hand）来形容木钝的触觉，莎士比亚悲剧里的盲人也说：“假如我能用触觉瞧见你（see thee in my touch）。”培根说，音乐的声调摇曳使人好像感到光芒在水面浮动一样。近代意大利美学家克罗齐在《美学原理》中对通感也从一个特定的角度作了论述："又有一种怪论，以为图画只能产生视觉印象。腮上的晕，少年人体肤的温暖，利刃的锋，果子的新鲜香甜，这些不也是可以从图画中得到的印象么？它们是视觉的印象么？假想一个人没有听触嗅味感觉，只有视觉感官，图画对于他的意味何如呢？我们所看到的而且相信只用眼睛看的那幅画，在他的眼光中，就不过像画家的涂过颜料的调色板了。"（克罗齐：2012）总之，人的各种感官之间，在一定条件下、一定结构中，是完全可以被打通的；这无论对文学艺术的创作者还是对其转述、翻译者，都颇具启示性。

在中国丰富的文化典籍中，其实早有"通感"要素的存在。例如，文人们惯于用眼去品尝滋味，用耳朵去听钟声之"湿"；惯于诗中见画，画中听声，而这些与西方艺术家将建筑视为"凝固的音乐"、将音乐称为"流动的建筑"、将舞蹈视为"活动的雕塑"等等，在深层次的感觉上，其实如出一辙。我们所缺乏的，可能是对这种"通感"宝藏的挖掘、比较与翻译，而《典籍中的"通感"》恰恰提供了这种可能性。

二、层次结构法的解析

在著名语言学家乔姆斯基（Chomsky）的转换生成模式中，把句子分析为一系列受规则制约的相关层级，即有短语结构规则生成潜在或深层结构（deep structure）、受音韵规则和词素规则所约束的表层结构（surface structure），以及通过与另一种潜在结构依相关规则所发生的转化（transferring）（Chomsky, 1965）。著名翻译学家奈达（Nida）将乔氏的模式加以改造，融合到了他的翻译研究中，认为原语文本的表层结构实则为深层结构的基本成分，而这些成分在翻译过程中被“转移”了，然后根据语义和文体的特点重新建构了译语文本的表层结构（Nida and Taber, 1969：33）。

具体到对于中国典籍里“通感”论述的理解与翻译，则不妨在理解乔氏与奈氏框架精髓的基础上，进一步加以改造如下：

层次结构法（Hierarchical Structuring）

A 原语	语言层次	B 译语
	↓　↑	
分析　↓		↑　编码
	理解层次	
	↓　↑	
融化　↓		↑　重组
	通感层次	

语言表达淡化

感知彼此交融

如上所述，在此结构中，除了语言的因素，更有理解与通感的功能，且对于原语的分析与融化的过程，直接影响着其相应的重组与编码的结果；故译语的质量，其实取决于变化中的语言功能与各种感知相互作用的程度。

在［2］中，“目不能坚，手不能白”、“譬如耳目鼻口，皆有所明，不能相通”、“鼻目易处，不知香臭”及“臣闻目无尝音之察，耳无照景之神”等之论，可谓仍在语言层次，故可较为平实地译为“the eye cannot detect hardness and the hand cannot detect whiteness”；“It is precisely like the ears, eyes, nose, and mouth, which each has their own sensibilities and discernments that are not interchangeable”；“If the nose and eyes are detached from each other, then fragrant and ill smells can hardly be differentiated”；“It is said that eyes are unable to relish sounds, and ears lack the ability to see”等。

到了［3］，则逐渐进入“通感层次”；如前所述，其语言表述的突出特点是“淡”与“融”。何谓“神秘宗侈陈之高境”？这里的“神”不是神圣，“高”则是指有见识，故不妨分别译为“heightened stage”和“mystic appreciation”。至于“‘视听不用耳目’、‘神合于无’者，神会而不以官受”的翻译，因其文言甚为简约，故可稍加释义：首先，加一句“he will perceive things differently”，将不同于“常世所识”之意淡然而止；然后将“神合”以 the spirit has melted things together 译出，而“神会”，则又不必特意突现为 divine understanding，而只将其“俗化”为常人的理解，译为 a higher level of awareness；“不以官受”译为 beyond the sensory sphere。同时，为了使行文更为“通融”，故不应终止于此，而宜以代词 where 接引下文：where the highest learning perceives with the spirit, the middle with the mind, and the lowest with sensory organs...。

［4］则是在“通感层次”上的延伸，分为“列子”（Taking *Liezi* as an example）和“张湛”（According to Zhang Zhan）两部分论述。对于前者的前一部分“而后眼如耳，耳如鼻，鼻如口，无不同也”的翻译，可不必太“实”，如译成 eyes don’t have to be like ears, eyes don’t like nose and nose doesn’t like mouth...”，而宜“通融”为“my eyes, ears, nose and mouth then all seem to be interchangeable and mingled together, differentiating none of them”；对于后一部分“心凝形释，骨肉都融”的翻译，则要添加不少成分，方能使行文“贯通”：首先加上一句常识性的解释“With this kind of sensation”，再作出铺垫“I have been elevated to a stage”，最后落到实处“where my mind concentrated and my body relaxed; bones and flesh are totally fused”，其中的“融”未译成较为理论化的 blend、be in harmony、melting 等，而采用了更为形象化的 fused，以求通俗与具体。

对于后者，即张湛的评论，“夫眼耳鼻口，各有攸司。今神凝形废，无待于外，则视听不资眼耳，嗅味不赖鼻口”，其中的“攸司”，可理解为 be in charged；“待”为 rely、need；“资”为 support，而“则”不妨以 As a result 述之。故整句不妨译为：With the eyes, ears, nose, and mouth each being in charged in a different sense, the mind is contemplated and the body left out, so that anything external is no longer needed. As a result, sight and hearing are no longer supported by eyes and ears, smell and taste are no longer dependent on the nose and mouth either.

在［5］、［6］中，引用了大量的佛经典籍中的相关论述，乍看起来很难翻译，但若参照梵文与英文的对译辞典及佛经的英汉字典，许多问题便会化解。例如，查到相关的术语 Surangama Sutra、Ananda、Aniruddha、Upananda、Gavampati、Sunyata、gatha 等之后，翻译中的障碍就完全可以推倒。

在［7］、［8］、［9］中，其论述可谓是到达了“通感层次”的高峰，故其相应的翻译亦应更加“淡定”与“通达”。例如，“‘佳人抚琴瑟，纤手清且闲；芳气随风结，哀响馥若兰’，岂非‘非鼻闻香’？”其中的“芳气”，并非一般的 fragrance, 而译为 fragrant tune 更加贴切；“哀响”之“馥”，则可译为 the lugubrious resonance 和 aromatic，看似平常之语，但与“鼻闻香”相结合、相贯通，便显得非同凡响：Is this not a case of scenting without using her nose（岂非“非鼻闻香”）？

再如，“隔竹卷珠帘，几个明星，切切如私语”，其中的“明星”（bright stars）可以“私语”（whispering to one another），故接下来的译文不妨顺势而成：Are these not exemplifications of “hearing sounds with the eyes（岂非“眼里闻声）”？以与前句形成贯通、呼应之势。

最后，道家的“内通”，可以译为 inversion、internal connection、contemplation 等，而佛家的“互用”，亦可用 mutual benefits、reciprocal function 等，而所以分别选择了 internal travelling 和 interchangeable application，主要是想体现其中“平实”与“贯通”的特质。

其实，在西方，文学艺术家们早已运用大量的通感手法进行创作。例如，象征主义诗人波德莱尔的《恶之花》中有一首被称为象征派宪章的十四行诗《应和》：

自然是座庙宇，那里活的柱子，
有时说出了模模糊糊的话音；
人从那里过，穿越象征的森林，
森林用熟识的目光将他注视。
如同悠长的回声遥遥地汇合，
在一个混沌深邃的统一体中。
广大浩漫好像黑夜连着光明——
芳香、颜色和声音在相互应和。
有的芳香新鲜若儿童肌肤，
柔和如双簧管，青翠如绿草场，
——别的则朽腐、浓郁、涵盖了万物，
像无极无限的东西四散飞扬，
如同龙涎香、麝香、安息香、乳香
那样歌唱精神与感觉的激昂。

（引自金元浦，2003)

这里，人的感官之间是相通的；视觉、听觉、嗅觉、触觉在一起作用。声音在视觉中有光线颜色——“如同悠长的回声遥遥地汇合，在一个混沌深邃的统一体中。广大浩漫好像黑夜连着光明”；在嗅觉中有芳香——“芳香、颜色和声音在相互应和”。同时，颜色在嗅觉中有芳香，芳香在听觉中有声音，在触觉中有感觉，在视觉中有颜色——“有的芳香新鲜若儿童肌肤，柔和如双簧管，青翠如绿草场”。

所以，我们在翻译中国典籍中关于通感的论述时，可再少些顾忌，而更“通达”一些。例如，与“通感”息息相关的，对于刘勰《文心雕龙·神思》中的名句“寂然凝虑，思接千载；悄焉动容，视通万里；吟咏之间，吐纳珠玉之声；眉睫之前，卷舒风云之色：其思理之致乎？”有学者翻译成：“When we silently focus our concerns, thought may reach to a thousand years in the past; and as our countenance stirs ever so gently, our vision may cross（通）ten thousand leagues. The sounds of pearls and jade are given forth while chanting and singing; right before our eyelashes, the color（色）of windblown clouds unfurls. This is accomplished by the basic principle of thought（理）.”（宇文所安，2003：207）

其中的“silently focus our concerns”、“a thousand years”、“our countenance stirs”、“ten thousand leagues”等，显然是有些“过实”了；因为在“通感层次”上，就作者、译者和读者之间而言，其实可以预留更多彼此“通融”的空间，故不妨译为：“When we are solitarily contemplating, our mind may reach out to events thousands of years ago; as we are sobering up, a clear vision may appear to the endless horizon. When a person is on a creative mood and murmuring out, the noises are as pleasant to hear as the sounds of pearls and jade; the colorful scene may also merge to the creator's eyes accordingly. Are those not generated by the rules of mighty thinking?”

换言之，在突破了“语言层次”的羁绊之后，更多需要着眼的是在“分析”基础之上的“融化”，即钱锺书所讲的“化境”、“得意而忘言”，进而在更深结构上的“重组”与“编码”，必然不应只是“形似”的，而更应是一种“贯通”的意境。

参考文献

① ［意］克罗齐著．美学原理［M］．朱光潜译．北京：商务印书馆，2012.

② ［匈］富兰兹·李斯特著．李斯特论肖邦［M］．张泽民等译．台北：世界文物出版社，1993.

③ 金元浦主编．文艺心理学［M］．北京：中国人民大学出版社，2003.

④ ［美］克雷奇等著．心理学纲要（上册）［M］．周先庚等译．北京：文化教育出版社，1980.

⑤ ［美］宇文所安著．中国文论：英译与评论［M］．王柏华陶庆梅译．上海：上海社会科学出版社，2003.

⑥ Aristotle. *Nicomachean Ethics* [M].Translated by D. P. Chase. New York: E. P. Dutton, 1992.

⑦ Chomsky, N. *Aspects of the Theory of Syntax* [M]. Cambridge, MA: MIT Press, 1965.

⑧ Nida, E. A. and C. R. Taber. *The Theory and Practice of Translation* [M]. Leiden: E. J. Brill, 1969.

原 文

天府文化的和谐与包容

“天府”，指地理位置优越、特产丰富、人文发达的区域。历史上，秦灭巴蜀后，四川盆地的富饶，巴蜀之地的地理优势，使得秦国在严重打击了楚国的同时，也在无形之中瓦解着山东六国的合纵联盟，为其统一天下提供了战备基础。西汉时继续开发巴蜀，使其繁荣兴盛，富甲一方，因而“天府之国”成了四川的美誉。[1]

在此自然与人文基础上形成的巴蜀文化，即为天府文化，它是西学进入成都后对于古蜀文化的继承与更新；既是历史上天府之国文化的总结，也是当今成都市域文化的特征。[2]

以天府地区为中心的这种特殊文化的形成，是各种文化不断碰撞融合的发展过程，充满了和谐与包容性。“创新创造、优雅时尚、乐观包容、友善公益”是新时代天府文化理念的核心。[3]

天府之国所以能够成为道教的发源地，在于天府文化视人与自然为一体，注重人与人之间的和谐统一。蜀人张道陵，正是受到天府文化的浸润，由此顿悟，创立了天师教（早期道教的一派），为天府文化注入了和谐基因，使天府之国成为治世中的繁盛之乡，乱世中的安民之地。[4]

蜀人治学，往往儒释道兼容，并提出了“漫汗通观儒释道，从容涵化印中西”，海纳百川，融为一体。例如，三星堆文化就是与相邻的中原文化、滇文化相互影响和渗透而成，同时又与相距遥远但有经济文化交往的东南亚文明、中东文明，甚至欧洲古代文明，有着绵延不绝的关联。[5]

几千年来，天府人民把“天人合一”的和谐观发挥得淋漓尽致，在工程上，最典型的体现在驰名中外的都江堰。它巧妙地利用了天然地势和水流，科学地解决了江水的自动分流、排沙、引水的难题，收到了“行水灌田，泄洪平灾”的功效。2000年11月，被联合国教科文组织列入“世界文化遗产名录”。[6]

其实，天府文化是以成都城市文化体系为主体、兼容南北文化的多元文化复合体。在人文方面，体现在对于东南西北各方众多移民的吸纳与包容，而每次移民不是简单的人口地理位置的移动，而是其背后的文化交流与融合，更丰富了天府文化的特色与内涵。[7]

在地理上，蜀道的内外勾连，入蜀与出蜀的交相呼应，使得巴蜀文化善于汲取其他地域的文化特点，而其他地域的士人来到蜀中之后，亦可受到这片古老土地上异样文化的滋养，得以取长补短，融会贯通，相得益彰。因而，许多蜀中士人，之前也许默默无闻，一旦出川，特别是来到当时的政治、文化中心后，往往能崭露头角，出类拔萃。[8]

如今，天府文化已经融入到了“一带一路”国家战略的发展之中，与世界文化有着多层次的互动交流，并在此基础上，日益展开着与丝绸之路经济带沿线欧亚各大城市在众多领域的广泛合作。[9]

相应地，天府文化的这种和谐与包容性，形成了其特有的开明、开放的文化传统，使得天府人民生性乐观，勤劳勇敢，风趣幽默，无论遇到怎样的灾难与挫折，都能坦然面对，百折不挠，始终以一种客观而积极的态度面对人生。[10]

译 文

The Harmonious and Inclusive Nature of Tianfu Culture

Literally, "Tianfu" refers to a region with superior geography, rich specialties and well-developed culture. Historically, after conquering Bashu, Qin state precisely used the basin's abundance and geographical advantage to defeat Chu state severely as well as naturally breaking up the vertical alliance of the six states in the Shandong region, so as to consolidate its foundation to unify China. The Western Han Dynasty (206 BC-25 AD) continued to explore Bashu, boosting its prosperity and abundance. Thus ever since, Sichuan has been reputed as *Tian fu zhi guo* (the land of abundance).[1]

Based on the natural and human conditions of Bashu, Bashu culture had evolved and gradually progressed and been renovated into Tianfu culture after Western learning entered Chengdu, China, consummating the local culture and characterizing the unique city.[2]

The materialization of this special culture, (full of harmony and inclusivity,) centered on the Tianfu region was actually formed through the constant collision and integration of various cultures. Furthermore, the ideology of "promoting innovation, elegance, optimism, inclusiveness and kindness for the public good" became the core value of Tianfu culture in the new age.[3]

Regarding man and nature as one and emphasizing harmony among people, saw Taoism born in the Tianfu region. Inspired by and immersed in the Tianfu culture, Zhang Daoling, a local figure, founded the Tianshi Religion (a faction of early Taoism), which injected a harmonious element into the Tianfu culture and made it the land of prosperity and peace in a troubled world.[4]

Academically, Tianfu scholars have always tried to accommodate Confucianism, Buddhism and Taoism under the banner of "balancing the three beliefs to allow the learning of China and the West to complement each other" , so as to be assimilative and comprehensive. The Sanxingdui culture, for example, was a result of the mutual influence and infiltration of the neighboring cultures from Central Plains and Yunnan, while it also experienced lasting interaction effects through economic and cultural exchanges with remote civilizations in Southeast Asia, the Middle East and even ancient Europe.[5]

For thousands of years, the people of Tianfu have brought into full play the concept of "harmonizing man with nature", embodied in the globally known irrigation project of Dujiangyan. This project aimed to make good use of the natural terrain and water flow, scientifically solving the problems of automatic diversion, sediment discharge and diversion of the river water, effectively "irrigating the land with water and preventing disasters by discharging floodwater", resulting in it being listed as a "World Cultural Heritage" by UNESCO in November 2000.[6]

In fact, Tianfu culture is a multicultural complex that takes the urban cultural body of Chengdu as its core, while being compatible with northern and southern cultures as well. Its humanity is reflected in the tolerant absorption of numerous immigrants from places all over the country. With each wave of immigration, people not only simply moved geographically but also brought cultural exchange and integration with them, further enriching Tianfu's cultural characteristics and connotations.[7]

Geographically, concerted actions are taken between inside and outside Bashu culture connected by the Shu Road, making it liable to access cultural traits from other regions. Also, scholars coming from other regions are easily nourished by the exotic culture on this ancient land, melting the merits as one and complementing each other. So many obscured figures, once going out of Sichuan, especially after arriving at the political and cultural centers of the time, they often stand out and excel.[8]

Nowadays, Tianfu culture has been integrated into the development of China's "Belt and Road Initiative", interacting with other cultures in the world at multiple levels. On the ground, it's expanding the cooperation with the major cities along the Eurasian economic belt of the Silk Road in many fields.[9]

Consequently, with this harmonious, inclusive and distinctively open cultural tradition, the Tianfu people are naturally endowed with an optimistic and humorous personality apart from their diligence and courage. Encountering whatever disasters and setbacks, they always seem to be calm and indomitable in confronting life with an objective and positive attitude.[10]

解　析

语义·逻辑·等值

——首届“天府杯”翻译大赛汉英译文点评

由四川省翻译协会主办，重庆翻译学会、“一带一路”东南亚非政府组织联盟中国区共同指导；《英语世界》杂志社、云南省翻译工作者协会、贵州省翻译工作者协会、杭州师范大学协办，《译苑新谭》编辑部和西南民族大学承办的首届“天府杯”翻译大赛，历时5个月，共有千余人参加，经初筛、复评、终评，于2022年10月落下帷幕。现就其汉译英部分，作一点评。

一、挖掘深层语义

翻译一般从词语层面入手，但词汇不是孤立的，需在多种选择中挖掘其深层涵义，找出最恰当的“那一个”。

就题目“天府文化的和谐与包容”而言，参赛者一般都译成了 Harmony and Tolerance of Tianfu Culture。之所以不妥，其一，这里的“天府文化”讲的是其性质，故不只是 culture；其二，“包容”一定是 tolerance 吗？tolerance 的本义是 the willingness to accept or tolerate somebody or something, especially opinions or behavior that you may not agree with, or people who are not like you，强调的多是被动的容忍，如 The managers all took the opportunity to denounce the attacks and plead for tolerance.（经理们都借此机会谴责这些攻击，并且恳请予以宽容。）；Similarly, those who are able to view the world with amused tolerance are often equally forgiving of their own shortcomings.（同样地，那些能够以幽默宽容的眼光看待世界的人，往往也会原谅自己的缺点。）；Most of their remarks were kindly made—with tolerance rather than bitterness—and frequently were softened by the fact that the students were speaking about some, not all, instructors.（他们的大多数言论都是善意的，其中带着宽容而不是怨恨，并且经常因为学生谈论的是部分而非所有老师，语气变得更为缓和。）等。然而，此处的深层涵义是积极的融合，因而更宜用 inclusive，该词的本义为 covering or intended to cover all items, costs, or services，如

The academy is far more inclusive now than it used to be.（该学院如今比过去更为兼收并蓄。）; The party must adopt more inclusive strategies and a broader vision.（该党必须采取更广泛的策略和更远大的视野。）等。因而，题目可译为 The Harmonious and Inclusive Nature of Tianfu Culture。

［1］中，"人文发达"一般似可译成 advanced human culture/humanity，但此处是指整体文化而言的，故不妨为 well-developed culture。"西汉时继续开发巴蜀，使其繁荣兴盛，富甲一方，因而'天府之国'成了四川的美誉"，较为典型的参赛译文，如 In Western Han dynasty, Bashu has been continuously explored, and has become prosperous and rich beyond other regions, thus Sichuan was called "The land of abundance" /Western Han Dynasty witnessed that Sichuan continued to develop Bashu, making it prosperous and rich, so that "The Land of Abundance" became Sichuan's reputation./During the Western Han due to the continued development of Bashu, Bashu became better than other places, prosperous and wealthy so Sichuan enjoyed the reputation of the "Land of Abundance" 等，其中的画线部分或拘泥于原文的字面意思而显得冗赘，或未能充分译出原文的内涵。特别是，"富甲一方"若已经在 prosperous、rich、wealthy 等词语中表达，则可不必再用 beyond、better than other 等加以比较，而 reputation 可用其动词形式 repute，以更为精练；同时，在翻译中国朝代时，应标示出其年代，以便译入语读者了解其时间背景，而中文名称等汉语拼音，亦宜用斜体表示，因而该句可译为：The Western Han Dynasty（206 BC-25 AD） continued to explore Bashu, boosting its prosperity and abundance. Thus ever since, Sichuan has been reputed as *Tian fu zhi guo* (the land of abundance).

在［3］“以天府地区为中心的这种特殊文化的形成”中，“形成”绝大多数都顺理成章地译成 formation，这个词指一般事物形态，且多用于物质形态，如 This spongy tissue serves as a source of calcium for eggshell formation.（这种海绵状组织是形成蛋壳的钙质来源。）; Scientists do not know exactly how this process prevents ice crystal formation.（科学家们还不清楚这个过程是如何阻止冰晶形成的。）; That's the key to understanding planet formation.（这是理解行星形成的关键。）等，因而用在这里不合适。可以考虑用 materialization，它的本义为 the process of coming into being or becoming reality，强调的是实际效果，如 What is the essence of the materialization of education?（教育实效问题的本质是什么？）; the ways of the materialization of images（关于审美意象具体化的方法论）; Realize that your physical experience and environment is the materialization of your beliefs.（应当认识到，人们的世间经验和环境都是其信念具体化的结果。）等。而“以……为中心”很多人没有译出来，其实可穿插在句子中，译为 The materialization of this special culture, (full of harmony and inclusivity,) centered on the Tianfu region...。该段最后的“核心”，参赛者大都译成了 central concept、cultural concept，其实，结合题目并通观全文，会发现此处讲的是天府文化理念中的“和谐”与“包容”核心价值，即 the core value，类似的：“该

书的核心内容是，城市由人创造，并不断演化，形成一个有机系统。”（The core value of this book is that the city, built by people, has been evolving and growing into an organic system.）；“中国画的核心内涵是文化价值的终极体现。”（The core value of Chinese painting is the ultimate embodiment of cultural values.）；“志愿服务的精髓是奉献精神。”（The core value of volunteerism is the spirit of contribution.）；“该小说的核心思想是挖掘人性的救赎。”（The core value of this novel is to explore the salvation of humanity.）等。同时，“新时代”，参赛译文多用了 new era，但若是强调与以往的对比，则更多用 new age，如“让过去的就过去吧，一个新时代开始了。”（Let bygones be bygones, and a new age has begun.）；“总之，若没有一种新的可持续提供动力、可移动的能源，就没有新机械化时代的产生。”（The new age of machinery, in short, could not have been born without a new source of both movable and constant power.）；“屹立在古老的建筑之上，它像一座城堡，又确是一个新时代的前哨，这可能意味着一种新文明，也可能是一种新野蛮。”（It towered above the older buildings like a citadel, which indeed it was, the outpost of a new age, perhaps a new civilization, perhaps a new barbarism.）等，因而，此处不妨译为：...became the core value of Tianfu culture in the new age。

［4］中，“（创立了天师教……，）为天府文化注入了和谐基因”，是一句比喻，但许多人译得很实，如 which injected the gene of harmony into Tianfu culture、injecting the gene of harmony into Tianfu culture 等，而实际上，由于人体免疫系统的排异性，

基因只能由父母遗传给孩子，而不能从外部注入另一个人的体内，故可将其变通为 element，即 ...which injected a harmonious element into the Tianfu culture。

［9］中的“一带一路”，仍有许多人译成 Belt and Road strategy/construction，以往分析过，strategy 的本义是 a general plan or set of plans intended to achieve something over a long period of time，带有“预谋”的意思，会让人产生误解，从而加以抵制；而 construction 的本义为 the building of things such as houses, factories, roads, and bridges，过于实用、狭义，不宜用于一种主动、宏观的国家方针，而 initiate 的本义则是 actively start something or cause it to happen，带有主动性而又不强加于人，其名词形式 initiative 正符合中国对于该倡议的提出。类似的用法很多，如 United Nations peace initiative（联合国的和平倡议）; He proposed a new diplomatic initiative to try to stop the war.（他提出了一个新的试图阻止战争的外交倡议。）; On this issue, the country has seized the initiative.（在这一问题上，该国为首倡者。）等，故“天府文化已经融入到了‘一带一路’国家战略的发展之中”，宜译为 Tianfu culture has been integrated into the development of China’s “Belt and Road Initiative”。

此外，一些字面意思，不必刻板求译，而可在语义深层的融合中表达。如［7］中的“每次移民不是简单的人口地理位置的移动，而是其背后的文化交流与融合，更丰富了其文化特色与内涵”，其中有明显的递进语气，not only simply...but also...，这一点大都能够译出，但“背后的”若一定要译成 behind it/them

便显生硬、刻板，因为参考译文 people not only simply moved geographically but also brought cultural exchange and integration with thcm, further enriching Tianfu's cultural characteristics and connotations 的画线部分，已包含了这层涵义，不必再画蛇添足。

二、疏通内在逻辑

一些惯用因果关系的翻译，在新的语境中，也会发生变化，所以不可用固定模式一成不变地套用。

[4] 中的“天府之国所以能够成为道教的发源地，在于天府文化视人与自然为一体，注重人与人之间的和谐统一”，因其中有“所以能够……”，故很多参赛者自然用了句式 The reason why (the land of Tianfu...)，或 Because Tianfu culture values..., it is possible for...，这固然不能认为是错译，但分析起来，天府文化的这种性质形成了道教发源地的条件，故可将条件从句作为状语提前译出，即 Regarding man and nature as one and emphasizing harmony among people，将结果句放后面：it saw Taoism born in the Tianfu region，以更加自然、简练。

“蜀人张道陵，正是受到天府文化的浸润，由此顿悟，创立了天师教（早期道教的一派）”，参赛译文大都顺其语序译出，如 Zhang Daoling, a Shu native, was infiltrated by Tianfu culture. After experiencing an epiphany as a result, he founded Tianshi Religion (an early Taoist school). / Zhang Daoling, a native of Shu, was influenced by the Tianfu culture, from which he had an epiphany and founded an early school of Taoism—Tian-Shi Taoism./Zhang Daoling, a native of the Shu, established the Celestial-Master Taosim (one of the early Taoism schools) with the sudden enlightenment coming from the nourishing of Tianfu culture. 等，这些译法固然不错，但不够地道；"受到天府文化的浸润"是因，"张道陵……创立了天师教"是果，按照英语表述习惯，可将因作为状语提前译出，如 Inspired by and immersed in the Tianfu culture，而将果接在其后，即 Zhang Daoling, ...founded the Tianshi Religion。

[5]中，"例如，三星堆文化就是与相邻的中原文化、滇文化相互影响和渗透而成，同时又与相距遥远但有经济文化交往的东南亚文明、中东文明，甚至欧洲古代文明，有着绵延不绝的关联"，其中的画线部分，一般都译成了 For example, the Sanxingdui culture is influenced and permeated with the neighboring Central Plains culture and Yunnan culture, and at the same time has an endless relationship with the Southeast Asian civilization, the Middle East civilization, and even the ancient European civilization that are remote but have economic and cultural exchanges/which were not only far away from each other but also had economic and cultural interactions. 等；实际上，其内在的逻辑是，这种"绵延不绝的关联"是通过"经济文化交往"而发生的，故不妨将其整合为：The Sanxingdui culture, for example, was a result of the mutual influence and infiltration of the neighboring cultures from Central Plains and Yunnan, while it also experienced lasting interaction effects through economic and cultural exchanges with remote civilizations in

Southeast Asia, the Middle East and even ancient Europe.，进而揭示出其内在的逻辑关系。

［6］中，“几千年来，天府人民把‘天人合一’的和谐观发挥得淋漓尽致，在工程上，最典型的体现在驰名中外的都江堰”，较为典型的参赛译文，如 Through the ages, the locals of the land of abundance have demonstrated most fully the harmonious outlook on “the unity of heaven and man”. In engineering, as the most typical example, the world-wide famous Dujiang Yan./For thousands of years, people in Chengdu have performed thoroughly and vividly in the practice of the harmony between man and nature. The most representative example in project is Dujiangyan, a water conservancy system./Over thousands of years, Tianfu people exert the concept of “heaven and people are united as one” and one of its engineering representatives is Dujiangyan Irrigation System. 等，其中“最典型的体现”，如画线部分译文，虽在字面上非常接近，但这里的深层涵义是都江堰就是天府文化的一个名片或象征，故不妨用动词 exemplify、embody、symbolize 等，简练而生动，同时“都江堰”仅仅音译是不够的，故应根据该句内在逻辑作相应的浓缩与扩展：For thousands of years, the people of Tianfu have brought into full play the concept of “harmonizing man with nature”, embodied in the globally known irrigation project of Dujiangyan.

［10］中的“……使得天府人民生性乐观，勤劳勇敢，风趣幽默”，其中的“生性”大多数参赛译文只译成 naturally，固然不错，但程度不够，不足以表现“天府人”独特的性格，而此

处用 be endowed with（a particular desirable ability, characteristic, or possession when they have it by chance or by birth）更合适，同时将其前置，以示强调，而不平均用力：...the Tianfu people are naturally endowed with an optimistic and humorous personality apart from their diligence and courage.

［1］中，“历史上，秦灭巴蜀后，四川盆地的富饶，巴蜀之地的地理优势，使得秦国在严重打击了楚国的同时，也在无形之中瓦解着山东六国的合纵联盟，为其统一天下提供了战备基础”。大部分参赛译文都处理成 In the history, after the Qin State annexed the Ba State and Shu State,.../Historically, after Qin destroyed Bashu, due to.../Throughout the history, after Qin demolished Bashu, due to the richness of...等，但实际逻辑关系是“灭巴蜀后”作为状语，可置前起引导作用，“秦”置后，与后面的句子形成“主—谓—宾”结构：Historically, after conquering Bashu, Qin state precisely used the basin's abundance and geographical advantage to defeat Chu state severely as well as naturally breaking up the vertical alliance of the six states in the Shandong region, so as to consolidate its foundation to unify China.

此外，有时为强调内在的关联，亦可用增词、增译的方法，如［8］中的“在地理上，蜀道的内外勾连，入蜀与出蜀的交相呼应，使得巴蜀文化善于汲取其他地域的文化特点”，参赛者一般将画线部分译成 In geography, the Shu Dao is linking inside and outside, the echo of entering Shu and leaving Shu made Bashu culture be good at absorbing the cultural features from other regions./

Geographically, the roads of Shu link up Shu and the outside, two opposite directions of entering and leaving echoing each other./ Geographically, the internal and external links of the Shu Road, into and out of Shu echo, so that the culture of Shu is good at drawing on... 等，而其中的“内外”、“出入”实则指的是其多面连接、多重影响的状态，故不妨译为：Geographically, concerted actions are taken between inside and outside Bashu culture connected by the Shu Road,... 尽管有些拟人化。

三、追求整体等值

翻译中，有些词语、句式，若仅仅局限于具体词义，难免会“只见树木，不见森林”，陷入琐碎，难达整体效果。

对于［2］中的“在此自然与人文基础上形成的巴蜀文化，即为天府文化，它是西学进入成都后对于古蜀文化的继承与更新；既是历史上天府之国文化的总结，也是当今成都市域文化的特征”，对于其中的画线部分，参赛译文大都按字面意思作了相应的转述，如 The Bashu culture, formed on basis of this kind of nature and cultural environments, is thus dubbed as the Tianfu culture. It is an inheritance and renewal of the ancient Shu culture after the Western studies were transmitted to Chengdu. Moreover, it is both a summary of the historical culture of “Heavenly Land of Plenty”, and an epitome of the current Chengdu metropolitan culture./ Bashu culture, formed on the basis of nature and humanity, is Tianfu culture, and is also the inheritance and renewal of ancient Shu culture after western learning was introduced to Chengdu; It is not only the summary of the culture of the Land of Abundance in history, but also the characteristics of present urban culture in Chengdu. / The Bashu culture formed on the basis of this natural and humanistic basis is the Tianfu culture, which is the inheritance and renewal of the ancient Shu culture after the Western school entered Chengdu; It is not only a summary of the culture of the country of Tianfu in history, but also a characteristic of the culture of Chengdu today. / The Ba-Shu culture formed on this natural and humanistic basis is the Tianfu culture, namely is the inheritance and renewal of the ancient Shu civilization after Western learning entered Chengdu; it is not only the summary of the culture of the land of Tianfu historically but also the characteristic of the metropolitan culture of Chengdu nowadays. 等等。

分析起来，“在……基础上形成的”一般情况下固然可以译成 formed on basis of，但此处重点讲的是天府文化的性质，故在形式上可以放开些，不妨将其译为状语 Based on the natural and human conditions of...，引出后面的主要部分。而“巴蜀文化”蜕化成为“天府文化”，故应释译出这一过程：...had evolved and gradually progressed...been renovated into...，尽管在书面上与原文拉开了一些距离，但在本质上则更加吻合。同时，提到“总结”，历来惯于与 summary 相搭配，然而，有时又需根据上下文加以变通，特别是这里指的是其历史发展上的一个高峰，虽然原文似乎并没有与此相对应的词，但通观整个语境，不妨用 consummate，其本义为 complete in every detail。此外，“文化特征”也未必要用名词 the characteristics of culture，用动词 characterizc 会更为直截了当，如参考译文：Based on the natural and human conditions of Bashu, Bashu culture had evolved and gradually progressed and been renovated into Tianfu culture after Western learning entered Chengdu, China, consummating the local culture and characterizing the unique city. 其实，类似的译法并不少见，如“市场商品丰富多彩”，如果只在字面层次，很容易将画线部分译成 The market has a colorful display of commodities，但就整体意思而言，这里表述的并不是外在的形式，而是其实质内容，故更宜译为 This market has an adequate supply of commodities. 再如，时政语“三严三实”，官方译语是“Three Stricts and Three Honests”（Be strict in morals, power and disciplining oneself; be honest in decisions, business and behavior）；其实不妨将其实质提炼成 The Campaign to Promote Integrity，甚至 The Integrity Initiative，虽然二者字面距离拉大了，但实质内涵更靠近了。有时，就是同义语，也需进行某些升华，如我在外文局工作时，清楚地记得沙博理先生（Sidney Shapiro）将老舍《月牙儿》中的“妈对我很好，而且有时候极庄重地说我：‘念书！念书！’”译为：She was so good to me , always urging, “Read your books, study hard”. 当问及为何要“窜改”后一句时，他说“这才叫翻译”！

在［5］，“蜀人治学，往往儒释道兼容，并提出了‘漫汗通观儒释道，从容涵化印中西’，海纳百川，融为一体”，其中的中国传统俗语表述句式（画线部分），亦应从意境入手，而不可受具体对象的羁绊，如“生意兴隆通四海，财源茂盛达三江”，若按词义层面渲染成 Business is thriving, reaching out to the five continents of the world; Revenues are accruing, flowing in from the four corners of the earth，对于译入语读者，未必产生相应的效果，甚至不知所云，而究其实质，应为 Business booms far and near, profits net there and here——语言上似乎不对等，但内涵上却更为等值。同样的，“自古而今，马在中华民族文化中都是美好寓意的代表，如：马到成功、万马奔腾、兵强马壮等等”，其中的“马”不必刻意译成 to win success immediately upon the arrival of the horses; ten thousand horses gallop forward; strong soldiers and sturdy horses，而可贯通寓意，综合性地将全句译为 Since ancient times, the horse has been bestowed goodwill implications in Chinese culture. When the word *ma* (horse) is used in an idiom, it usually means instant success and powerful strength. 然而，此次参赛译文对于原文中的画线部分，大都仍采取了第一种译法，如 Man explored the Confucianism, Buddhism and Taoism, and remained calm to include the culture of Indian, Chinese and Western/widely understand the cultures of Confucianism, Buddhism and Taoism, and to absorb and adapt to them with a calm attitude, so as to confirm the different cultures of China and the West/Man Khan looking at Confucianism and Buddhism, calmly encompassing the Indian Chinese and Western 等，应当说，不是错译，但如上所述，有些过分囿于具体概念或象征，实则，可从立意层次，

更加精练地译为 Academically, Tianfu scholars have always tried to accommodate Confucianism, Buddhism and Taoism under the banner of "balancing the three beliefs to allow the learning of China and the West to complement each other", so as to be assimilative and comprehensive. 尽管在词语层面与原文不够对称，但这里追求的是二者整体内涵的等值，即钱锺书讲的翻译中的"得意而忘言"。

此外，该次翻译大赛还暴露另外两个共性问题：一是翻译软件的使用。翻译软件不是不可以用，但不可百分之百地用，需要经过起码的人工编辑与加工，否则便失去个人参赛的意义。二是标注段落符号，以便于参赛者和评阅者对照查看原文和译文，但仍有参赛者无视于此，以致造成混乱。

作为一种地方翻译大赛，首届"天府杯"取得的成绩值得肯定。通过及时总结，不断改进，相信之后的大赛会更加出彩。

原 文

辨明病机方能防病治病

中医认为，人生病的过程，如同发矢，病因似机，疾病发展似箭发以后的势。《神农本草经》说，“欲疗病，先察其源，先候病机”。病机既包括致病原因，也包括疾病发生后不同阶段的病理变化。[1]

中医的病机学说是研究疾病发生的原因、发生、发展和转归的机制、一般规律及其临床联系的综合性理论，与藏象、经络学说相渗透、印证，成为辨证论治体系的理论基础；而病机的辨析，既有病性，又有病位。[2]

病性即病理性质，或病理变化的本质属性。辨证论治首先要从整体上或宏观上把握病变之属性，这是中医临证的基本要求。只有准确辨识病性，方可确立基本治疗原则和治疗方法。疾病的基本病性主要包括阴、阳、寒、热、虚、实，表现实寒、虚寒、实热、虚热等交叉复合关系。[3]

疾病的病位主要在五脏、六腑、经络、表里，也可在上中下三焦等。人体是以五脏为中心，配以六腑，通过经络系统外合五体、五官、九窍，从而组成有机联系的整体，完成机体统一的机能活动。因此，辨别疾病病位所属应以“五脏”为核心。辨识病位不仅要确定五脏所属，还应进一步分析各脏腑气、血、阴、阳病机变化，如肝气郁结、脾气亏虚、心血不足、肺阴亏虚、肾阳虚衰等。[4]

此外，还需注重“病势”——病机转化的趋势，即疾病发生、发展、转归等过程中病情的轻重缓急。同一病邪可多向转化。[5]

破坏人体相对平衡状态而引起疾病的原因就是病因。病因是多种多样的，诸如气候的异常、疫疠的传染、精神刺激、饮食劳倦、持重努伤、跌仆金刃外伤，以及虫兽所伤等，均可导致疾病的发生。此外，在疾病过程中，原因和结果是相互作用着的，某一病理阶段的结果在另一阶段则可能成为原因，如痰饮和瘀血等，既是脏腑气血功能失调所形成的病理产物，反过来又能成为某些病变的致病因素。[6]

疾病的产生，首先是身体虚弱，又感受了虚邪贼风，两者结合，才会得病。身体强壮，四时之气也正常，就不容易生病。邪气根据其不同性质，侵袭人体不同部位。一般而言，虚邪贼风侵袭人体，先从皮肤开始，向里传到络脉、经脉、腧穴、冲脉，再向里到肠胃、募原，表现出各种各样的证候。[7]

尽管疾病的种类繁多，临床征象错综复杂，千变万化，各个疾病都有各自的病机，但总离不开邪正盛衰、阴阳失调、气血失常、经络和脏腑功能紊乱等病机变化的一般规律。对于医者，需辨明病机，方能防病、治病。[8]

译 文

Syndrome Differentiation: the Prerequisite to Prevention and Treatment of Diseases

Traditional Chinese medicine (TCM) believes that the process of getting sick is like firing an arrow—the etiology is the motivator causing the disease to develop its potential along the way. *Shen Nong's Herbal Classic* notes that "In order to cure a disease, the first thing is to detect the source and pathogenesis" . "Pathogenesis" here includes the cause of disease and pathological changes at subsequent stages.[1]

Being a comprehensive theory, the pathology of TCM is based on the mechanisms, general patterns and clinical experiences of the causes, occurrence, involvement and prognosis of diseases, laying the foundation for syndrome differentiation and treatment. Analyses of pathogenesis in TCM, on the other hand, involve searching for the nature and location of a disease.[2]

The nature of pathology in TCM is the qualification of the essential attribute of pathological changes. Clinically, in terms of TCM treatment, it requires holistic judgement and grasp of the pathological changes. In other words, the basic treatment principles and methods have to be based on accurately identifying the nature of the disease, which can be defined in terms of *yin*, *yang*, cold, heat, deficiency and excess, manifested in many kinds of intricate relations, such as dominating-*yin* with declining-*yang*, dominating-*yang* with declining-*yin*, excess-cold, deficiency-cold, excess-heat, deficiency-heat and so on.[3]

Diseases are mainly located in the five *zang* organs, six *fu* hollow organs, meridians, exterior and interior muscles, as well as upper, middle and lower *San Jiao*. According to TCM, the human body is centered on the five *zang* organs, assisted by the six *fu* viscera, five body constituents and nine orifices connected through collaterals, together making the body an organic whole in performing its functional activities. Therefore, in identifying the disease location, we should not only determine the attributes of the five *zang* organs, but also the changing conditions of their related *qi*, blood and pathological *yin* and *yang*, such as liver-*qi* stagnation, spleen-*qi* deficiency, heart blood deficiency, lung *yin* deficiency, kidney *yang* deficiency and so on.[4]

Meanwhile, attention must also be paid to the *bing shi*, or the pathological trend, namely the occurrence, involvement and transformation of the disease in order of priority. Normally, the same pathogen can lead into many directions, resulting in a variety of diseases.[5]

The etiology is defined in TCM as the disruption of proper balance of the human body that causes diseases or sickness. The disruptions can be caused by various factors, such as abnormal climate, severe infectious diseases, heavily-burdening injuries, dietary fatigue, falling down, or injury by metals, as well as bites by insects or animals. Meanwhile, the causes and effects of diseases are interrelated. By which it is meant that an effect at certain pathological stage may be the cause of another disease at a different pathological stage. For example, phlegm and blood stasis are not only the pathological effects caused by the dysfunction of *qi* and blood in *zang-fu* organs (viscera), but may also become fatal factors for some lesions later.[6]

The emergence of disease, initially caused by physical weakness, is followed by the "evil wind" of deficiency from outside. It's hard to get sick when you have a robust body living normally through four seasons. The evil wind invades different parts of the body in a specific order, penetrating from the skin to meridians, collaterals, acupoints, vital channels, and then getting deep into the intestines, stomach and *Muyuan*, manifesting a variety of symptoms.[7]

Various types of diseases, though complicated clinically, are categorized by their different pathogeneses, relating to some general etiological rules, such as variation of positive versus negative pathogenic factors, imbalance of *yin* and *yang*, disorders of *qi* and blood, dysfunction of meridians and *zang-fu*. In preventing and treating diseases or sicknesses, it is important for medical practitioners to analyze and identify these specific pathogeneses.[8]

解 析

中医语境下的辨析与变通

——兼评第七届“岐黄天下杯”世界中医翻译大赛英语组参赛译文

为进一步弘扬中医药优秀文化，推进中医药国际化进程，提高中医药对外宣传的质量和翻译水平，世界中医药学会联合会于2023年成功举办了第七届“岐黄天下杯”世界中医翻译大赛。大赛的规模和语种都进一步扩展。作为该大赛的终评专家之一和原文译者，现就其英语组的某些典型参赛译文，作一点评、分析。

一、中医词语辨析

就题目“辨明病机方能防病治病”而言，参赛者一般译成 Only By Identifying The Pathogenesis Can We Prevent And Treat Diseases，其中的“辨明”都顺理成章地译成 identity、identify 或 identifying，其本义为 be able to recognize someone/something or distinguish them from others，意思似乎不错，但原文在中医里从“辨证论治”而来，其英译文通常为 treating diseases/illness based on syndrome differentiation、syndrome differentiation and treatment，而中医的“病因辨证”为 etiological analyses and differentiation 等，故此处更宜用 differentiate、differentiation 或 differentiating。当然，在某些中医语境里，又非绝对不可用 identify，如［4］中“辨别疾病病位所属”，指具体定位，不妨译为 in identifying the disease location；［8］中，就更宽泛意义而言的“对于医者，需辨明病机，方能防病、治病”，不妨译为 In preventing and treating diseases or sicknesses, it is important for medical practitioners to analyze and identify these specific pathogeneses，但作为该中医篇章的主旨标题，更宜译为：Syndrome Differentiation: the Prerequisite to Prevention and Treatment of Diseases。

［2］中，“中医的病机学说”，许多都译成了 the pathogenesis theory of Traditional Chinese Medicine，其中 pathogenesis 是名词，这里应用其形容词 pathogenetic。不过，这里直接用 pathology 更为简洁，因为 pathology 本身就具有 theory 性质，如：“中医学深受中国传统哲学的整体观影响，其病机学说也是整体观的。”（Traditional Chinese medicine was highly affected by the holistic concept of viewing things of Chinese classical philosophy, so as its pathology.）等。特别是结合下文的“研究疾病发生的原因、发生、发展和转归的机制、一般规律及其临床联系的综合性理论”，就不妨译为：...the pathology of TCM is based on the mechanisms, general patterns and clinical experiences of the causes, occurrence, involvement and prognosis of diseases...。

［3］中，“病性”可以简单地译成 nature of disease /illness

吗？参阅相关的工具书便知，更确切的译法是 the nature of pathology；而［5］中的"'病势'——病机转化的趋势"，较为典型的参赛译文有："tendency of disease"—the trend of patho-mechanism conversion、the "disease momentum"—the trend of pathogenetic development、its tendency of progression—the trend of disease alteration 等，应当说，均未能尽传其意。鉴于该词是中医特有词汇，可先存其原形 *bing shi*，后续释译为 or the pathological trend。同时，该句中的"轻重缓急"之意大都没有译出，如 its course in the process of onset, development and outcome/which means the severity of patients' condition over the course of the occurrence, advancement, and outcome of disease/the severity of the disease in the process of disease onset, progression, ending and so on 等，有的试图译出层次，如 ...development and outcome according to the urgency of the case/That is, mild or severe, urgent or non-urgent conditions, during the disease occurrence, development, and prognosis，但难免冗赘，不如 ...involvement and transformation of the disease in order of priority 简单明确。

此外，［4］中的一些典型中医概念，亦是译法纷繁。"五脏"、"六腑"，在通常意义上，似可译成 the vital organs of the human body/the viscera internal organs of the body（heart, liver, spleen, lungs and kidneys）等，但如学术界多年所探讨的，中医所讲的"心、肝、脾、肺、肾"并不能与西医的 heart、liver、spleen、lungs、kidneys 画等号，而有着其特殊含义，因而更确切的译法应为 the five *zang* organs, six *fu* hollow organs；"五体"、

“九窍”为 five body constituents and nine orifices 等。至于“上中下三焦”的译法，历来更颇具争议。这一独具中医特色的概念，可解释为“是脏腑外围最大的腑，有主持诸气、疏通水道的作用。分上焦、中焦、下焦三部分”（原一祥等，2000），因而就其本义，似可翻译成 It is the largest one outside all the viscera and bowels within the body cavity consisting of the upper-energizer, middle-energizer and lower-energizer. Its main function is to control the *qi* movement and to circulate the passage of water；但是由于“三焦”没有具体位置，故在翻译中多作模糊处理（如 the largest one 等），或加释译：In fact, “*san jiao*” does not describe a physical organ, which is normally included in the “body part” radical in the TCM dictionary. Like the heart in TCM, it has “a name but no form”. It is rather the sum of the functions of transformation and interpretation of various densities and qualities of substance within the organism, “circulates the way and pathways of liquids and controls the beginning and ending of *qi*”。因而，也产生了多种译法，如 three bodily regions of fluid-transport、three hearts、triple energizer 等，参考译文的 upper, middle and lower *San Jiao* 是一种折中，是较易接受而又不失中医本色的译法。

其实，由于中医概念深植于中国传统文化，对其翻译的辨析是一个延续至今的探讨过程，如“中国按摩”是要沿用西方的译法 Chinese massage，还是用更具中医治疗性质的译法 *Tui Na*（Chinese massage）？“天行赤眼”，可以完全按中医原形译成 heavenly red eyes 吗？还是应比照西医，变通为 epidemic keratoconjunctivitis？同样，“针灸学”是简单地译为 acupuncture，还是应附加有学科性质的后缀 -logy，形成 acupunctology？进而，针灸中的“得气”，仅仅是 arrival of *qi*，还是更有实质意义的 having a sense of acupuncture feeling？总之，其要旨是，在保持中医本色与参照西医科学术语及西方接受程度之间找到适当的平衡。

二、中医话语变通

应当说，中医话语是渗透中国传统文化、同时又受到西方现代医学词汇影响的一种叙述，因而翻译时须在保持其本色的基础上，根据英文的表述习惯作出许多变通。

整个第［2］段，“中医的病机学说是研究疾病发生的原因、发生、发展和转归的机制、一般规律及其临床联系的综合性理论，与藏象、经络学说相渗透、印证，成为辨证论治体系的理论基础；而病机的辨析，既有病性，又有病位”，是典型的中医表述方式，参赛译文大都按其语序、逻辑关系翻译，如 The pathogenesis theory of traditional Chinese medicine is a comprehensive theory that studies the general rules, clinical connections and mechanism of disease causes, occurrence, development, and prognosis. It permeates into and confirms with visceral manifestation channel and channel theory, becoming the theoretical foundation of the pattern in treatment. Thus the differentiation of pathogenesis involves both the disease character and disease location. /The theory of pathogenesis in TCM is a comprehensive study that researches the causes of diseases, the mechanism of diseases' occurrence and progression as well as clinical outcome, general laws and clinical correlations. It is deeply integrated with and certified by the theory of Visceral Manifestations and the theory of Meridians and Collaterals, serving as the theoretical foundation of the syndrome differentiation and treatment system. The identification of pathogenesis comprises both the nature and the location of diseases. 其中画线部分是问题所在。分析起来，英文的惯用句式对于中医的某些表述并不相称，需作调整。如，"综合性理论"，不一定作宾语，而可作为状语前置，即 Being a comprehensive theory；"相渗透、印证"，不一定要译得那么"实"，而可融于 based on 和 foundation 之中；而"既有病性，又有病位"，是又回转到"病机"话题而言的，故应岔开一笔，用 on the other hand 引出。因而，整句不妨译为：Being a comprehensive theory, the pathology of TCM is based on the mechanisms, general patterns and clinical experiences of the causes, occurrence, involvement and prognosis of diseases, laying the foundation for syndrome differentiation and treatment. Analyses of pathogenesis in TCM, on the other hand, involve searching for the nature and location of a disease.

［6］中，"破坏人体相对平衡状态而引起疾病的原因就是病因。病因是多种多样的，诸如气候的异常、疫疠的传染、精神刺激、饮食劳倦、持重努伤、跌仆金刃外伤，以及虫兽所伤

等，均可导致疾病的发生”，较为典型的参赛译文，如 The cause of disease that disrupts the relative balance of the human body is called the etiology. Etiologies are diverse, including... / The cause that destroys the relative balance of the human body and causes disease is the pathogenic factor. The pathogenic factors can be diverse, such as... / Factors that disrupt the relative balance of the body and lead to illness are the causes of disease. Disease causes are multifarious, such as... / The causes that break relative balanced state of human body and lead to diseases could be the causative factors. Causative factors are diverse, such as... 其中，“（引起疾病的原因）就是”分别译成 is called、is、are、could be，而此处的含义是“在中医里认定的”，因而应更加确定：is defined（in TCM）；而“……就是病因。病因是……”之间的接续，参赛译文多用的是“...the etiology. Etiologies...” / “...the pathogenic factor. The pathogenic factors...” / “...the causative factors. Causative factors...”，而中医所讲的病因，是指对人体平衡的破坏（the disruption of proper balance of the human body），因而 the disruptions 应成为强调的重点，并作为后句的主语；且“多种多样的”意为“可由多种因素所引起”，故宜为被动语态 can be caused by various factors...。

［3］中的“辨证论治首先要从整体上或宏观上把握病变之属性，这是中医临证的基本要求。只有准确辨识病性，方可确立基本治疗原则和治疗方法”，其中蕴含一种因果关系，参赛译文一般都“顺理成章”地处理成 ...this is the basic requirement for/...which are the essential prerequisite that/that constitutes the fundamental conditions.../the first step in...is to...; only by...can...,以及 Only when the nature of the disease is accurately identified, can the foundational treatment principles and methods be established...等，其实，提到"基本要求"，不一定总是用名词 basic requirement、essential prerequisite、fundamental conditions，而若用动词，有时会更加简练、明确，如 to be based on...；同时，"只有……方可……"的因果关系也已暗含其中，不必再刻意译出；同时，还应有语气上的转折，整句可译为 In other words, the basic treatment principles and methods have to be based on accurately identifying the nature of the disease, which can be defined in terms of...

［4］中，"人体是以五脏为中心，配以六腑，通过经络系统外合五体、五官、九窍，从而组成有机联系的整体，完成机体统一的机能活动"，一般容易译成 the human body combines the five bodies, the five sense organs and the nine orifices through the meridian system to form an organic whole and complete the functional activities of the body system./The body takes the five zang organs as the centers, with the assistance of the six-fu organs, through the meridian system to link five body constituents, five sense organs and nine orifices to realize an organic whole./ The unity of the body is realized through the five-zang organs, with the assistance of six-fu organs and externally integrates the five body constituents, five sense organs and nine orifices through the communication of the meridian system. 意思固然都不错，且译文大体可以接受，但画线部分仍值得关注、改进。如"以五脏为中心"的意思很容易被埋没，而

即使是介词短语（takes the...as the centers）亦不如动词 centered on 精准；类似的，“配以（六腑）”，译成 with the assistance of 不如 assisted by 精准；“经络系统外合”，用 externally integrates、link、communication 等，似都偏拘泥于原文，可作相应变通；至于“统一的机能活动”，参赛译文多有漏译外，有的即便宾语用了 functional activities，其谓语动词用 complete 也并不合适，不如用 perform 更恰当；同时，还应强调其中医性质，故整句可增译为：According to TCM, the human body is centered on the five *zang* organs, assisted by the six *fu* viscera, five body constituents and nine orifices connected through collaterals, together making the body an organic whole in performing its functional activities.

此外，一些通常的表述，在中医语境下，亦可能有所不同。如［7］中的“一般而言”，大都被译成了 generally speaking、in a general sense、overall 等，但结合上文可知，此处恰恰是“具体位置”之意，因而应为（The evil wind invades different parts of the body）in a specific order。再如，［8］中的“尽管疾病的种类繁多，临床征象错综复杂，千变万化，各个疾病都有各自的病机”，一般都按部就班译成 Although diseases have voluminous varieties, clinical signs are intricate, with myriad changes, and each disease has its own pathogenesis, they never deviate from the universal rules pathogenetic change.../Although diseases are various and no matter how complicated and changeable their clinical manifestations are, each disease has its own pathogenesis 等，但可否将三处画线部分综合考虑？且中医里的“临床征象”未

必完全等同于西医的 clinical manifestations，因而可用其副词形式 clinically 连接前二者；以 be categorized by 划分“各自的病机”，同时对其中的让步状语从句亦可作相应变通，如参考译文：Various types of diseases, though complicated clinically, are categorized by their different pathogeneses, relating to some general etiological rules...，以更符合英文的表达习惯。

三、中医细节表述

同时，参赛译文在一些中医文本翻译的细节上，亦多少存有疏僻。

“中医”概念在参赛译文中仍有不同译法和形式，如 Chinese Medicine、Traditional Medicine of China、Traditional Chinese Medicine 等，而根据世界卫生组织的规范术语，实为 traditional Chinese medicine，即不必大写；而对其缩写形式，许多参赛者处理成 TCM（Traditional Chinese Medicine），实则应在其首次以全名出现后，将缩写放在随后的括号中，即 traditional Chinese medicine（TCM），而在下文中均以 TCM 表述。

对于书名《神农本草经》，亦出现多种译法，如 Astheorizedinthe Shennong’s Herbal Classic of Materia Medica、“Shennong Bencao Jing” (Shennong’s Classic of Materia Medica)、Shen Nong Ben Cao Jing (Shen Nong’s Classic of Materia Medica)、Shennong’s Classic of Materia Medica 等，其中不乏拉丁文，然而就现在流行的译法，不妨为 *Shen Nong’s Herbal Classic*，但应不用引号，而为斜体。

文中的“医者”，指“中医医生”，许多人仍译成 Chinese medical doctor，以往多有论述，doctor 这一概念在西方有特定含义：A person who has been trained in medical science, whose job is to treat people who are ill/sick or injured, and it normally refers to someone who can perform surgery（Martin A. Elizabeth, 2000）。因而“中医医生”不等于 Chinese doctor；TCM 在西方归属于 alternative medicine，其定义为：The various systems of healing, including homeopathy, herbal remedies, hypnosis, and faith healing, that are not regarded as part of orthodox treatment by the medical profession, especially when offered by unregistered practitioners. ...The extent to which individual registered practitioners indulge in or spurn these therapies varies enormously but is governed by the overriding principle that shared care is only permitted if the registered practitioner remains in overall control...（Martin A. Elizabeth, 2000）（译文：[替代疗法] 包括顺势疗法、草药、催眠法及信仰疗法等各种治疗体系，被医学界摒除在正统医学之外，特别是那些未注册的行医者。由于注册行医者对种种疗法的接受或排斥程度的差异会很大，因而他们都要服从这一项硬性规定：即只有在医院的统筹主导下，才能进行与另类医学的配合治疗……）（其中下画线为笔者所加）。因而，文中的“医者”应译为 practitioner。

同时，有关中医特有术语的音译，应均用斜体，如“阴阳”（*yin* and *yang*）、五脏六腑（five *zang* organs, six *fu* hollow organs）、腧穴（*shu* points）、募原（*Muyuan*）等。

此外，各种翻译大赛中的通病，即使用软件翻译的痕迹也依稀可见。不是不可以使用翻译软件，但一定要做必要的编辑、加工、再译；特别是如中医这样专业、有特色的原文，任何翻译软件都不可能完全胜任，否则也便失去了翻译大赛的意义。

参考文献

① 原一祥等．汉英双解中医大辞典［Z］．北京：人民卫生出版社，2000.

② Martin A. Elizabeth. *Oxford Concise Medical Dictionary* [Z]. New York: Oxford University Press, 2000.

原 文

灵魂的追问

古往今来，悠悠数千年，人类的文明有了巨大的进步，但是困扰人类的基本问题，似乎依然如旧：人从哪里来？要到哪里去？世界的本质是什么？人生的根本意义何在？这些问题永远无解，但却永远被追问，原因就在于只有人类独具灵魂。[1]

在古希腊的雅典城，专门有一群“智者”，在公共场合向人们回答各种各样的人生问题，后人称他们为“哲学家”。因那时人类的学问还没有分类，故哲学就是包罗万象的学问。词根上，“哲学”（philosophy）源于拉丁文的 philo（爱）和 sophy（Sophia, 智慧），故其意为“爱智之学”。至今，西方许多科学学科的博士学位仍冠以“哲学博士”（PhD），而牛顿的物理学名著，亦是《自然哲学的数学原理》。可见，哲学渗透着人类科学精神的实质，那便是对于终极存在、终极价值、终极知识的无穷尽的追问，至于结果如何，反倒次要。[2]

有道是，一个人只有经过哲学性质的启蒙，才能真正具有“自我”，故 17 世纪法国大哲学家笛卡尔提出了著名的“我思故我在”的命题。[3]

一般认为，有两大哲学启蒙：一是仰望星空，二是直面死亡。在人生的某个时刻，或许是在夏天的夜晚，在一片寂静中仰望星空，顿感苍穹之浩大，自我之渺小。面对茫茫宇宙，不免唏嘘自身在世间的真实处境。尽管有了达尔文的进化论，但那只是假说，不乏难解之谜；马斯克的人类移民火星计划，似乎仍十分遥远。另一次启蒙，是意识到了死亡，特别是随着年龄的增长，真正懂得了其实每个人都是向死而生。[4]

既然每个人的终极结果是死亡，那么活着到底意义何在？从某种意义上讲，没有意义。但是从哲学含义中所揭示的世界观、人生观、价值观里又可寻找到某种意义，即是要从无意义中活出意义——活出人生的真谛。[5]

孔子说："未知生，焉知死？"其实，此话应当倒过来，"惟知死，方知生"，即只有弄懂了死亡这回事，才能真正活出人生意义。苏格拉底说，学习哲学就是"预习死亡"，这便是此后人生哲学、价值取向、道德伦理的立论根基。物质不灭，本质永恒。人的灵魂并不会随着肉体而消失，于是导致了西方哲学对于"终极关切"的追求。[6]

固然，哲学是一种高端智慧，但智慧并不等于哲学。智慧要能解决问题；哲学的"实用性"可以很强，也可以很弱。哲学提出的终极问题，至今大都未得到解决，但这并未导致哲学的消亡。[7]

其实，哲学是一种灵魂的升华，只接受理性的权威。在人类智慧的早期，哲学曾是"科学的科学"；在当今，哲学仍与科学有部分交叉，亦有矛盾所在。[8]

牛顿将自己的著作冠以哲学之名，因其中有探究"终极问题"的成分，但囿于科学成果的限制，他最终只能求助于"来自上帝的第一推动力”。这种哲学与科学间的矛盾、困惑，延续至今。[9]

纵观历史，人类的文明总是在种种矛盾与困惑中发现、发展的，其中的动力便是灵魂的追问。[10]

译 文

Constant Inquiries About the Soul

Throughout thousands of years of history, human civilization has made tremendous progress, and yet the fundamental questions that perplex humanity seem to remain unchanged. Issues such as "Where do we come from?" "Where are we going?" "What is the essence of the world?" "What is the fundamental meaning of life?" are eternally unanswerable but perpetually asked. This is simply because only humans are endowed with a soul which distinguishes them from other beings.[1]

In ancient Athens, there was a group of "wise men" (sophists) who answered various life questions in public settings, later referred to as "philosophers" . Since human knowledge had not yet been classified at that time, "philosophy" encompassed all fields of study. Etymologically, "philosophy" comes from the Latin words *philo* (love) and *sophy* (or *sophia*, wisdom), thus meaning "the love of wisdom". Even up to today, many scientific disciplines in the West confer the degree of "Doctor of Philosophy" (PhD). Newton's famous work on physics, for example, was entitled *Philosophiae Naturalis Principia Mathematica* (Mathematical Principles of Natural Philosophy) showing that in the West philosophy permeates the essence of the human scientific spirit, which is the unceasing inquiry into ultimate existence, values and knowledge, with the actual results being secondary.[2]

It's said that only through philosophical enlightenment can a person gain a true sense of ego. In this connection, the great 17th-century French philosopher Descartes proposed the famous proposition "ego cogito ergo sum" (I think, therefore I am).[3]

It is generally believed that there are two major sources of philosophical enlightenment: gazing at the stars and facing death. At certain points in life, perhaps on a quiet summer night, looking up at the starry sky, one cannot help but thrill at the vast cosmos and the tiny self. Confronted with the gigantic Creation, one may inevitably ponder where to locate the ego in eternity. Despite Darwin's theory of evolution, it remains a hypothesis with many unresolved mysteries; Musk's plan for human colonization of Mars still seems very remote. The other enlightenment comes with the realization of death, especially as one ages and truly understands that everyone is born to die.[4]

Given that everyone's ultimate end is death, what is the true meaning of living then? In a sense, it seems to be meaningless.

However, viewed from the philosophical viewpoint integrated with the macrocosmic prospects of world, life and values, one can surely dig out some kind of meaning for life. In other words, the essence of life is to live meaningfully out of meaninglessness.[5]

Confucius said, "It's hard enough to know life, let alone death" . As a matter of fact, this saying should be reversed, "Only when you know death, can you truly understand life" , which means that a meaningful life only follows the enlightenment of death. Socrates said that learning philosophy is "preparing for death" , which laid the foundation for life philosophy, value orientation and moral ethics in the West. While matter is indestructible, the essence of substance remains permanently. The assumption that the soul does not perish with the body leads to the Western philosophical pursuit of "ultimate concern" .[6]

Certainly, philosophy is the promoted wisdom, but wisdom does not equate to philosophy. With wisdom, one should be able to solve certain problems. With philosophy, however, people may be either powerful or powerless to resolve issues confronting them. The ultimate questions raised by philosophy have almost all remained unsolved today, and yet they have not resulted in the collapse of the discipline itself.[7]

In a way, philosophy could be seen as an elevation of the soul, accepting only rationality. In the early stage of human wisdom, philosophy was treated as "the science of sciences" . Today, philosophy still intersects with science, though there are conflicts.[8]

Newton rightfully entitled his work as philosophy, since it incorporated the exploration of certain "ultimate questions". Confined by the limited scientific achievements in his age, however, he ultimately resorted to the "first mover from God". This kind of contradiction and confusion continue to today.[9]

Throughout history, human civilization has in fact always discovered and developed amid various contradictions and confusions, motivated by inquiring about the soul.[10]

解 析

在比较语境中释译

本文的题目是“灵魂的追问”，其实“灵魂”在中西文化里有着不尽相同的含义。应当说，在中国传统儒家文化里，对于灵魂的认识是个弱项，因为它更注重现世的道德修养和家庭伦理，而只有在礼仪和祭祖中，才重视灵魂的存在。西方则不同，受到希腊古典哲学和基督教的影响，灵魂涉及人的本质、意识、道德、生死、未来等问题的探讨，因而在“灵魂追问”这一点上，主要是从西方哲学意义上出发的。

根据西方哲学词典解释，**Soul**: Creek: *psyche* and Latin: *anima*, originally the breath of life. An entity, the presence of which in a body causes the body to possess life and in the absence of which the body is dead. The soul gives the body the faculty of cognition and, in the case of man, thought. The soul gives the power of self-motion. By analogy, the changing world is sometimes claimed to be a living thing and to have a world soul. (Bunnin, 2001: 942)（**灵魂**：希腊文为 *psyche*，拉丁文为 *anima*，原义指“生命的气息”。灵魂是这样一种实体，它在躯体中时便具有生命，不在时便意味着死亡。灵魂赋予躯体认知和活力，特别是思想。相应活生生变化着的世界，也应具有某种“世界灵魂”。）总之，灵魂在西方哲学中探讨的，不仅仅是对人类精神的定义，更是对存在、意识和终极问题的不断追问与深刻思考。正是在这个意义上，“灵魂的追问”并没有译成 Constant Inquiries of the Soul，而是译为 Constant Inquiries about the Soul，更能体现“灵魂”在这一语境中的性质，其中带有某种诠释成分。

“诠释”一词源自希腊文 Hermeneuia，有“说出”（to say）、“解释”（to explain）、“翻译”（to translate）三重含义。西方近代诠释学的发展，与翻译有着密切关系，如施莱尔马赫（Shleiermacher）的诠释学，和他以德文翻译柏拉图作品密切相关。当然，翻译与诠释并不等同，但翻译可具有和借助诠释的某种性质和方法来从事，简称“释译”，这可体现在词语、句式、表述等各个方面。

[1] 中，“（这些问题永远无解，但却永远被追问，）原因就在于只有人类独具灵魂”，似可按字面意思译成…the reason is that only human beings have souls，但这并不能完全体现“灵魂”的属性，特别是在西方，对于人所具有的真正独具特性的含

义，故参考译文中，将此意另开一句：This is simply because only humans are endowed with a soul which distinguishes them from other beings.，加以强调。

该文中有几处“自我”概念（如［3］、［4］中等），翻译中亦应加以区别与斟酌，而这又应是跨中西文化视野的。

如西方哲学词典所释：**Self:** The subject or bearer of mental attributes such as experience, consciousness, thoughts, beliefs, emotions, intentions and sensations. It is the human agent which deliberates and initiates actions, and which bears responsibility for one’s action. It is the referent of the first-person pronoun. It is sometimes used as a synonym for person. However, person is associated in different ways with bodily form and with public or social role, while the self is more related to inner part of a person. Sometimes the term is used interchangeably with terms such as the pure ego, unity of consciousness, subject and, in a loose sense, soul or mind. The self is a unity which integrates all experiences, beliefs and feelings of an individual and which enables an individual to have identity as the same person at different times. The self is characteristically taken to be the subject of self-consciousness, which includes itself or its states among the objects of its own consciousness.（Bunnin, 2001: 907，其中画线部分为笔者所加）（**自我：**体验、意识、思想、信念、情感、意图和感觉等心理属性的主体或载者；是谋划、发起行为并对其负责的始作俑者。它是第一人称代词的指称对象，有时又被用作人称的同义词。然而，人称与身体

形态以及公共或社会角色有不同的关联，而“自我”更多地与个人内在部分相关。有时该术语与诸如纯粹自我、意识统一、主体等术语可互换使用，而在宽泛意义上，与灵魂或心灵等术语也有关联。自我是一个统一体，它整合了个体的所有经验、信念和感受，从而使个体能够在不同时间以相同身份存在。自我在本质上被视为自我意识的主体，其中包括自身或其状态在自身意识中的对象。）如画线部分所示，“自我”概念可有不同的英文词或词组表达，取决于不同的语境。

相关的，庄子在《齐物论》中提出了“至人无已，神人无功，圣人无名”的命题，之后展开论述：“人之生也，固若是芒乎？其我独芒，而人亦有不芒者乎？”、“其寐也魂交，其觉也形开”、“非彼无我，非我无所取”等，概括而言，阐述了这样几个“自我”概念：“经验的自我”、“身体的自我”、“心理的自我”、“机心的自我”，翻译成英文时，不可一概而论，而需甄别其细微差异，如可分别译为 the empirical self、bodily form、psychic ego、calculative identity 等。

同样，［3］中的“（才能真正具有）自我”，没有简单地用 the self，而是用了 a true sense of ego，以体现经过哲学性质启蒙后的自我程度；而对于法国哲学家笛卡尔的“我思故我在”的著名命题，为准确起见，可先引用其原文，特别是英文的 ego 源于法文，而该法文源于拉丁文，由此更可看清其脉络；当然其词义又有所演化、扩展，如在弗洛伊德的经典精神分析理论中，ego、id、superego 三个核心概念相互作用，构成了人格的基本架构。同时，列出其英文：I think, therefore I am，尽管其中既没有 self

和 ego，但其本义在比较语境中不言自明。

接下来，［4］中的“顿感苍穹之浩大，自我之渺小”，其中的“自我”不妨译为 the tiny self，以对应 the vast cosmos；“（面对茫茫宇宙，）不免唏嘘自身在世间的真实处境”则将其译为 the ego，即 one may inevitably ponder where to locate the ego in eternity，以更显其深层含义。

［7］中，关于哲学的“实用性”，是否可直接译成 practicability？这里又涉及对哲学性质的理解。从物质层面的应用性而言，哲学确实没有像工程学、医学等学科那样直接和显而易见的实用价值，但在更高层次上，哲学对人们的思维方式、价值观念和生活态度产生影响，训练人们的批判性思维和逻辑分析能力，这对于解决实际问题又非常重要，因而不可简单而论，故用了 ...may be either powerful or powerless to resolve issues confronting them，特别是结合前面的“智慧要能解决问题”，用了近乎排比的句式 With wisdom, ... 和 With philosophy, ... 以体现其可能“很强”与“很弱”的两面性。

［5］中，“从哲学含义中所揭示的世界观、人生观、价值观里又可寻找到某种意义，即是要从无意义中活出意义——活出人生的真谛”，对此，如果译成 A certain meaning can be found in the worldview, outlook on life, and values revealed in philosophical meanings, that is, to live out meaning from meaninglessness—to live out the true meaning of life. 意思固然不错，但囿于原文形式，内容并未能充分表达，故参考译文将“世界观、人生观、价值观”加以融合、概述为 ...integrated with the macrocosmic prospects of world, life and values，而将“从无意义中活出意义——活出人生的真谛”整合为一句：In other words, the essence of life is to live meaningfully out of meaninglessness.，以更突出其实质。

同时，基于对原文的整体把握和语境的比较分析，在释译中还可通过变换、变通、增译、减译等方式，进行多种处理。

原文中多处出现关于“宇宙（世界）”的表述。据西方哲学词典解释：**Cosmos:** Etymologically *kosmos* means good order, but its meaning is extended to refer to the ordered universe, for the Greeks observed that the major cosmic events are marked by their regular order. For them, order meant arrangement, structural perfection and beauty.（Bunnin, 2001: 540）（**宇宙：**希腊文 *kosmos* 在词源学上指“良好秩序”，其意后扩展为“有秩序的宇宙”，因在古希腊人看来，主要的宇宙事件都是有规则的，而规则意味着组织和结构完美。）［4］中表宇宙之意的有“苍穹”、“宇宙”、“世间”，参考译文中分别对应了 cosmos、Creation、eternity，第一个是其辞源上的词义，第二、第三则是渗入文化、宗教含义的引申义，可视为同义语表述，以避免重复。其实，还可用 Universe、Space、Outer space 等，取决于不同学科和语境。

同段中的“向死而生”，可有多种译法，如 born towards death、born into death、born towards life through death、birth into death、birth towards death、life towards death、life into death、embracing death as part of life 等，而参考译文用了 everyone is born to die，主要是为了契合此处的语境和句式。

［7］中，“哲学提出的终极问题，至今大都未得到解决，但

这并未导致哲学的消亡"，其中的"消亡"并非简单意义上的 die out、wither away、extinct、subduction、disappear 等，而是要从学科的性质上来理解。一般来讲，哲学探讨的问题涵盖了存在、世界、本质、知识、价值、道德、思维等，这些往往超出了一般人的认知和理解范畴，即使高深的哲学研究似乎也不能给予最终、彻底的答案，但其价值在于提供了思考的框架和方法，同时启发了诸如科学、数学、物理、天文、政治学等学科的发展，因为它鼓励人们思考抽象、基础性的问题，促进对人类经验和存在的深刻理解。所以，作为一种思维方式和探索人类智慧的工具，"哲学"曾经是人类最古老的科学，随着当代科技的发展，其本身作为一门学科，并不会被学术、知识界所唾弃，正是在这个意义上，参考译文将该句译为 ...and yet they have not resulted in the collapse of the discipline itself，也可说是对其中"消亡"一词翻译的一种变通。

［1］中，"这些问题永远无解，但却永远被追问"，其中的两个"永远"，在译文中似可不必重复，因而译为 Issues such as... are eternally unanswerable but perpetually asked，以免显得呆板。

［10］中，"人类的文明总是在种种矛盾与困惑中发现、发展的，其中的动力便是灵魂的追问"，此"动力"是名词，可有多种对应的英文词，如 motivation、power、drive、momentum、incentive、impulse 等，但此处的句式适宜用动词，而 drive、power、impulse 等都不十分确切，故将该句译为 ... motivated by inquiring about the soul。

［4］中的“面对茫茫宇宙，不免唏嘘自身在世间的真实处境”，其中的“唏嘘”没有译成 sign at，而是用了 thrill at，以示 stronger feeling，特别是对于青少年时期的自我。同样，［6］中的“即只有弄懂了死亡这回事，才能真正活出人生意义”，其中的“弄懂”没有用 knowing、understanding、comprehending、realizing 等，而是用了 enlightenment，以表其中 more knowledge and greater understanding 之意。

同在［6］中，“未知生，焉知死？”若只按字面意思译成 Not understand life, how can you understand death? 显然不够。对于这类文言文警句，需作颇多增译，如 How can you know about death when you do not know about life?/If you do not understand life, how can you understand death?/How can we know about death when we do not yet understand life?/If we are ignorant of life, how can we comprehend death? 特别是最后一句，使用了 ignorant 和 comprehend 两个词，增加了其哲学色彩。然而，参考译文为 It's hard enough to know life, let alone death，着重译出前后句之间的递进含义。

类似的，如孔子的名言“道不同，不相为谋”，不宜简单译成 Different ways do not conspire with each other，而应增加画线部分：People following different principles do not take counsel with one another；“刚、毅、木、讷，近仁”不宜译成 Strength, determination, simplicity, and reticence are close to benevolence，而应增译为 He who possesses the four qualities of firmness, resolution, simplicity and discretion in words is close to benevolence. 等。

仍在［6］中，“人的灵魂并不会随着肉体而消失”，这是一个在哲学、科学、宗教意义上都极具争议的话题，如柏拉图在《理想国》中提出了“灵魂永恒”论，而亚里士多德的“功能论”则认为灵魂会随着肉体的死亡而消失；现代科学对灵魂的研究主要集中在神经科学和心理学领域，认为意识和心灵现象可归因于神经系统的活动，而灵魂的概念被视为超自然现象等，故对此句不宜简单译成 the soul does not perish with the body..., 而应增译为 The assumption that the soul does not perish with the body（leads to the Western philosophical pursuit of “ultimate concern”），如此方能确切表达出该命题的性质。

［9］中，“牛顿将自己的著作冠以哲学之名”，增译为 Newton rightfully entitled his work as philosophy，表明的是一种肯定的态度；而“囿于科学成果的限制”译为 Confined by the limited scientific achievements in his age，后面加上了 in his age，以更加明晰、准确。

同时，释译中的增译又往往与减译相辅相成，如［2］中的“哲学渗透着人类科学精神的实质，那便是对于终极存在、终极价值、终极知识的无穷尽的追问”，不宜简单根据原文译成 philosophy permeates the essential nature human scientific spirit, it is the endless inquiry into ultimate existence, ultimate value, ultimate knowledge，而可释译为 ...in the West philosophy permeates the essence of the human scientific spirit, which is the unceasing inquiry into ultimate existence, values and knowledge, with the actual results being secondary，其中 in the West 是增译，指明其哲学主体、性

质，而 ultimate existence, values and knowledge 则是一种浓缩式减译，以更精练。

同理，[8] 中的“只接受理性的权威”，可将 authority 省去，译为 ...accepting only rationality，减词而并未减意。

总之，翻译过程是“先进后出”，即先沉浸原文之中，整体把握原意及相关背景知识，融会贯通后，再跳出原文，摆脱其羁绊，“得意而忘言”，以自己的理解重新组织语言，在不同语境的比较中进行“释译”，当变则变，增减自然，从而求得最佳等值效果。

参考文献

① Bunnin, Nicholas. *Dictionary of Western Philosophy: English-Chinese* [Z]. Beijing: People Publishing Press, 2001.

附　录

原文

杭州散记*

描述杭州，既有“上有天堂，下有苏杭”的俗语，又有白居易“忆江南，最忆是杭州”和苏东坡“欲把西湖比西子，淡妆浓抹总相宜”这样的千古名句。[1]

杭州是南宋故都、文化名城，孕育了良渚文化、吴越文明，最是温柔富贵。她是浙江首府，现代都市，美丽、时髦、新潮，具有包融气质；她又是江南的代名词，被马可·波罗称为“世界上最华贵的天城”。[2]

杭州是联合国最佳人居奖得主，她新的城市定位是：历史文化名城、创新活力之城、著名旅游胜地、一流国际大都市……很少有一座城市像杭州这样汇集了如此多不同的身份。[3]

西湖之精致，钟灵毓秀，是柔美山川的杰作。近年来，西湖西进，杨公堤成为与苏堤平行的又一跨湖卧波彩带。西溪湿地开发，原生态的水乡景致秀丽多彩。小河绕人家，轻轻盈盈。[4]

三台山的茶楼近水依山，幽中藏雅，飞檐翘角，亭阁宛然。被桂花汁浸得丹红的米藕，咬一口，软软粘连，满口清香。杭州的女孩与生而来着一股仙气，清水出芙蓉，天然去雕饰。西泠桥

* 选自王建华主编的《微观杭州》(商务印书馆，2016年)。

边枫树林，秋来霜红雾紫，鲜艳夺目。[5]

太子湾的潮湿阳光，从肩头流过，落下一地芬芳。一首诗，一阕词，一座桥，一尊塔，一匹绸，一叶茶，都是那样的精美、雅致，展示着当代中国城市的高端品质。[6]

杭州“三面云山一面城”，山、水、城、人最为协调相配。引入了钱塘江活水的西湖，更为清澈，周围的山，可远观亦可近昵，在西湖水的滋养下，灵秀无比。[7]

一个拥有洲级规模高铁站、地铁与高铁齐飞的城市，竟还保留着一条绿皮火车站，为职工和居民通勤。[8]

杭州的居民和农民的收入之比为全国最低，生动诠释着城乡协调发展的真谛。[9]

虎跑寺的弘一法师，了断俗念，青灯古佛，与凡尘就此别过；司徒雷登本是美国人，却生于此，葬于此，魂归杭州。[10]

众多百年老店坚守着濒临灭绝的手工技艺，代代相传，而梦想小镇和“西溪创意产业园”的创业机会，带给年轻人无限的希望。[11]

随处可见的免费自行车租借点，是杭州新的风景线。斑马线前车让人，已成为公众的习惯，也谱写出城市和谐文明的新篇章。[12]

到武林门会同学，查了地图却也坐错了车，懒得再查，就问一美女。“可以百度的，”她说。但并不等我自己搜，她就拿出手机了，然后带我过去，到了路口，她说朝前走就是了，还担心地看着我，唯恐我不明白。[13]

这种礼遇，已不是第一次。若是碰到赋闲的老年人，他们甚至会带你过去。杭州景美，人心更美。[14]

宿舍后面有一条小吃街，里面有大大小小的各种小吃和饭店。每次过来吃饭，总能看到夫妻档，而卖鸡蛋灌饼的河南老夫妇，总是夸他家的鸡蛋饼独门秘制，无人能比。[15]

二层小阁楼的特色面馆，每每过去总是座无虚席；一胖一瘦夫妻的水果摊，推销的水果总是那么讨人喜欢，幸福就是简简单单一起相伴的日子。[16]

译　文

Hangzhou Sidelights

In portraying Hangzhou, there is the old saying "Up there is paradise, down on earth here are Hangzhou and Suzhou". There are also the eternal poetic lines from the Tang Dynasty's Bai Juyi "Hangzhou is the most memorable city whenever someone recalls the area south of the Yangtze River", and "West Lake, resembling the ancient beauty Xi Zi, is always stunningly attractive whatever she adorns" as depicted by Su Dongpo, a well-known poet of the Song Dynasty.[1]

As the ancient capital of the Southern Song Dynasty, Hangzhou bred Liang Zhu culture and Wu Yue civilization, transforming itself into the wealthiest and most elegant place in China. As the capital of Zhejiang province, it became synonymous with Jiangnan (the area south of the Yangtze River), modern, gorgeous, fashionable and inclusive, "the most magnificent city in the world" in the words of its adoring Marco Polo.[2]

Also, as the winner of the United Nation's Best Residential Award, Hangzhou's new position is a famous cultural center, innovative city, well-known tourist resort, first-class international metropolis... Few cities have so many different identities.[3]

Highly delicate and endowed with the fine spirit of the universe, the West Lake is a masterpiece of gently beautiful mountains and rivers. Recently, as it extends westwards, its Yang Gong Causeway has become a marvelous complement to the Su Causeway. In exploring the West Creek Wetlands, the colorful landscape of their original ecology is revealed. Nearby, the brooks flow gently around houses.[4]

The tea houses on Mount Santai's peaks and rivers are structured as pretty pavilions with upturned eaves. Trying a soft and sticky lotus cake of rice flavored with osmanthus, one will be overwhelmed by its delicacy. Local girls are endowed with natural elegance, simple and ingenuous. In autumn, the maple forest adjoining the Xiling Bridge forms a fascinating scene of red leaves against purple mists.[5]

The moist sunshine in the Prince Harbor Park flows over people's shoulders with its encircling fragrance. A poem, a bridge, a tower, a bolt of silk, a tea leaf... are all so exquisite and gorgeous, manifesting the high quality of this Chinese city.[6]

Hangzhou is a city with cloudy mountains on three of its sides with the fourth opening to the air. In a way, the mountains, water, city and people are perfectly harmonious. The Qiantang River's living water is drawn into the West Lake, limpid against its montane backdrop, which is in turn nourished by the water, making it unparalleledly picturesque, accessible both from near or afar.[7]

A city with a continental-scale high-speed rail station, subways and high-speed rail lines, still retains a green train station, convenient for workers and residents to commute.[8]

Its ratio of income between residents and farmers is the lowest in the country, vividly illustrating the true meaning of coordinated urban-rural development.[9]

The Running Tiger Temple is where Master Hongyi cast off worldly desires and became a monk in this austere scenery. John Leighton Stuart, originally an American, was born and eventually buried here.[10]

Many century-old stores keep practicing their handicrafts which were passed down through the ages and are now on the verge of extinction. The Dream Town and the West Creek Industrial Park provide opportunities for young people to start a business with unlimited hope.[11]

The ubiquitous free bike rentals are part of Hangzhou's new landscape. Cars yield to pedestrians at zebra crossings by habit, which is another nice addition to the city's harmonious civilization.[12]

On the way to Wulinmen to meet my classmates, I consulted the map but still took the wrong route. As I didn't feel like rechecking it again, I asked a pretty girl instead. She said, "You may check the Baidu Map on your phone." Having said that, she took out her phone and found the place for me, and then took me to the intersection. "It's right up there," she said, with great concern. I felt totally relieved by her effort.[13]

This was not my first time receiving such courtesy. If you meet old people idling around, they may even take you there. Indeed, Hangzhou has beautiful scenery with nice people.[14]

Behind our dormitory there is a snack street, which has all kinds of snacks and restaurants. Whenever you go there to dine, you will find husband-and-wife operations, and the old Henan couple always boast of their egg-filled savory pancakes, which are made exclusively by their family's secret recipe.[15]

On the second floor of a building there is a noodle shop with a special flavor, which is always filled to its capacity. A fruit stall, run by a fat man and his thin wife, has products selling well among the buyers. Happiness is actually a simple life with a good company.[16]

原 文

让非遗绽放更加迷人的光彩*

非遗的每一次精彩亮相、每一次引人瞩目，既是人们对技艺之美、匠心之美的再认识，对传统之美、生活之美的再感知，也是感悟中华文脉、增强文化自信的过程。

在“云游非遗·影像展”上，新鲜“玩法”解锁中国非物质文化遗产之美；在“百年百艺·薪火相传”中国传统工艺邀请展上，观众近距离感受非遗文化的魅力；7000余家非遗店铺、6万余种非遗产品参与线上线下销售活动……前不久，以“人民的非遗人民共享”为主题，各项非遗展示体验活动纷纷开展，非遗变得更加触手可及。[1]

近年来，从赫哲族伊玛堪说唱到古典民族史诗《格萨（斯）尔》说唱，从西湖边的绿茶制作工艺到潮绣、潮瓷、潮剧和工夫茶，从海南黎锦到青藏高原的编织藏毯……丰富多彩的非遗与现代生活相融相通，成为文旅消费的“新秀”、群众欢迎的“潮流”。巧夺天工的匠心之作引得观众连连惊叹，世代传承的古老技艺赢得广阔市场，淳朴丰富的民俗节庆留住心中乡愁，非遗展

* 选自《人民日报》（2021年6月25日9版）。

现着中华民族文化的博大精深、源远流长，更在创新中激发出强大的生命力。[2]

非物质文化遗产是中华优秀传统文化的重要组成部分，是我国各族人民宝贵的精神财富，体现着中华文明5000多年的继往开来，需要进行系统性保护、传承与发展。不久前，第五批国家级非物质文化遗产代表性项目名录公布，一批具有重大历史、文学、艺术、科学价值的非遗项目列入了名录予以保护。截至目前，国家级非遗代表性项目已达1557项。我国已建立起了具有中国特色的国家、省、市、县四级的名录体系，共认定非遗代表性项目10万余项。这既是非遗代表性项目名录体系建设的成果，也是中华文明与世界其他文明交流对话的重要资源。[3]

习近平总书记强调："要加强非物质文化遗产保护和传承，积极培养传承人，让非物质文化遗产绽放出更加迷人的光彩。"非遗从来不是孤芳自赏的"老物件"，不是华丽空洞的"招牌"，而是祖祖辈辈留下来的智慧结晶，是有生命力的"活化石"，是可见、可亲、可参与的现实生活。非遗的每一次精彩亮相、每一次引人瞩目，既是人们对技艺之美、匠心之美的再认识，对传统之美、生活之美的再感知，也是感悟中华文脉、增强文化自信的过程。[4]

非遗"活"起来、"火"起来，正是推动传统文化创造性转化、创新性发展的生动映照。"非遗进校园""非遗进景区""非遗购物节"等活动广泛开展；文旅部在国家级贫困县设立的非遗扶贫就业工坊，成为帮助群众增收致富的"金钥匙"。[5]

在一些地方，非遗保护被写入村规民约，助力乡村振兴……

越来越多的非遗从田野巷陌中“走出来”，传承与发展的生命力就蕴藏在人们的看见、了解与热爱中。这些启示我们，让非遗“见人见物见生活”，才能更好促进经济社会发展，不断惠益人民福祉。[6]

一个民族的复兴需要强大的物质力量，也需要强大的精神力量。不久前，文旅部发布了《“十四五”非物质文化遗产保护规划》，明确了加强非遗调查、记录和研究，加强非遗项目保护等6个方面主要任务。让更多璀璨明珠照亮前进征程，让凝聚在亿万中华儿女内心深处的自信化为更深沉、更持久的力量，中华民族伟大复兴的步伐必将更加豪迈。[7]

译　文

Making Our Intangible Cultural Heritage Shine More Brilliantly

Each wonderful appearance of our intangible cultural heritage on the world stage is an eye-catching event, recreating craftsmanship and artistic appreciation, re-recognizing the beauty of tradition and life, as well as furthering our understanding of the Chinese context and enhancing our cultural confidence.

Ways to promote intangible cultural heritage are diverse: In the exhibition of "Intangible Heritage in the Cloud" , the beauty of Chinese intangible cultural heritages is revealed quite refreshingly; while at the Invited Exhibition of "Quality Chinese Crafts Inherited from Previous Generations in the Centennial" , the audience experiences their charm at close quarters. Meanwhile, more than 7,000 stores selling intangible cultural heritage artefacts and 60,000 types of these products have participated in online and offline sales...Recently, themed as "Sharing intangible cultural heritage among the people" , various experiential programs have been launched, translating the intangible into the tangible.[1]

In recent years, rich and colorful Chinese intangible cultural heritages, ranging from Yimakan rap of the Hezhe ethnic group to the rap of the classical national epic *Gesar*; from the green tea-making techniques by the West Lake to Chaozhou embroidery, porcelain, opera and *Kongfu* tea; from Hainan's Li Brocade to woven Tibetan carpets from the Qinghai-Tibet Plateau... are all mingled into modern life, becoming the "rookie" of cultural tourism consumption and a popular trend. Marveling at the master-craftsmanship of the work, the audience are deeply impressed. A vast market for the ancient skills inherited from generation to generation has been developed, and nostalgia derived from rich, unsophisticated folk festivals has endured in people's hearts. Clearly, intangible cultural heritage embodies a long history of profound Chinese culture, inspiring great innovative vitality.[2]

These intangible cultural heritages are an important part of China's splendid traditional culture, a valuable spiritual treasure of the people of all its ethnic groups, symbolizing the five thousand years of Chinese civilization both inherited from the past and committed to the future, which require further systematic protection, inheritance and development. Not long ago, the fifth list of representative national intangible cultural heritages was published, including quite a number of items with significant historical, literary, and scientific values for protection. So far, China has established a national, provincial, municipal and county-level directory system with Chinese characteristics, with a total of more than 100,000 typical intangible cultural heritage items identified and 1,557 projects at national level approved. China has thus put in place fairly extensive list, which could prove to be important resources as China interacts with other civilizations in the world. [3]

General Secretary Xi Jinping has stressed that "We should reinforce the measures to protect and inherit intangible cultural heritages and actively cultivate inheritors, so as to make them more charming and magnificent" . In fact, intangible heritage is never an "antique object" enjoyed by a happy few, nor a flashy "signboard" ; instead, it's a "living fossil" full of life, crystalized wisdom left over from generation to generation, visible, amiable and participating in our daily lives. Each wonderful appearance of our intangible cultural heritage on the world stage is an eye-catching event, recreating craftsmanship and artistic appreciation, re-recognizing the beauty of tradition and life, as well as furthering our understanding of the Chinese context and enhancing our cultural confidence.[4]

The effective way to creatively transform and develop traditional Chinese culture is to make our intangible heritages more vivid and popular. Extensively activities that have already been carried out, such as "Intangible Culture on Campus", "Intangible Culture in Scenic Areas", "Intangible Heritage Shopping Festivals", as well as the Intangible Heritage Poverty Alleviation Workshops in poverty-stricken counties at national level, have all become "golden keys" to help people increase their incomes and wealth.[5]

In some places, protection of intangible cultural heritage has been written into village rules and regulations to boost rural revitalization. As more and more "invisible relics" become visible in the fields and alleys, it has increasingly become clear that the vitality of intangible cultural heritage is rooted in people's sensibility, comprehension and passion, which have inspired us that only by making intangible heritage a living figure/thing in our daily lives, can we better promote economic and social development, and continuously benefit people's well-being.[6]

The revival of a nation requires not only material strength but also great spiritual power. Not long ago, the Ministry of Culture and Tourism issued *Regulations on the Protection of Intangible Cultural Heritage in the 14th Five-Year Plan*, specifying six major tasks, including reinforcing the investigation, and research into and recording of intangible cultural heritage as well as protection for its projects. In that way, let's release more of our brilliant intangible cultural heritages as bright pearls, illuminating the journey ahead, agglomerating deeper and more lasting strength from inner confidence in the hearts of hundreds of millions of Chinese people, so as to rejuvenate our nation even more heroically.[7]

原 文

刻下今天，抗拒遗忘*

我们知道自己是容易忘记的。有心人能坚持写下日记，日日记录，到时回头还能翻回去，某一年某一天，字字句句都在纸上，能唤起记忆。也有人记忆超群，过了多少年，还能细数某时某地某事，让人惊叹。但大部分的我们呢？我曾记过一阵日记，从开始的日日记，到后来的隔日记，再到后来的不知隔多少日记，终于有一天把日记本尘封在写字台的某个抽屉角落里了。我也曾与好友仔细回想，在何时何地哪一个场合第一次遇见，却相顾茫然。[1]

这样的无从查考，这样的相顾茫然，并不算得上如何特殊。[2]

生活的大部分形态，总是碎片化的。一时在东，一时在西，纷繁复杂，并不是那么容易记住的。我们记住了海潮翻腾，侧耳又听见大江大河奔涌怒吼；记住了大江大河的浪高声宏，耳边又传来远处的人声鼎沸……热点似乎一个接着一个，连时尚流行都以百倍的速度在此起彼伏，每个似乎都在沸点上翻滚。可新的记忆总是一页页压过旧的，遗忘总在这样不知不觉的侧

---

* 选自《人民日报2016年散文精选》（人民日报出版社，2017年）一书中，虞金星的散文《刻下今天，抗拒遗忘》。

耳、挪移间发生。[3]

而更多时候，生活的形态，又是屡屡重复的。连古人都说，“年年岁岁花相似”，相似的花，相似的叶，总是最不容易区分的。我们记忆里，只留下似曾相识的影子。提过的话题要再提，理过的逻辑要再理，连听过的故事，也总在天南海北再听到相似的讲述。“仙桂年年折又生”，如果枝头还是避着风头的朝向，连挂着的果子上的疤痕都一般，谁又能分清是哪一年、哪一月种下的树呢？[4]

若说世上事尽是重复，无疑太消极。而太阳每天都是新的，又高估了普通人心里的饱满度。我们在光与影里穿行，日久年深。有这样一个日子，我们停下来，做一个特别的标记，把它从漫长的旅途里区别出来，想想过去，看看前程，也是对自己的一种关怀。在意义被怀疑、被消解的时候，有这样的庄重的一刻，反观静照，在一片喧腾和琐碎里执着地找到那份属于自己的历史感，也是一种觉醒。[5]

译 文

Recording Today to Avoid Forgetting

We are apt to forgetting. Some people keep writing diaries. Their daily labor on paper yields them tangible memories whenever they wish to recall them in chronological detail. Surely, there are a few people with remarkable memories, capable of recounting certain things at certain locations and times even after many years. But what about most of us? I once kept a diary for a while, beginning with a daily diary, then a later interval diary, and still later an "unknown interval" diary. Finally, one day I sealed the diary in a corner of my desk drawer. I have tried to recall carefully with my friends when, where, on which occasion we first met, but we just looked at each other in a haze.[1]

It's not unusual to have such a memory blank, not having recorded anything on paper.[2]

Most parts of our lives are recalled in fragments. Sometimes, it's really hard to remember the whole lot sequentially: you may retain the tumultuous tides of the seas, while still getting some impression of the roaring of certain great rivers and the shouts of crowds in the distance. Hot spots seem to come one after another, like fashion trends rising and falling at an incredible speed, each seemingly tumbling out at boiling point. As new memories always overwhelm the old ones, oversight occurs in such an imperceptible diversion.[3]

Moreover, the routine of life also constantly repeats itself. As the ancients said, "Flowers bloom similarly year in and year out" . Indeed, similar flowers and leaves are the hardest things to distinguish, just like the things shadowed in our memories. Similar topics, logic, even stories may have been mentioned, rationalized and told repeatedly somewhere and at some time in the world. "Branches of bay trees are snapped and healed every year" , so if they are all subject to the direction of the wind, the scars on the hanging fruits will be average, and who can then tell in which year and month the tree was planted?[4]

While it may sound a bit negative to say that things in the world are nothing but repetitions, they do overly satisfy us ordinary beings, if we say "the sun is renewing itself daily for us" . Traveling through lights and shadows, we pause at certain phases to make special marks, distinguishing them within a long journey, which is also a kind of self-comfort when looking back and looking forward. It is quite inspirational to find such a sense of history in a solemn moment during the time of bustle and rush when meanings and memories have faded away.[5]

原 文

当我们纪念屈原时，我们在纪念什么？*

屈原大夫提倡“美政”，主张对内修明法度，对外联齐抗秦，后遭贵族排挤，被流放至沅湘流域。但他像战士一样，坚守自我理想，践行君子之道，绝不允许世俗的秽气玷污自己高洁峻美的人格，绝不允许一丝松懈与放弃出现在自己的生命意志中[1]

屈原用自己的名字反映追求的道德标准。据《离骚》开篇，“父亲把我的名取为正则，把我的字叫作灵均”。“正则”即正直、正派，恪守做人原则；“灵均”指聪颖、智慧、公平、公正。在《橘颂》中，他又以橘树的“独立不迁”体现自己的人格情操：为了心中美好的理想，绝不同流合污，纵然死去也不后悔。他仿佛生活在楚国的高空，鸟瞰着世间纷纭的一切，心中洞明，却无能为力。[2]

屈原的千古之志，在于其文学作品和政治抱负无不站在人民的立场上。他的伟大之处，在于始终怀着强烈的忧国忧民的悲悯之心，始终怀着强烈的爱国之情。[3]

他的事迹和作品之所以能和民众日常生活结合在一起，并成

---

* 本文为2024年第三十六届韩素音国际翻译大赛汉译英竞赛原文。

为一个重要传统节日的主要纪念对象，就是因为他的言行流露着对祖国、对人民、对故土文化无限的爱，其中深深蕴藏着民族精神和文化的持久力量。“国无人莫我知兮，又何怀乎故都？”屈原亦曾考虑过“何不去国”的问题，但他最终没有去国远游，这正体现了他对精神和文化的坚守。[4]

而今，每逢端午节，中国各地都突出祭祀屈原的主题，歌颂屈原正道直行、爱国爱民的精神，通过讲述端午节与屈原的故事、开展诗词吟诵和进行赛龙舟等活动，引领公众学习传统文化，厚植家国情怀。[5]

今天我们纪念屈原，是纪念屈原代表的传统中国士人直面生死、敢向未知勇猛叩击的“天问”精神。在长诗《天问》中，屈原从天地离分、阴阳变化、日月星辰等自然现象，一直问到神话传说乃至圣贤凶顽和治乱兴衰的历史故事，并从设问中表达自己的宇宙观念、历史观念和政治主张。不唯书，只唯实，敢于怀疑，敢于批判，这样的探索精神令人叹服。[6]

中国行星探测任务名为“天问”，实际上表现了中国人对既有传统观念的批判精神和对科学真理的探索精神。没有对旧有观念的批判，就难以产生新的科学思想。《天问》给今人的启示，不仅是要怀疑传统的偏见和凝固的史观，更要在不断的批判和追问中，寻求思想突破和科技创新。[7]

“屈原”作为一种精神符号对中华民族共同体意识的构建，从过去到现在以至未来都发挥着非比寻常的作用。倘若没有屈原这样一位伟大的先贤，那么整个中国士人群体势必会缺少一种精神的力量，而中国历史也会失掉不少悲壮的色彩。[8]

文明弦歌终不绝，屈子精神永流传。守正不守旧，尊古不复古，这是我们对传统文化充满自信的表达。[9]

译 文

The Essence of Commemorating Qu Yuan

Qu Yuan (340 BC-278 BC), a high-ranking official of the Chu State, championed the principles of "benevolent rule" . He believed a state should be governed by a wise ruler and virtuous officials, with perfected laws and regulations. He allied with the Qi State to resist the expansion of the Qin State. However, his vision and reforms were opposed by the nobility, leading to his exile to the Yuan and Xiang River Basin. Yet, Qu Yuan remained steadfast, embodying the virtues of a gentleman. He upheld his ideals and maintained his noble character, refusing to let worldly corruption tarnish his spirit or weaken his resolve.[1]

Qu Yuan's name itself reflects the moral standards he pursued. As the opening of *Li Sao* states: "My father named me Zheng Ze and characterized me Ling Jun" , symbolizing integrity, uprightness, and honesty alongside intelligence, fairness, and justice. In *Orange Ode*, Qu Yuan likened his personality to the orange tree, embodying "independence and steadfastness" . He declared he would never regret chasing his vibrant dreams, nor would he ever align himself with evil—even at the cost of his life. Standing above the chaos of his time, he possessed a clear vision of the challenges his state faced but found himself powerless to enact change.[2]

Qu Yuan's enduring aspirations were reflected in both his literary works and political ideals, which aligned with the will of the people. His deep compassion and unwavering patriotism for his country and compatriots elevated him to the status of a revered figure in Chinese history.[3]

His boundless love for his homeland, its people, and its culture is a testament to his national ethos and enduring cultural influence. This devotion, immortalized in his works and the stories surrounding him, became intertwined with the lives of the people and a centerpiece of traditional festivals. Despite lamenting "Since no one understands me domestically, why should I still miss my hometown?" and contemplating leaving his country, he ultimately chose to stay. This decision highlighted his remarkable perseverance and unshakable belief in his principles.[4]

Today, the Dragon Boat Festival honors Qu Yuan by celebrating his unwavering integrity and patriotic spirit. The festival recounts his historical legacy through poetry recitals, dragon boat races, and activities that promote traditional culture and cultivate patriotism.[5]

Nowadays, the essence of commemorating Qu Yuan lies in

preserving his spirit of "Inquiring the Heavens" , a hallmark of traditional Chinese intellectuals who courageously confronted life, death, and the unknown. In his long poem *Inquiring the Heavens*, Qu Yuan explored a wide range of natural phenomena, from the origins of heaven and earth to the cycles of *yin* and *yang*, the sun, moon, and stars. He also delved into myths, legends, and historical accounts of sages and demons, reflecting on the rise and fall of dynasties. Through his questions, Qu Yuan expressed his cosmological, historical, and political insights. Unconfined by conventional thought, his realistic and critical inquiries remain admirable.[6]

The Chinese planetary exploration mission, aptly named Inquiring the Heavens, embodies this same spirit of questioning and exploration. It reflects the necessity of critically examining traditional concepts to advance scientific understanding. Without challenging outdated ideas, the generation of new scientific breakthroughs becomes nearly impossible. Inspired by *Inquiring the Heavens*, we are reminded to contest traditional biases, question entrenched historical narratives, and seek innovations in thought, science, and technology.[7]

As a spiritual icon, Qu Yuan exemplifies the profound connection between the shared destiny of the Chinese nation and its historical, present, and future endeavors. Without such an extraordinary scholar, the nation would lose a significant part of its spiritual power, and Chinese history would feel far less heroic.[8]

As the vibrant song of civilization continues, the spirit of Sage

Qu endures through generations. We take pride in our traditional culture, cherishing its principles of righteousness and reverence for the past, while striving to adapt and innovate rather than return to antiquated ways.[9]